NO LONGER STRANGERS

*Rediscovering the Chosen People
and the Jewish Roots of Christianity*

No Longer Strangers

*Rediscovering the Chosen People
and the Jewish Roots of Christianity*

Dr. Richard Booker

© Copyright 2002 by Sounds of the Trumpet, Inc.

All rights reserved. This book is protected under the copyright laws of the United States of America. This book may not be copied or reprinted for commercial gain or profit. The use of short quotations or occasional page copying for personal or group study is permitted and encouraged. Permission will be granted upon request.

Scripture quotations are taken from The New King James Bible, copyright © 1982, Thomas Nelson, Inc., Nashville, TN.

Special thanks to Michael Washer for supplying the art work for the front cover.

ISBN: 0-9615302-7-8

Printed in the United States of America

Acknowledgments

My love and deepest gratitude to the following:

My colleagues who were kind enough to take the time to read the manuscript and write an endorsement. Thank you for your encouragement and support. Also, to Pastor Bron Barkley for his excellent editing skills and valuable suggestions and Rick Ladage for his composition assistance.

To my wife and covenant partner in life, Peggy, who has faithfully served the Lord with me and whose great sacrifices have enabled me to fulfill God's call for my life. There are many great women in the world, but Peggy surpasses them all. May her rewards be great—well done, good and faithful servant.

Endorsements

"...This well-researched book will challenge believers of every stripe and will provide a new appreciation of Gentiles for Jews and of Paul's intriguing words, "no longer strangers." I highly recommend this study."

Dr. Marvin Wilson
Professor of Biblical Studies, Gordon College
Wenham, Massachusetts

"*No Longer Strangers* is an excellent introduction to Jewish roots covering the essentials in an easy reading format. I highly recommend it as a teaching text."

Dr. Ron Moseley
President of Arkansas Institute of Holy Land Studies

"...*No Longer Strangers* is an insightful contribution which introduces the Jewish roots of the Christian faith to a broad audience....Every Christian needs to read this book and discover the authentic context of Jesus' teachings and the beginnings of Christianity."

Dr. Brad Young
ORU Associate Professor of Judaic Christian Studies
President and Founder of the Gospel Research Foundation

"*No Longer Strangers* introduces Christians to Judaism and its formative influence upon the first-century Jesus Kingdom Movement, later called the Church. It is a comprehensive but concise and clear treatment of the subject and well serves the multitudes of believers awakening to their rich Hebrew heritage."

Dwight Pryor
President, Center for Judaic-Christian Studies

"*No Longer Strangers*, is a must for every serious student of the Bible and Church history...Richard Booker brings a lost legacy to the Church with his clear explanations of the things we need to understand about the Jewish roots of Christianity."

Clarence Wagner
International Director, Bridges for Peace

No Longer Strangers

"Therefore remember that you, once Gentiles in the flesh—who are called Uncircumcision by what is called the Circumcision made in the flesh by hands—that at that time you were without Christ [Messiah], being aliens from the commonwealth of Israel and strangers from the covenants of promise, having no hope and without God in the world. But now in Christ [Messiah] Jesus you who were once far off have been brought near by the blood of Christ [Messiah].

"For He Himself is our peace, who has made both one, and has broken down the middle wall of separation, having abolished in His flesh the enmity, that is, the law of commandments contained in ordinances, so as to create in Himself one new man from the two, thus making peace, and that He might reconcile them both to God in one body through the cross, thereby putting to death the enmity.

"And He came and preached peace to you who were afar off and to those who were near. For through Him we both have access by one Spirit to the Father.

> *"Now, therefore, you are no longer strangers and foreigners, but fellow citizens with the saints and members of the household of God"* (Ephesians 2:11-19).

Contents

Chapter 1   **Introduction** 1
                 The Abrahamic Curse and the Church ... God Is Doing a New Thing ... Words of Confirmation ... The Institute for Hebraic-Christian Studies ... Personal Study Guide

Chapter 2   **The Jews: A People Who Won't Go Away** 11
                 Who Are the Jews? ... Jewish Mother or Jewish Father? ... When Is a Jew a Jew? ... Whose Judaism? ... Proselytes ... Jewish Groups According to Geography and Culture ... Jewish Denominations ... The Immortal Jew ... Personal Study Guide

Chapter 3   **The Jewish People in the First Testament** 25
                 In the Beginning ... The Call of Abraham ... Abraham's Covenant Descendants ... The Hebrews Enslaved in Egypt ... From Egypt to the Promised Land ... From Moses to Samuel ... The Monarchy ... The Divided Kingdom and the Exile ... The Return ... Personal Study Guide

Chapter 4   **The Jewish People Between the Testaments** ... 39
                 The Greek Period Under Alexander (333–323 BC) ... The North Against the South ... Antiochus IV (Epiphanes) (175–164 BC) ... Antiochus Epiphanes and Jerusalem ... The Maccabees (167–142 BC) ... Rededicating the Temple ... Judah(s) Maccabees (164–160 BC) ... Jonathan (160–143 BC) ... Simon (143–134 BC) ... The Hasmonean Successors ... John Hyrcanus (134–104 BC) ... Aristobulus I (104–103 BC) ... Alexander Jannaeus (103–76 BC) ... Salome Alexandra (76–67 BC) ... Aristobulus II (67–63 BC) Versus Hyrcanus II ... Jerusalem Falls to Pompey (63 BC) ... Herod Antipater and John Hyrcanus II (63–40 BC) ... Antigonus (40–37 BC) ... Herod (37–4 BC) and the Romans ... Herod's Reign ... Personal Study Guide

Chapter 5 **The Jewish People in the New Testament Era** .. 63
Jesus of Nazareth—King of the Jews ... Jesus' Mission ... Jesus the Jew ... Jesus' Ministry ... Jesus' Crucifixion, Resurrection, and Ascension ... The Spread of Christianity ... Herod's Divided Kingdom ... Herod Philip (4 BC–AD 34) ... Herod Antipas (4 BC–AD 39) ... Archelaus (4 BC–AD 6) ... Herod Agrippa I (AD 37–44) ... Herod Agrippa II (AD 49–70) ... Personal Study Guide

Chapter 6 **The Jewish People and Rome** 79
From Republic to Emperor ... The Roman Caesars ... Augustus (27 BC–AD 14) ... Tiberius (AD 14–37) ... Caligula (AD 37–41) ... Claudius (AD 41–54) ... Nero (AD 54–68) ... Galba/Otho/Vitellius (AD 68–69) ... Vespasian (AD 69–79) ... Titus (AD 79–81) ... Domitian (AD 81–96) ... Nerva (AD 96–98) ... Trajan (AD 98–117) ... Hadrian (AD 117–138) ... The First Jewish Revolt ... The Second Jewish Revolt ... Rabbinic Judaism ... Personal Study Guide

Chapter 7 **Christian Anti-Semitism** 103
The Jewish Revolts ... The Gentile Church Fathers ... The "Christ-Killers" ... The Allegorical Interpretation of Scripture ... Constantine ... The Council of Nicea ... The Day of the Sun ... Renouncing One's Identity ... A Flood of Pagans ... Augustine (AD 354–430) ... The Crusades ... Anti-Semitic Hysteria ... The Inquisition ... The Reformation ... The Russian "Pogroms" ... Protocols of the Learned Elders of Zion ... The Holocaust ... Hitler's Youth ... Germany's Humiliation ... Hitler's Defeat and Rise to Power ... The Night of Broken Glass ... Hitler's Death Camps ... Christians and the Holocaust ... Personal Study Guide

Chapter 8 **Judaism and Christianity** 137
The Place of Grace in Judaism and Christianity ... The Place of Faith in Judaism and Christianity ...

Faith and Works in Judaism and Christianity ... Creed or Deed? ... Law and Grace ... The Meaning of *Torah* ... The Purpose of the *Torah* ... The Essence and Blessings of *Torah* ... *Torah* in the New Testament ... The *Torah* and Gentiles ... The *Torah* Misinterpreted ... Problem Passages ... New Testament Statements About the *Torah* ... The *Torah* and Christians ... Personal Study Guide

Chapter 9 Basic Jewish Beliefs and Christianity 159
Basic Jewish Beliefs ... The Thirteen Principles ... The Hebrew Scriptures ... *Torah* ... *Nevi'im* ... *K'tuvim* ... Jewish Views About the *Tanakh* ... God ... *Shema Yisrael* ... *Adonai Eloheynu* ... *Adonai Echad* ... Man and Sin ... Salvation (Atonement) ... The Messiah ... The Messiah as Prophet ... The Messiah as Priest ... The Messiah as King ... Personal Study Guide

Chapter 10 Basic Jewish Practices and Christianity 187
The Synagogue ... *Kippah* ... *Tzitzit/Tallit* ... *Tefillin* ... *Mezuzah* ... *Mikveh* ... *Kashrut* (*Kosher*) ... The Jerusalem Council ... Personal Study Guide

Chapter 11 Jewish Life Cycle 221
Covenant of Circumcision *(Brit Milah)* ... Redemption of the Firstborn *(Pidyon Haben)* ... Bar/Bat Mitzvah ... The Jewish Wedding ... Death and Mourning ... Personal Study Guide

Chapter 12 Jewish Religious Cycle—the Sabbath 245
The Great Divide ... The Sabbath ... Jesus and the Sabbath ... Paul and the Sabbath ... Personal Study Guide

Chapter 13 Jewish Religious Cycle—the Feasts 255
The Jewish Calendar ... The Feasts ... Passover ... Unleavened Bread ... Firstfruits ... Pentecost ... Trumpets ... Atonement ... Tabernacles ... Hanukkah ... Purim ... Personal Study Guide

Chapter 14 The Time to Favor Zion **281**
　　　　　　Secular Zionism ... Replacement Theology Zionism
　　　　　　... Biblical Zionism ... Regathering Zion ...
　　　　　　Redeeming Zion ... Restoring Zion ... Favoring
　　　　　　Zion in the Latter Days ... Personal Study Guide
Epilogue: The Hebraic Roots of Christianity . . **301**
Selective Bibliography **305**
Selective Index of Names and Subjects **311**
Vision and Resource Materials **317**
Book Order Form **319**
Book Order Form **321**

Chapter 1
Introduction

One of the most profound statements in the Bible is in Genesis 12:3. The Lord had just directed Abram (later called Abraham) to leave his pagan country (Babylon) and go to a new land where God would bless Abram and make his descendants a great nation. Later God would make a covenant with Abram in which He promised to redeem the world through one of Abram's descendants.

Because the Lord established His plan of redemption with Abram, He promised to bless those who bless Abram but curse those who curse him. The obvious reason is that those who would seek to destroy Abram and his descendants would hinder the redemptive purposes of God.

The Lord said to Abram, "I will bless those who bless you, and I will curse him who curses you; and in you all the families of the earth shall be blessed" (Gen. 12:1-3). History has shown time and again this to be true. Nations that have blessed the Jewish people have prospered, while those who have persecuted them have suffered.

The Abrahamic Curse and the Church

Unfortunately, the Christian Church has not blessed the Jewish people. It has persecuted them. One of the reasons for this tragic past is that the early church fathers in the second, third, and fourth centuries stripped Christianity of its Jewish roots. The result of this action was that the Church established anti-Semitic policies of hatred and violence towards the Jewish people. Without its Jewish root, the Church embraced Greek and Roman concepts and practices.

It was with this knowledge of hate shown by Christendom towards the Jewish people that Adolph Hitler was able to write in

Mein Kampf, "Hence today I believe that I am acting in accordance with the Almighty Creator: by defending myself against the Jew, I am fighting for the work of the Lord."[1] Hitler knew that European Christendom would not resist his plans to destroy the Jews because of its own anti-Semitic past.

While many Christians say they are not responsible for this terrible past, we still suffer the consequences of the sins of our church fathers, even though we personally did not participate in the Crusades, the Inquisition, the Holocaust, etc. The Church collectively has been under the dark cloud of the curse of Abraham for seventeen hundred years.

Hatred of Jews and Israel is not a thing of the past. It is once again raising its ugly voice like the Philistine giant of Bible times who threatened the very existence of Israel and the Jewish people. In order to have the blessing of Abraham promised by God, Christians must repent of our anti-Semitic past. We must stand with the Jewish people against the dark forces of evil which would seek to destroy both communities. Evil that is not opposed will spawn even more evil.

When Christians are educated in the Jewish roots of their faith, they will understand the great debt Christianity owes to the Jewish people. They will want to bless, comfort, love, and support the Jewish people and the nation of Israel as commanded in the Bible. The curse of Abraham will be lifted off the church and the blessings of God will come to corporate Christianity in the form of spiritual renewal and enrichment.

God Is Doing a New Thing

While Christians must never forget the past, this is a new day for thousands of Gentile believers around the world who are discovering that biblical Christianity has its roots in Jerusalem and biblical Judaism.

---

1. Adoph Hitler, *Mein Kampf*, translated by Ralph Manheim (Boston: Houghton Mifflin Co., 1971), 65.

Introduction

Our Christian roots are not in Athens, Rome, Geneva, Wittenburg, Aldersgate, Azuza Street, Nashville, or Tulsa. Our spiritual roots are in Jerusalem, and the Lord is calling us back to our roots. This realization has created a desire in the hearts of Christians to learn about the Jewish heritage of our faith.

This happened in my own life in 1974 when the Lord gave me spiritual insight regarding the connection between the Hebrew Scriptures (the Old Testament) and the New Testament. I saw that the two Testaments told one basic story and that it was impossible to correctly understand the New Testament without a good knowledge of the Hebrew Scriptures.

I left my successful business career in 1979 and, along with my wife, Peggy, traveled extensively throughout the United States teaching the Bible in churches and conferences. Over the years, I came to realize that one of the greatest needs among Christians is for them to understand their Hebraic/Jewish roots.

There were 2,000 years of Hebrew history, culture, language, traditions, and customs that formed the root of Christianity. The more Christians learn about our Hebraic/Jewish roots, the more fruitful and blessed we can be in our lives.

While Christians in America view life with a Western mind and worldview, the Bible was written by Abraham's descendants who had an Hebraic culture, language, and worldview. This presents a real challenge. We have a Middle Eastern Book that we seek to understand from our Western culture.

Our Western perspective can easily cause us to misunderstand the Bible. Furthermore, our mind has been more influenced by Greek philosophy than biblical, Hebraic thought. This is why we must study the Hebraic/Jewish roots of Christianity.

When we read the Bible through Hebrew eyes, our understanding becomes much richer, deeper, and clearer with more detail than we could ever imagine. We see truths that we are unable to see with our Western eyes, no matter how pure our motives and intense our desires.

Jesus and His early followers were deeply rooted in the rich Hebraic soil of their ancestors. They thought, taught, and lived out of this soil. God planted Christianity in this soil, and we must return to it in order to be biblically nourished.

As this understanding became clearer in my mind, Peggy and I sought the Lord for several years about what this could mean for our lives and ministry. We believed God had a change in store for us, and that somehow, it related to helping educate Christians in the Hebraic/Jewish roots of the faith.

Words of Confirmation

Finally, on the night of November 13, 1995, the Lord impressed on two of his servants, each with over fifty years' experience in ministry, to share the following words to us. Both words were spoken as prophetic utterances. The setting was a Bible school where I had taught for seven days on the Feast of the Lord. I have included these words below, without editing, just as they were given. The first word given was as follows:

"For the Lord would say unto you, Richard and Peggy, that a greater anointing and a greater open door stands before you. For the Lord says, As you have been faithful in small things, I will bless you in greater things. And you shall minister to thousands where you have ministered to hundreds. And where you have ministered to tens, you shall minister to hundreds. For the Lord has said for the hour of your message has come for you to go forward.

"And be not discouraged by the opposition and disinterest that you may find among My people, says the Lord. For there are those who care nothing about the message you bring. Yes, I say unto you that I see their hearts.

"But I have raised you up for such an hour as this in which you must take the message that I have burned and branded into your soul. And you will give it forth without seeking to please man or win the favor of man. And though there be only a fraction of the people who will hear it, you shall still give My message. For it is better that you be faithful with few things than you miss the perfect plan of God among many.

"For the Lord says unto you, For this day and for this hour and for this moment have you been born and you have come into the kingdom for such a time as this. And I will give you wings like eagles, yes swift as an eagle, says the Lord. And you shall indeed see the fulfillment of the prophetic word that you did speak this night.

"For the Lord has said, I have put within you, not only the teaching ministry, but I have put within you the word, the sure word of prophecy. And I will stand behind you to confirm it so that not one word shall fall to the ground. I planted in your heart a love for My people and for Israel. And that love shall be used by the Holy Spirit to draw many of My people to Me, says the Lord. For you shall be as a bugle call to Israel."

This word was immediately followed by the second word which was like a confirmation of the first one.

"The Lord further says, I shall cause that you shall plant seeds. You shall drop one here and drop one there. For many times you have thought, are we really planting anything at all? But know that you are planting.

"And you shall plant seed among my Church, says the Lord. Seeds among those that before thought they were Israel, not knowing that I had a true people Israel and that I have a parallel people, My own Church. And you shall drop the seed into them to straighten out their thinking. You shall put a seed into them to cause them to have a love for the nation of Israel. You shall plant a seed into them which will cause the two to become one. Yes, you shall break down the middle wall of partition that flesh has built and that tradition has built.

"And know not but that one day when you sow the seed, it shall fall upon ground and bring forth another Haym Salomon (a Jewish man who financed the American Revolution). It shall bring forth another Haym Salomon that you know not of who shall bless with finances, not only My people Israel, but will bless My Church with multitudes in the end times, says the Lord. For there are those who have the millions. Yes, you shall plant the seed in one of them unknowingly and the millions shall be loosed for My kingdom in the end times, says the Lord."

The Institute for Hebraic-Christian Studies

After hearing these words, Peggy and I fasted for twenty-one days to seek God about what this could mean for our lives. Months later, the Lord impressed on my heart and mind to begin a new work in Houston to be entitled the Institute for Hebraic-Christian Studies (IHCS).

The vision of IHCS would be to educate Christians in their Hebraic/Jewish roots; build bridges of love, understanding, and mutual respect between the Christian and Jewish communities; and continue our support of the state of Israel.

After sharing this vision with others, I was encouraged to establish IHCS, which I did in 1997. We had our very first meeting to announce our existence at the Holocaust Museum in Houston. This was on April 3, 1997. It's certainly unusual for a Christian organization to have its initial birthing at a "Jewish" Holocaust Museum. But we are living in a time when the Lord is doing some unusual things

We were encouraged that three hundred Christians attended—plus leaders from the Jewish community, as well as Messianic Jews. These people represented communities of faith that had been alienated from each other for centuries, Yet, they were all in the same room sharing a common interest to build relationships of love, understanding, and mutual respect. After touring the Museum, we sang songs about Jerusalem, and I shared the vision of IHCS.

In May, June, July, and August, we were able to bring four well-known conservative, Christian scholars to Houston to speak on the Hebraic/Jewish roots of Christianty. We called this series

Introduction

the "Dr. G. Douglas Young Visiting Scholar Series" named after the pioneering Christian Zionist who established the Institute for Holy Land Studies located in Jerusalem, and later the Bridges for Peace organization. Approximately one hundered people attended each of the lectures.

In September, we began hosting an Erev Shabbat (Eve of Sabbath) celebration event once a month. The theme for each month was based on the Jewish calendar and some Christian connection to the Jewish people throughout history.

The celebration included exhuberant Davidic praise and worship, exciting Hebraic dance, colorful Feast of Tabernacles-type pageantry in anticipation of the soon coming of Messiah, and teaching on the Jewish roots of Christianity.

I had no idea how many people would attend such an event. I hoped for 200-300. My faith was so small. The Lord had bigger and better plans. Naturally I was overwhelmed when 800 people filled up the auditorium even before our scheduled time to start. We have had successful meetings every month since that awesome beginning.

In addition to these powerful and exciting celebration events, we established a nine-month course of study on the Jewish roots of Christianity. The Lord blessed us with seventy hungry students the first year, with seven graduating in the first class with a diploma in Hebraic-Christian Studies.

With God's favor, our gifted and anointed IHCS team is already ministering nationally and internationally. We are truly humbled and grateful that the Almighty has called us to participate in His last great work of binding together the hearts of Jews and righteous Gentiles for the redemption of Jerusalem.

This does not happen by itself. Jews and Gentile believers must discover their common heritage. The purpose of this writing is to inform Christians about their Hebraic/Jewish roots. The intention is not to make Gentile Christians into Jews or put Christians "under the law" but to help us better understand one another. While we recognize that Christendom and Judaism have some theological differences, we do not have to agree on theology to love one another. For if we can't love one another, what good is our theology?

Now is the time for Gentile Christian believers and Jews to start communicating with one another with love, understanding, and mutual respect. May the Lord open our minds and hearts to understand the new prophetic season in which we are living.

Introduction

Chapter 1—Personal Study Guide

1. Why did God promise to bless those who bless Abraham but curse those who curse him?

2. What do we mean when we say the Church is under the "curse of Abraham"?

3. What is the "new thing" God is doing with Christian-Jewish relationships?

Chapter 2
The Jews: A People Who Won't Go Away

In his book *What is a Jew?*, Rabbi Morris Kertzer tells the following story:

"A number of years ago, I invited a Japanese army officer, who was studying in the United States, to attend a religious service which I was conducting.

At the end of the service, as we were walking home, he asked me, 'What branch of Christianity does your church represent?'

'We are Jews,' I answered, 'members of the Jewish faith.'

"My Japanese friend was puzzled. He was a Shintoist, but he had read the Christian Bible.

"But what are 'Jews'?

" 'Do you remember the Israelites in the Bible—Abraham and Moses and Joshua?' He recalled those stories. 'Well, we are those Israelites.' Major Nishi gasped in amazement. 'What! Are those people still around? ' "[2]

Frederick the Great of Prussia once challenged Count Nicholas von Zinzendorf to defend the Bible. Zinzendorf was the founder of the Moravian Christian movement which is best known in history for its prayers and piety.

Zinzendorf knew that the long history of the Jewish people was the best proof of the accuracy of the Bible. He replied in two words: "The Jew!"[3]

Yes, those people are still around! There is simply no other explanation for the survival of the Jewish people down through the ages. They are a people who won't go away. But who are the Jews?

---

2. Rabbi Morris Kertzer, *What is a Jew?* Revised by Rabbi Lawrence A. Hoffman (New York: Macmillan Publishing Company, 1993), xii-xiii.
3. John Phillips, *Exploring the World of the Jew* (Neptune, NJ: Loizeaux Brothers, 1993), 7.

Who Are the Jews?

According to the Bible, the Jews descended from Abraham. He is the first person in the Bible called a "Hebrew" (Genesis 14:13). He was originally named Abram, but God changed his named to Abraham after making covenant with him (Genesis 17:5).

We are not sure of the etymology of the word, "Hebrew." Some believe it is derived from a Semitic word which means "to cross over" or to "migrate." This refers to the fact that Abram crossed over the Euphrates when he left his home for the land God promised him.

"The word *Jew* comes from the Hebrew *Yehudi*, a word originally referring to members of the tribe of Judah [*Yehudah*]."[4] The word means to "praise." God created a unique people out of the human race who would live for His praise on the earth. While the Jews often failed to live up to their high calling, they did give the world the revelation of the one true God.

One of Abraham's descendants was called Jacob. God changed Jacob's name to "Israel" (Genesis 32:28). His descendants were called "The Children of Israel," or the "Israelites." The land God promised to Abraham and his descendants was also called Israel, as it is today.

Eventually, the word "Jew" became the common name for Abraham's natural descendants from Isaac and Jacob.

The word "Judaism" refers to the tradition, culture, religion, and way of life of the Jewish people with its roots in the Bible as opposed to the Gentile worldview and way of life.

Jewish Mother or Jewish Father?

Even though the Jews have been around for centuries, there is still much confusion as to what makes a person a Jew. There is an ethnic understanding and a religious understanding.

---

4. David Rausch, *Building Bridges* (Chicago: Moody Press, 1988), 19.

In Bible times, Jewish physical descent was identified with and passed on through the father. God made His covenant with Abraham and gave him the covenant seal and sign of circumcision indicating that God's covenant people would be physical descendants through the father (Genesis 12-17). This was the original ethnic understanding.

However, over time, Jewish traditional law established that the mother would be the designated parent determining if the child was considered a Jew. Why this change from the father to the mother? There were several reasons.

First, the ancient Jewish sages realized that the identity of the father could be questionable, but not so with the mother. Furthermore, the mother was usually the primary parent providing care, nurture, and the earliest religious orientation to the child.

As a result, Jewish legal tradition accepted the mother, rather than the father, as the designated parent determining the physical or ethnic identification of the child as a Jew. Thus, if the father is a Jew but the mother is not, the child is not considered Jewish. If the mother is a Jew but the father is not, the child is considered Jewish.

In more recent times, some of the Jewish religious denominations such as the Reform and Reconstructionists have accepted the father or the mother as the designated parent, if the father publicly affirms his Jewish identity and raises the child as a Jew. This more liberal view has caused serious problems within the Jewish community because the Orthodox and Conservative Jewish denominations do not accept it.

This means children can be raised as Jews in a Reform tradition only to discover later that the Orthodox denomination does not recognize their Jewishness. If they wanted to marry into an Orthodox or Conservative family, they would be required to convert to the Jewish faith even though they believed they were Jewish.

A similar circumstance is found in Christianity when a Protestant wants to marry a Catholic. Traditionally, the Catholic

Church required the Protestant to convert to Catholicism, even though the Protestant considered himself or herself to be a Christian.

When Is a Jew a Jew?

The Bible also makes a distinction between a person who is a natural descendant of Abraham and one who is a spiritual descendant of Abraham. A person could be born into a Jewish family and have Jewish blood running in his or her veins yet not be a spiritual heir of Abraham. In order to be a spiritual heir of Abraham, the natural born Jew had to worship the God of Abraham. And this worship had to come from their heart.

The great declaration of faith of Judaism is as follows: "Hear, O Israel: The LORD our God, the LORD is one! You shall love the LORD your God with all your heart, with all your soul, and with all your strength" (Deuteronomy 6:4-5).

There were natural-born Jews in Bible times, just as there are today, who did not worship the God of Abraham. There were also natural born Jews who were religious but not true worshippers in their heart. They were not fulfilled or completed in their Jewishness. They were either secular or religious, but they did not have a personal relationship with the God of Abraham. The same is true today of Gentiles who "attend church" but do not have a personal relationship with God.

As Moses observed this lack in the lives of many of the Jews who followed him, he rebuked them with these words, "Therefore circumcise the foreskin of your heart, and be stiff-necked no longer" (Deuteronomy 10:16).

Later, Moses said, "And the LORD your God will circumcise your heart and the heart of your descendants, to love the LORD your God with all your heart and with all your soul, that you may live" (Deuteronomy 30:6).

The prophet Jeremiah also lamented the poor spiritual condition of the people and warned them, "Circumcise yourselves to the LORD, and take away the foreskins of your hearts..." (Jeremiah 4:4).

While many would heed the voice of Moses and the prophets, others hardened their hearts. John the Baptist gave the same rebuke to some of the Jewish leaders of his day.

John said, "Therefore bear fruits worthy of repentance, and do not think to say to yourselves, 'We have Abraham as our father.' For I say to you that God is able to raise up children to Abraham from these stones" (Matthew 3:8-9).

Jesus spoke of this circumcised heart in terms of a spiritual birth. He said to one of the leading Pharisees named Nicodemus, "...Most assuredly, I say to you, unless one is born of water [natural birth] and the Spirit, [spiritual birth], he cannot enter the kingdom of God. That which is born of the flesh is flesh, and that which is born of the Spirit is spirit. Do not marvel that I said to you, 'You must be born again'" (John 3:5-7).

This was not some strange or new teaching from Jesus. He was only clarifying what the prophets said centuries before. For example, the LORD spoke these words through the prophet Ezekiel, "I will give you a new heart and put a new spirit within you; I will take the heart of stone out of your flesh and give you a heart of flesh. I will put My Spirit within you and cause you to walk in My statutes, and you will keep My judgments and do them" (Ezekiel 36:26-27).

The apostle Paul had this natural/spiritual Jew concept in his mind when he wrote, "For he is not a Jew who is one outwardly, nor is circumcision that which is outward in the flesh; but he is a Jew who is one inwardly; and circumcision is that of the heart, in the Spirit, not in the letter; whose praise is not from men but from God" (Romans 2:28-29).

With these words, Paul certainly did not mean that a natural Jew was not a descendant of Abraham. He was simply making the same point that Moses, the prophets, and Jesus made regarding the necessity of worshipping God from your heart.

Paul believed that the only way a Jew could be a true spiritual heir of Abraham and be complete and fulfilled was by having a circumcised heart towards God. As stated earlier, this is also true for Gentiles.

Whose Judaism?

There is also the religious understanding of who is a Jew. From this understanding, a person is a Jew if he accepts the faith of Judaism. But whose Judaism? Once again, there is controversy since the Orthodox Jewish denomination does not recognize the legitimacy of the other Jewish denominations.

The Orthodox only recognize their own tradition as valid Judaism. Therefore, if a person raised in a non-Orthodox tradition wants to immigrate to Israel, he or she must undergo an Orthodox conversion in order to be considered a Jew according to the religious meaning of Jewish.

Proselytes

A person who is not born into a Jewish family may become Jewish by converting to Judaism. While converts will still physically be non-Jewish from birth, they are considered to be Jews by the fact of their religious conversion and identification with the Jewish people. The classic example of this in the Bible is the story of Ruth.

Ruth was a Moabite who left Moab with Naomi, her mother-in-law, and embraced the God of Abraham, Isaac, and Jacob. Her well-known words to Naomi recorded in the Book of Ruth are:

"Entreat me not to leave you, or to turn back from following after you; for wherever you go, I will go; and wherever you lodge, I will lodge; your people shall be my people, and your God, my

God. Where you die, I will die, and there will I be buried. The LORD do so to me, and more also, if anything but death parts you and me" (Ruth 1:16-17).

In Orthodox Judaism, a male who wants to convert to Judaism must be ritually circumcised. Both males and females must be immersed in a *mikveh*.

From a Christian perspective, the *mikveh* is like a baptismal pool in which the convert washes as a symbolic act of ritual purification. Furthermore, the convert is considered spiritually "reborn" in the waters of the *mikveh*.[5] Moses, the prophets, Jesus, Paul, and Orthodox Judaism are in complete agreement regarding the necessity of a spiritual new birth.

Jewish Groups According to Geography and Culture

From the time of the Middle Ages, Jews have been identified as belonging to two major groups, with a third now receiving more recognition. These groupings are based on geographic and cultural considerations. They are: 1) Ashkenazim, 2) Sephardim, and 3) Edot HaMizrach.

Ashkenaz was a grandson of Japheth and greatgrandson of Noah (Genesis 10:1-3; 1 Chronicles 1:4-6). The word Ashkenaz means "Germany" and refers to those Jews who descended from the Jewish communities of Germany, central Europe, and eastern Europe, including Russia and Poland. They had their own language, Yiddish, which was a combination of Hebrew and Old German.

The majority of American Jews are Ashkenazi. They fled here in the nineteenth century as a result of czarist persecution in Russia. These same Russian Jews laid the basis for the modern state of Israel. For most of its history, Ashkenazi Jews have been the majority of the population of Israel. They have also been the financial and political power in Israel.

---

5. Rabbi Wayne Dosick, *Living Judaism* (New York: HarperCollins, 1995), 69.

The word Sepharad means "Spain" and refers to Jews who descended from the Jews of Spain and Portugal. They too had their own language, called Ladino. Sephardic Jews were expelled from Spain in 1492. They fled primarily to the Middle East and North Africa, with some eventually making their way to the Americas.

There are many inhabitants of Central and South America, Mexico, and the southwestern United States who are descendants of Sephardic Jews, yet are not aware of their ancestry.

The third cultural or geographic grouping of Jews is Edot HaMizrach. Edot HaMizrach means "eastern or oriental" and refers to the Jews who lived in Persia, Yemen, Ethopia, and other Near Eastern countries. They are the smallest and least influential of the three groupings.

Because they have lived near the land of the Bible, their culture is much closer to that of the Bible than that of the Ashkenazi and Sephardi Jews. While all three of these groups are Jews, they differ widely in their culture, customs, religious practices, etc.

It has been a challenge for the state of Israel to learn to recognize the value of each group and how to blend the best from each for the benefit of Israeli society. This is especially true with so many immigrants coming to Israel from the former Soviet Union as well as with the many Ethopian Jews who have come to Israel in recent years.

Jewish Denominations

Just as there are different Protestant Christian denominations, there are also different Jewish denominations. As with Christianity, each group reflects a different view and interpretation of Judaism and the Jewish way of life. They have their family squabbles just as we do in the Christian world.

Traditionally, there are three major Jewish religious groups. These are: 1) Orthodox, 2) Reform, and 3) Conservative. A fourth group, which is not recognized by the others at this point, is

Messianic Judaism. Messianic Jews believe that Jesus is the Messiah. This is the fastest-growing branch of Judaism today. A smaller group which denies the existence of a personal God is called Reconstructionist. As with Christianity, these groups range from a very strict interpretation of what it means to be Jewish while others are very liberal in their understanding and practices.

Orthodox Judaism is the traditional, mainstream branch of Rabbinic Judaism that has survived down through the centuries. We might think of them as the "fundamentalists." They believe the Hebrew Scriptures and the Oral *Torah* to be the Word of God. Orthodox Jews seek to keep the commandments of God as interpreted by the rabbis throughout the centuries.

While most Orthodox Jews believe in participating in the secular society in which they live, the "ultra-Orthodox" separate themselves in order to preserve their way of life. The most charismatic of this group is the *Hasidic*. The *Hasidim* are easily recognized by their dress—which includes large, round black hats, long black coats, beards, and sidecurls.

Reform Judaism is a product of the French Revolution, which occurred in the latter part of the eighteenth century. It dramatically improved the condition of Jews living in western Europe.

The eighteenth century in Europe became known as the Enlightenment. It was a period of social, religious, economic, and political upheaval. Jews were accepted as national citizens of the country in which they lived, rather than as Jews who were to be shunned by Gentile society. As a result of this new attitude, many Jews sought to assimilate into their societies by reinterpreting traditional Judaism so it would be more compatible with the "new world." This development led to Reform Judaism.

Reform Judaism began in Germany and was brought to the United States in the nineteenth century. It is the liberal branch of Judaism. Reform Judaism does not believe that the *Torah* is the divinely-inspired Word of God nor does it believe in a physical, personal Messiah. Reform Judaism rejected rabbinic teachings as being binding on their understanding of Judaism. Reform Jews turned away from traditional Jewish practices and rituals such as keeping kosher dietary regulations, wearing ritual garments, etc.

Reform Judaism emphasizes the ethical teachings of Judaism and how to practice them in a way that is compatible with the society in which they live. They seek to assimilate in order to eliminate cultural distinctions between Jews and non-Jews.

Conservative Judaism was established as a backlash against Reform Judaism. The leaders of this movement believed that change was necessary for Judaism to survive but that Reform Judaism was too radical of a change. They wanted more moderate reforms.

Conservative Judaism seeks a meaningful balance between Orthodox beliefs and Reform practices. They accept the *Torah* as the Word of God while they reject the more strict Orthodox traditions. They seek to live out traditional Judaism but in a more contemporary way.

A large percentage of the six million Jews living in the United States are secular. Of those who claim a denominational preference, approximately eleven percent are Orthodox, thirty percent are Reform, and forty percent are Conservative.[6]

The newest, most controversial, and fastest growing branch of Judaism is Messianic Judaism. Messianic Jews believe that Jesus is the Messiah and want to follow Him while maintaining their Jewish heritage, culture, and identity. They want to worship Him in a Jewish way without taking on the Gentile forms and expressions of worship.

Before Israel retook Jerusalem in 1967, there were only a few thousand Messianic Jewish believers. This dramatic fulfillment of Bible prophecy was a prophetic call to Jews around the world to return to their spiritual roots. In doing so, many have come to

---

6. Rabbi Yechiel Eckstein, *What Christians Should Know About Jews and Judaism* (Waco, TX: Word Books, 1984), 230-240.

believe that Jesus is the Messiah spoken of by the prophets in the Hebrew Bible.

The existence of thousands of believers in Jesus who have a Jewish ancestry, and who do not want to be "Christianized," is challenging centuries of tradition in both the Jewish and Christian communities. This is particularly true in Israel where thousands of Russian Jews practice a Jewish form of Christianity.

While many Jews consider the Messianic followers of Jesus no longer to be Jewish and treat them with disdain, this is not a new problem. The very same situation developed in the New Testament when tens of thousands of Jews embraced Jesus as the Messiah. Some of the more prominent Jewish religious leaders in Jerusalem at that time sought to kill the disciples of Jesus.

However, Gamaliel gave the following wise counsel, "And now I say to you, keep away from these men and let them alone; for if this plan or this work is of men, it will come to nothing; but if it is of God, you cannot overthrow it—lest you even be found to fight against God" (Acts 5:38-39).

This is still wise counsel today for Jews and Christians who may not understand the Messianic Jewish followers of Jesus.

The Immortal Jew

In 1898, Mark Twain wrote in *Harper's* magazine:

"If the statistics are right, the Jews constitute but one percent of the human race. It suggests a nebulous dim puff of star dust lost in the blaze of the Milky Way. Properly the Jew ought hardly to be heard of; but he is heard of.

"He is as prominent on the planet as any other people, and his commercial importance is extravagantly out of proportion to the smallness of his bulk.

"His contributions to the world's list of great names in literature, science, art, music, finance, medicine, and abstruse learning are also way out of proportion to the weakness of his numbers....

"The Egyptians, the Babylonians, and the Persians rose, filled the planet with sound and splendor, then faded to dreamstuff and passed away; the Greek and the Roman followed, and made a vast noise for a time, but it burned out, and they sit in twilight now, or have vanished.

"The Jew saw them all and beat them all, and is now what he always was, exhibiting no decadence, no infirmities of age, no weakening of his parts, no slowing of his energies, no dulling of his alert and aggressive mind. All things are mortal but the Jew; all other forces pass, but he remains. What is the secret of his immortality?"[7]

We are all intrigued by secrets. One of the great secrets of the world is how the Jews have managed to survive living among the great sea of hostile Gentile nations. In the next chapter, we will learn the secret to their immortality. The Jews are a people who won't go away.

---
7. Phillips, 121.

Chapter 2—Personal Study Guide

1. Who are the Jews?

2. What is the difference between a natural-born Jew and a Spirit-born Jew?

3. What is the difference between Orthodox, Conservative, and Reform Judaism?

4. What is the difference between Ashkenazim, Sephardim and Edot HaMizrach Jews?

Chapter 3
The Jewish People in the First Testament

Mark Twain wanted to understand the secret of the immortality of the Jew. God revealed the answer to this secret in the Bible. As we will see, the Jews are God's chosen people. That is why they have survived their conquerors.

When the nations of the world have been judged by the Almighty, the Jews will still be around, and Israel will take her rightful place as the head nation on the earth. The Jews have a long history. Let's now learn about God's chosen people in the First Testament of the Bible beginning with the Book of Genesis.

In the Beginning

As a human father desires children, God, our heavenly Father, created human beings in His image and after His likeness so that mankind could know God and fellowship with Him (Genesis 1:27). Unfortunately, God's human children rebelled against their Creator (Genesis 3–5). The world became very wicked.

Moses writes, "Then the LORD saw that the wickedness of man was great in the earth, and that every intent of the thoughts of his heart was only evil continually. And the LORD was sorry that He had made man on the earth, and He was grieved in His heart" (Genesis 6:5-6).

God saw that man would not repent, so He destroyed the world with a great flood. Only Noah and his family were saved along with the animals God had told Noah to put in the ark. This was most likely between 2500 BC and 2400 BC (Genesis 6–8).

We learn in the Bible that Noah had three sons: Shem, Ham, and Japheth (Genesis 9) who repopulated the earth (Genesis 10).

As you can imagine, Noah's sons must have told the story of the flood many times to their descendants. Surely this would have caused them to fear the LORD and walk in His ways. However, when later generations were born, they did not have the same reverence for God. To them, the flood was just a story. Once again, the people rebelled against God (Genesis 11).

The Call of Abraham

Now, God would be perfectly just to judge mankind. However, God is not only just, He is also a merciful God. Instead of destroying mankind, God revealed Himself to one of Shem's descendants. His name was Abram, later Abraham. This was around the year 2090 BC.

Abram lived in Ur of the Chaldeans, which is called Babylon (Genesis 11:28). This is the land area of modern-day Iraq and Kuwait. The Bible tells us that Abram's father, Terah, served "other gods" (Joshua 24:2). The high god of the Babylonians was the Moon-god. Robert Morey writes, "The cult of the Moon-god was the most popular religion throughout ancient Mesopotamia. A temple of the Moon-god has been excavated in Ur by Sir Leonard Woolley. Haran was likewise noted for its devotion to the Moon-god."[8]

Robert Morey dug up many examples of moon worship in Ur which are displayed in the British Museum to this day. He and others have done extensive research connecting the ancient Moon-god of Babylon to the god of Islam, Allah. This is why the crescent moon is the symbol of Islam.

We don't know exactly how the one true God and Abram found each other, but the God of creation revealed Himself to Abram and called him to leave his pagan country and go to a new land that God would give to Abram and his descendants as an everlasting possession.

In Genesis 12 we read, "Now the LORD had said to Abram: 'Get out of your country, from your family and from your father's

---

8. Robert Morey, *The Moon-god Allah In the Archeology of the Middle East* (Newport, PA: Research and Education Foundation, 1994), 4-5.

house, to a land that I will show you. I will make you a great nation; I will bless you and make your name great; and you shall be a blessing. I will bless those who bless you, and I will curse him who curses you; and in you all the families of the earth shall be blessed" (Genesis 12:1-3).

We see that the Lord made three promises to Abram. He promised to give Abram a land, make him a great nation, and bless the world through one of Abram's descendants. Abram would be the father of a new, chosen people who would have a land as an everlasting inheritance for Abram and his descendants. Furthermore, one of Abram's descendants would be the Jewish Messiah and Savior of the world.

The LORD confirmed His word to Abram by making a sacred, blood covenant. This would be a literal, everlasting, unconditional covenant that God would keep in honor of His word to Abram. God then changed Abram's name to Abraham and required Abraham to be circumcised himself as the sign of the blood covenant (Genesis 15–17).

The LORD said to Abraham, "And I will establish My covenant between Me and you and your descendants after you in their generations, for an everlasting covenant, to be God to you and your descendants after you. Also I give to you and your descendants after you the land in which you are a stranger, all the land of Canaan, as an everlasting possession; and I will be their God" (Genesis 17:7-8).

God chose Abraham and his descendants as the human vessels through whom He would reveal Himself to a world that had once again strayed from Him. The LORD said to Abraham's descendants, "For you are a holy people to the LORD your God; the LORD your God has chosen you to be a people for Himself, a special treasure above all the peoples on the face of the earth" (Deuteronomy 7:6).

Abraham's descendants were to fulfill this sacred calling in three ways. First, they were to write down and preserve God's revelation of Himself to mankind (Exodus 24:1-8). The Jews faithfully did this by recording and protecting the Word of God, which eventually became known as the Bible.

Second, the Jews were to reveal the truth about God to the world through the laws God gave them and by their holy lives. As the Jewish people lived in obedience to God's divine instructions, they would be a light to the darkened pagan world, showing them the one true God and what He was really like (Exodus 19:5; Leviticus 11:44-45; 19:1).

Finally, the Jews would fulfill their divine call by bringing the Messiah into the world. As a Christian, my conviction is that Jesus of Nazareth is this Messiah for the Jews as well as the Savior for the Gentiles.

Because God made His covenant with Abraham, He decreed blessings on those who blessed Abraham and curses on those who cursed him. Biblical accounts and modern history have certainly substantiated this divine decree. All nations that have favored the Jews have been blessed by God. But nations that have opposed the Jews have fallen under God's judgment.

The Jews are immortal because God made an everlasting covenant with Abraham in which He promised to preserve a remnant of Abraham's seed down through the ages.

First Chronicles tells us the secret. It says that God will, "Remember His covenant forever, the word which He commanded, for a thousand generations, the covenant which He made with Abraham, and His oath to Isaac, and confirmed it to Jacob for a statute, to Israel for an everlasting covenant" (1 Chronicles 16:15-17).

Abraham's Covenant Descendants

Abraham had no children at the time God made His promises. His wife, Sarah, was too old to have children. Abraham thought he could help God fulfill His promises by having a child through Hagar, Sarah's Egyptian handmaid.

Abraham named the child Ishmael. The Arabs claim Ishmael as their ancestor.

However, this was not God's will. God promised to bless the union of Abraham and Sarah. God miraculously restored Sarah's body so that she conceived and bore Abraham a son named Isaac. God chose to continue His covenant promises to Abraham through Isaac, not Ishmael.

Genesis reads, "And Abraham said to God, 'Oh, that Ishmael should live before you!' Then God said, 'No, Sarah your wife shall bear you a son, and you shall call his name Isaac; I will establish My covenant with him for an everlasting covenant, and with his descendants after him' " (Genesis 17:18-19).

Isaac married Rebekah who bore him twin sons, Esau and Jacob. While these two brothers fought with each other, as siblings often do, God chose to continue His covenant through Jacob, as we learn in the following Scriptures.

God said to Jacob, "…I am the LORD God of Abraham your father and the God of Isaac; the land on which you lie I will give to you and your descendants. Also your descendants shall be as the dust of the earth; you shall spread abroad to the west and the east, to the north and the south; and in you and your seed all the families of the earth shall be blessed" (Genesis 28:13-14).

Later, God repeated His promise to Jacob and changed his name to Israel. We read in Genesis, "And God said to him [Jacob], 'Your name is Jacob; your name shall not be called Jacob anymore, but Israel shall be your name.' So He called his name Israel.

Also God said to him: 'I am God Almighty. Be fruitful and multiply; a nation and a company of nations shall proceed from you, and kings shall come from your body. The land which I gave Abraham and Isaac I give to you; and to your descendants after you I give this land' " (Genesis 35:10-12).

Israel had twelve sons who became the heads of the twelve tribes of Israel (Genesis 49:1-28). The nation of Israel began to come into existence from the offspring of these twelve sons.

One of the sons was named Judah. The LORD chose Judah as head of the family through which would come the kings of Israel (Genesis 49:10). One of these kings would be greater than the others. He would be the King of kings who would make Israel the greater nation God had promised Abraham.

One of Judah's descendants was King David (Genesis 38; Ruth 4:18-22). God chose David as head of the royal family through which He would fulfill His covenant with Abraham.

The LORD said to David, "When your days are fulfilled and you rest with your fathers, I will set up your seed after you, who will come from your body, and I will establish his kingdom. He shall build a house for My name, and I will establish the throne of his kingdom forever…And your house and your kingdom shall be established forever before you. Your throne shall be established forever" (2 Samuel 7:12-13,16).

In this amazing promise, God told David he would have a descendant who would rule over Jerusalem forever. The Jews have always considered this promise to refer to the Messiah who would be David's "Greater Son." The New Testament identifies Jesus of Nazareth as this "Greater Son of David" (Luke 1:30-33).

The Hebrews Enslaved in Egypt

When God made His covenant with Abraham, He told him that his descendants would be slaves in a strange country, but that He would deliver them in the proper time (Genesis 15:13-14). We learn that this strange country was Egypt. How did Abraham's descendants end up in Egypt?

One of Jacob's sons was named Joseph. Joseph made his brothers jealous, so they sold him as a slave to a caravan traveling to Egypt. Joseph suffered much personal tribulation in Egypt, but because he was able to interpret the pharaoh's dream, Pharaoh made Joseph the prime minister of Egypt.

Later, due to a famine, Jacob and his family moved to Egypt where Joseph cared for them. This was around the year 1876 BC.

The Jews prospered in Egypt. Their numbers grew so large that a new pharaoh felt threatened by them and made them slaves.

As time passed, the Jews cried out to God for deliverance. It was during this time that Moses was born about 1527 BC, during the reign of Thutmose I from 1539–1514 BC.[9]

After 430 years in Egypt (Exodus 12:40), God raised up Moses to deliver the Hebrews during the reign of Thutmose III. According to the dating system followed in this text, Thutmose III ruled from approximately 1482–1447 BC.[10]

Thutmose III was the pharaoh who oppressed the Hebrews. Dr. Gleason Archer writes of Thutmose III, "He alone, besides Ramses II, was on the throne long enough…to have been reigning at the time of Moses' flight from Egypt, and to pass away not long before Moses' call at the burning bush, thirty or forty years later. In character he was ambitious and energetic, launching no less than seventeen military campaigns in nineteen years, and engaging in numerous building projects for which he used a large slave-labor task force."[11]

His son, Amenhotep II (1447–1421 BC), was the pharaoh during the Exodus and was judged by God with the ten plagues. The last plague took the life of the firstborn son of Amenhotep II. According to this chronology, the Exodus from Egypt occurred in 1446 BC.

Dr. Archer says of Amenhotep II, "Amenhotep II, who doubtless hoped to equal his father's military prowess, seems to have suffered some serious reversal in his military resources, for he was unable to carry out any invasions or extensive military operations after his fifth year (1445 BC). The relative feebleness of his war

---

9. Gleason L. Archer, *A Survey of Old Testament Introduction* (Chicago: Moody Press, 1994), 236.
10. Ibid., 545.
11. Ibid., 245.

effort (by comparison to that of his father) would well accord with a catastrophic loss of the flower of his chariotry in the waters of the Red Sea during the vain pursuit of the fleeing Israelites."[12]

We further learn that Amenhotep II had a son named Thutmose IV who succeeded his father as pharaoh (1421–1412 BC). When Thutmose IV was a young boy he had a dream in which an Egyptian god appeared to him and promised him he would be the next pharaoh.

If Thutmose IV had been the oldest son of his father, there would be no need for a special promise since he would naturally succeed his father to the throne. The only reason for such a promise was that his older brother, the firstborn of Amenhotep II, died in the plague of the firstborn as recorded in the book of Exodus (Exodus 12:29).[13]

From Egypt to the Promised Land

The LORD parted the Red Sea to allow the Hebrews to escape from Egypt. During the journey to their Promised Land, God gave the Jews the *Torah* by which they would live and walk with Him.

We have traditionally called the *Torah*, "the Law." However, the better sense of the word is "instruction," "guidance," and "direction." The *Torah* was God's instruction to His people for godly living. It included moral instruction, which we call the Ten Commandments, civil instruction, religious instruction including a tabernacle, priesthood, and sacrificial system, as well as dietary instruction and instruction regarding purity.

It was only a few weeks' journey from Egypt to the Promised Land. However, it took the Jews forty years to make the trip. They failed to trust and obey God and murmured the entire way. God told them to conquer the land He had promised them, but instead of doing so, they sent in twelve spies to scout it out.

---

12. Ibid.
13. Ibid., 246.

Ten of the spies reported that the inhabitants were invincible. Only Joshua and Caleb were willing to go in and take the land as God had instructed them. But the people didn't listen. Because of their disobedience, God required them to wander in the desert for forty years until that entire generation died, except for Joshua and Caleb.

From Moses to Samuel

After Moses died, his successor, Joshua, led the people in victory and conquered the land God had promised them. This was about 1406 BC. The land was then divided among the tribes according to the inheritance God gave them. With the battle for Jerusalem at hand in our own times, we must take special note of the fact that God gave the land to the Jews as their everlasting possession.

The LORD told His chosen people to destroy the wicked inhabitants of the land as well as their idols. But the people didn't obey God. They started worshipping the heathen gods and living immorally. Everyone did what was right in his own eyes. It was the darkest hour in the young nation's history.

God chose to use the pagan enemies of Israel as a means of disciplining them to bring them to repentance. When the people were oppressed, they repented and cried out to God for deliverance. God sent judges to deliver them from their enemies. These judges were military leaders. There were thirteen of these deliverers.

At this time in the history of the nation, God ruled over Israel through these judges. It wasn't long after God delivered the people that they returned to their wicked ways. God would then allow them to be oppressed until they repented.

The last judge was Samuel, who guided the young nation during their transition from the period of judges to the monarchy. Samuel was a prophet of the LORD who kept the nation together during this difficult period. The people trusted Samuel. He expected his sons to succeed him. But because they were wicked, the people rejected them and demanded that Samuel appoint a king to govern them (1 Samuel 8).

The Monarchy

Although it was not God's desire for the people to have a human king like all the other nations, God directed Samuel to anoint Saul as the first king of Israel. Saul ruled from about 1050–1010 BC. He was proud and disobeyed God. But because of Samuel's influence, Saul did not lead the nation away from God.

During Saul's rule, God chose David as His king to succeed Saul. Samuel anointed David while David was still a young shepherd boy. Saul became jealous of David, so jealous that David had to live as an outlaw until Saul died. Although David often failed God, he loved God and sincerely wanted to please Him. In fact, the New Testament tells us that David was a man after God's own heart (Acts 13:22).

David united the tribes and was Israel's most-beloved king. As mentioned earlier, God promised David that one of his ancestors would rule over his kingdom forever (2 Samuel 7:12-13,16). David ruled from about 1010–970 BC and was succeeded by his son, Solomon, who ruled from approximately 970–931 BC.

Solomon was very wise and led Israel into her greatest period of glory. His most important accomplishment was building the Temple of worship in Jerusalem. But Solomon also brought disaster on the nation. Contrary to God's instructions (Deuteronomy 7:3-5), Solomon took many foreign wives who led him and the nation into idol worship from which they never recovered (1 Kings 11:1-13).

The Divided Kingdom and the Exile

In order to support his many wives and finance their idol worship, Solomon oppressed the people with excessive taxes and forced labor. They finally revolted in 931 BC, after Solomon's death. The kingdom had a civil war and was divided into north and south (1 Kings 12). This would have tragic consequences for the future of Israel and the Jewish people.

The northern kingdom was called Israel and consisted of ten tribes. The capital was Samaria. The northern kingdom lasted about 210 years until it was conquered by the Assyrians in 721 BC (2 Kings 17). It had nineteen kings who were of nine different families. All of these kings were evil and led the people into idol worship, which was why God brought them to defeat. The ten tribes were scattered throughout the Assyrian empire.

The southern kingdom was called Judah and consisted of the two tribes of Judah and Benjamin. Jerusalem was its capital. It lasted about 325 years until it was conquered by Babylon whose initial siege was in 606 BC. Jerusalem and the Temple were completely destroyed in 586 BC (2 Kings 24–25; 2 Chronicles 36; Jeremiah 52).

The southern kingdom had nineteen kings and one queen, all from the line of David. Some were good and some were evil. Although Judah honored the covenant more so than their brothers to the north, they too eventually turned away from God. This forced God to bring judgment on them as well. The elite were taken captive to Babylon while the poor stayed in the land.

God sent many prophets to warn His people to turn from their wicked ways. When they refused to repent, God was left no choice but to discipline them for their sins. Yet, He promised He would keep His covenant and restore them to their land.

The Return

Jeremiah prophesied that the Jews would be captive in Babylon for seventy years but that God would bring them back to their land at the end of their captivity (Jeremiah 29:10-14). After Persia conquered Babylon in 536 BC, Cyrus issued a decree allowing the Jews to return to their homeland and rebuild their Temple (2 Chronicles 36:22-23).

Zerubbabel led the first group of about 50,000 in 536 BC (Ezra 2). In spite of great obstacles, and with the encouragement of the prophets Haggai and Zechariah, Zerubbabel led the people in rebuilding the Temple of God in Jerusalem. It was completed in about 516 BC (Ezra 1–6).

Then in 458 BC, Ezra led a second expedition of about 2,000. He was a faithful scribe who kept the religious records, helped preserve the laws of God, and taught them to the people (Ezra 7–10).

The Persian king, Artaxerxes, appointed Nehemiah to be the governor of Judah. In 445 BC, he sent Nehemiah to Judah for the purpose of rebuilding the walls of Jerusalem. In spite of many obstacles, Nehemiah was able to rebuild the walls in only fifty-two days (Nehemiah 6:15).

John Phillips tells us of a new development, "Ezra and Nehemiah instituted the practice of reading aloud to the people the canonized books of the Old Testament. They also began the practice of interpreting the difficult passages. The average man no longer spoke Hebrew. Aramaic had replaced it as the language of culture and commerce, and that in itself made the common people dependent on the instruction of their more scholarly peers."[14] As we will see in the next chapter, this language problem set the stage for the development of a scholarly class of religious leaders in Israel.

The godly leadership of Nehemiah and Ezra brought spiritual renewal to the people. They reconfirmed their commitment to their God and the covenant He had made with them through their forefathers (Nehemiah 9–10).

The last prophet in the First Testament of the Bible was Malachi. He prophesied around 435 BC. Once again the people were turning away from God. Malachi rebuked them for their evil ways, exhorted them to keep God's laws, and promised a coming Messiah who would be announced by Elijah the prophet (Malachi 3:1; 4:5-6).

The New Testament presents John the Baptist as the one who came as the forerunner of Jesus. Jesus would be the Messiah for the Jews and Savior for the world (Matthew 17:11-13).

---

14. Phillips, 34.

Malachi brings the period of the First Testament to a close. Momentous events took place during the exile that prepared the Jews for their life between the Testaments. This is the subject of the next chapter.

Chapter 3—Personal Study Guide

1. What was the call of Abraham?

2. Who were Abraham's covenant descendants, including the names of the 12 tribes of Israel?

3. According to Dr. Gleason Archer, who were the pharaohs during the time of Moses and the exodus from Egypt? Name them and describe their importance.

4. Discuss the history of God's covenant people from the time of Moses to Samuel.

5. Discuss the history of God's covenant people from the time of the united monarchy to the divided kingdom and the exile.

6. Discuss the return of God's covenant people from captivity.

Chapter 4
The Jewish People Between the Testaments

The Persian Empire lasted from approximately 536–333 BC. This period ended the history of the First Testament and opened the time of the Jewish people between the Testaments. Great changes took place during this two hundred year period which would have a lasting impact on the Jews in the first century of the Christian era and beyond.

The Greek Period Under Alexander (333–323 BC)

The Persians established a great empire throughout the ancient Near East, including the land of Israel. It was a benevolent rule whose subjects enjoyed a reasonable amount of freedom and peace. Like other mighty empires before and after, it seemed like the Persian empire would last forever. However, it would soon succumb to one of the greatest military leaders of all time, Alexander the Great. Daniel foretold of Alexander in Daniel 2:32 (bronze belly and thighs), 7:6 (leopard), 8:5-8 (large horn), and 11:3-4 (mighty king).

In the middle of the fourth century, Philip of Macedonia was able to unite the various city states of Macedonia into one political power and made himself king of Greece. When he died, Philip was succeeded by his son Alexander, who was only twenty years of age.

As a young man, Alexander was tutored by the great Greek philosopher, Aristotle. Under Aristotle's training, Alexander came to believe that Greek culture was superior to all other cultures. He believed his mission in life was to spread Greek civilization, culture, and language to the rest of the world.

Alexander thought the unthinkable. Perhaps it was youthful zeal or prophetic vision, but he purposed to challenge the mighty Persian empire. Even though Alexander and his armies were greatly outnumbered, he defeated the Persian armies at the Battle of Issus in 333 BC.

Several years later the Persians regrouped, but Alexander defeated them once and for all at the Battle of Gaugamela in 331 BC. King Darius III abandoned his family and wealth and fled the battle. He was assassinated the following year by one of his own men.

Alexander conquered all of the Middle East, including Israel and Egypt, where he built the city of Alexandria in Egypt. The Jews submitted to Alexander's rule and were rewarded with considerable political and religious freedom. Alexander was able to established his empire in just ten years and certainly earned his name, "Alexander the Great."

As mentioned, Alexander wanted to spread Greek culture to the rest of the world. This process was called "Hellenism" based on the ancestral name of the Hellenic race of people that came to be known as Greece or Greeks. When Alexander conquered a city, he populated it with Greek citizens who established Greek city-states and the Greek way of life among the conquered people. They spoke Greek, thought Greek, and acted Greek. They worshipped Greek gods.

In each city they built a stadium for Greek games, a hippodrome for chariot races, a gymnasium for their wrestling matches, public baths and community center, theaters for plays, and temples for their gods.

Soon, the Greek language became the official language of the Mediterranean world and the Greek way of life the norm. Their emphasis on philosophy, literature, beauty, leisure, pleasure, and recreation was very attractive.

This caused great turmoil among the Jews in the empire and in the land of Israel. Some of the Jews were Hellenistic, and many prominent Jews embraced the Greek way of life in order to maintain their positions of influence and wealth.

The pious Jews were horrified. They were bitterly opposed to the Greek way of life. In the athletic events the young men performed nude. In fact the word gymnasium is derived from the Greek word *gymnos*, which means "naked."[15]

The Greek people worshipped the body and considered circumcision a form of mutilation. The young Jewish men were ashamed of their circumcision so they had an operation to disguise it. There was lewd behavior at the bath houses. Many of the Greek plays were immoral.

The true worshippers of YHWH couldn't worship the Greek gods. This clash of cultures set the stage for a later war between the pious Jews who kept the covenant with their God and those who embraced the Greek way of life.

Alexander believed himself to be the son of Zeus. But his untimely death of a fever in Babylon in 323 BC at the young age of thirty-three proved him to be mortal like the rest of us. Not expecting to die at such a young age, Alexander had not made the necessary arrangements for a successor. When his generals asked him to whom he left his empire, he answered, "To the strongest."[16]

The North Against the South

Alexander's four generals fought among themselves to see who would be the strongest. Lysimachus ruled in Thrace and Asia Minor (modern Turkey), Cassander ruled in Macedonia and Greece. Ptolemy I ruled in Egypt and Seleucus I in Syria.

Of these four generals, the two most important in the history of Israel are Ptolemy and Seleucus. They warred for control of the empire, and the little land of Israel was caught right in the middle. The outcome was settled temporarily in 302 BC at the Battle of Ipsus where Ptolemy I defeated Seleucus I.

The Ptolemies ruled the land of Israel from 301 BC to 198 BC. Egypt and Syria fought five major wars against each other

---

15. Daniel Fuchs and Harold Sevener, *From Bondage to Freedom* (Neptune, NJ: Loizeaux, 1995), 87.
16. Ibid., 80.

during this period of time. The Ptolemies won the first four wars with little change in territory. The Seleucids finally defeated them in 198 BC. These five battles were: 1) 274–272, 2) 260–252, 3) 246–241, 4) 221–217, and 5) 201–198 BC.

Their battles are mentioned in the book of Daniel (Daniel 11) where Ptolemy is called the "king of the south" (Egypt) and Seleucus the "king of the north" (Syria).

The Ptolemies established a rich and powerful dynasty in Egypt. Ptolemy I (323–285 BC) established Alexandria as his capital and built it into one of the greatest cities of his day. He and his descendants were among the wealthiest and the most powerful rulers of their times.

It is understood that Daniel 11:5 speaks of Ptolemy I and his son who succeeded him.

Judaism flourished in Alexandria under the Ptolemies, who established a great library and learning center in Alexandria.

Ptolemy II (285–246 BC) is thought to be the king spoken of in Daniel 11:6, who gave his daughter, Bernice, to be the wife of the Syrian king, Antiochus II, in order to make peace between the kingdoms.

Ptolemy II played a major role in the translation of the Hebrew Bible into Greek for the Greek-speaking Jews. This translation, called the *Septuagint*, was the Hebrew Bible (Old Testament) used by the Christians in the New Testament era

Many scholars believe Ptolemy III (246–221 BC) is referred to in Daniel 11:7-9 as the "branch who will enter the fortress of the king of the north." He was provoked to attack the Syrians in 246 BC to avenge the murder of his sister, Bernice, by the Syrians.

Ptolemy IV (221–203 BC) is referred to in Daniel 11:10-12. He was victorious in the fourth war with Syria against Antiochus III (the Great) in 219 BC. In spite of his victory, Ptolemy IV was weak in his resolve and character so that the Ptolemyies' rule in Egypt began to decline with his administration.

Ptolemy V (203–181) is considered by scholars to be the king Daniel spoke of in Daniel 11:14-17 in his battles against Antiochus the Great. Ptolemy V was only a boy when his father died. Antiochus the Great took advantage of this situation and attacked the Egyptians. He defeated them in a hard fought battle at Caesarea Philippi in 198 BC.[17] At this time, Ptolemaic rule over the land of Israel passed into the hands of the Syrians.

Ptolemy VI (181–145) fought against Antiochus IV (Epiphanes). Their battles are described in Daniel 11:25-30. In 168 BC, Antiochus marched his armies to Alexandria and was prepared to conquer the city when he was persuaded to turn back by Rome. Antiochus would turn and vent his anger and frustration against the Jews.

The remaining Ptolemaic kings were each weaker than their predecessors. The last and most famous in the line was Queen Cleopatra who ruled independently with the support of Julius Caesar and Mark Antony until her death in 30 BC. This ended the Ptolemaic dynasty, leaving Rome as the new superpower.

The Ptolemies did not have an aggressive policy of Hellenizing their subjects. The Jews in Israel were free to practice their ancient faith and enjoyed a relative measure of freedom, peace, and prosperity. Yet, they did pay tribute and were ruled by a foreign power.

Along with the political and military battles, a power struggle would develop among the Jews between the House of Tobias and the House of Onias for control of the priesthood in Jerusalem. This would dramatically influence future events and cause a war during the rein of Antiochus IV (Epiphanes).

---

17. Julius Scott Jr., *Customs and Controversies* (Grand Rapids, MI: Baker Books, 1995), 81.

Antiochus IV (Epiphanes) (175–164 BC)

As just mentioned, Antiochus the Great defeated Ptolemy V in 198 B.C. The Romans considered Antiochus a threat to their rising empire. They furiously attacked Antiochus near Greece and thoroughly defeated him. The result of this defeat was that the Romans forced Antiochus to sign a peace treaty called the Treaty of Apemea in 188 BC.

The Romans required Antiochus to make huge payments to them which completely depleted his treasury. The once proud Antiochus the Great was reduced to nothing more than a tax collector for the Romans.

Antiochus raised the taxes on his subjects and robbed their temples of all the treasures he could find. This included the Temple in Jerusalem.

As insurance that Antiochus would pay the tribute, the Romans took captive Antiochus's younger son who later became Antiochus IV (Epiphanes). He was held hostage for fourteen years until he was finally released by the Romans.

Antiochus the Great was succeeded by his son Seleucus IV (Daniel 11:14) who was assassinated by his minister, Heliodorus (Daniel 11:20). Antiochus IV defeated Heliodorus in battle and became king in 175 BC. Antiochus IV referred to himself as Epiphanes, which is a Greek name meaning, "god manifest." By taking this name, Antiochus was representing himself as a manifestation of Zeus. He issued coins with an image representing Zeus, but it was his picture on the coins.

Antiochus Epiphanes sought to Hellenize all the territories under his rule, including Israel and Jerusalem. He also had to pay off the remaining tribute to Rome.

Antiochus attempted to raise money by invading Egypt (Daniel 11:29). He also took control of the priesthood in Jerusalem and "sold" the office of the high priest to the highest bidder.

Antiochus invaded Egypt in 169 BC and soundly defeated the Egyptians. However, Rome did not approve of this war. They sent a delegation to Antiochus demanding that he immediately leave Egypt. In the face of Roman power, Antiochus had no choice but to comply.

This was a bitter defeat for Antiochus. He won the battle against Egypt but lost the war to Rome.

Antiochus Epiphanes and Jerusalem

As previously mentioned, Antiochus took control of the priesthood in Jerusalem and sold the office of the high priest to the highest bidder as a way of raising money. During this time, the bitter rivalry between the House of Tobias and the House of Onias for control of the office of high priest reached its peak.

The Onias clan were descendants of Zadok and the rightful high-priestly family (1 Kings 1:38-39; 1 Chronicles 29:22). They were Orthodox followers of the *Torah*.

The Tobiads were descendants of Tobiah who opposed Nehemiah in his attempt to rebuild the walls of Jerusalem after the return from Babylon (Nehemiah 2:10,19, 6:1). The Tobiads were Hellenistic. They had no legitimate claim to the office of high priest.

The feud between these rivals erupted during the reign of Antiochus Epiphanes. Onias III was the legitimate high priest, but he was loyal to the Ptolemies. Onias's brother, Jason, offered a huge bribe to Antiochus Epiphanes to be made high priest.

Antiochus Epiphanes was desperate for money to send to Rome. He gave permission to the pro-Syrian Hellenizers in Jerusalem to install Jason as the high priest. This appointment of the high priest by a pagan ruler incensed the pious in Jerusalem.

Jason became Hellenistic and did everything he could to make Jerusalem a Greek city. He built a gymnasium and sought to redesign Jerusalem according to the Greek model. Jewish priests dressed like Greeks and participated in Greek idolatry.

Jerusalem was becoming a pagan city. The Pious Ones, or *Hasidim*, were devastated. However, matters got worse. Another Hellenizer, Menelaus, offered Antiochus Epiphanes even more money for the office of high priest.

Menelaus was a Tobiad and not a member of the priestly line. This mattered not to Antiochus Epiphanes who appointed him as the new high priest, thus ending the succession of the Aaronic-Zadok priestly line. Menelaus was so thoroughly Hellenistic that he even assisted Antiochus Epiphanes in confiscating the Temple wealth.[18]

All of this turmoil was happening in Jerusalem at the same time that the Romans forced Antiochus Epiphanes to leave Egypt. The Jerusalemites heard a rumor that Antiochus Epiphanes had been killed in Egypt. They took this opportunity to revolt.

When Antiochus Epiphanes heard about this, he marched on Jerusalem to vent his rage and put down the revolt. This was in 168–167 BC. Daniel prophesied this in Daniel 11:30-31.

Antiochus Epiphanes believed that his problems with the Jews were caused by the Jewish religion, which he clearly planned to destroy by forbdding the Jewish people to practice their ancient faith. They could not practice circumcision, observe the Sabbath, celebrate the feasts, keep their dietary laws, study the *Torah*, or in any way worship their God.

Antiochus Epiphanes stopped the Temple ritual and ordered the burning of the *Torah*. He erected a statue of Zeus in the Temple bearing his own image. He built a new altar dedicated to Zeus on which he offered a sacrificial pig. He then poured the pig's blood over the *Torah*.[19]

---
18. Ibid., 82.
19. Fuchs and Sevener, 97.

The Jewish People Between the Testaments

Antiochus Epiphanes erected shrines and altars throughout the land and forced the people to make sacrifices as tokens of their acceptance of the Greek gods.

Those who disobeyed were either tortured or killed, or both. Their bodies were mutilated, and while still alive and breathing, they were crucified. The wives and the sons whom they had circumcised were strangled. The mothers were then crucified with the dead bodies of their children made to hang around their necks.

This period of time was one of the most gruesome in the long sad history of persecution of the Jewish people. Without God's intervention, they would have surely perished from the earth.

We learn of these events in the Apocryphal books of 1 and 2 Maccabees. First Maccabees reads: "Then the king wrote to his whole kingdom that all should be one people, and that all should give up their particular customs. All the Gentiles accepted the command of the king. Many even from Israel gladly adopted his religion; they sacrificed to idols and profaned the sabbath.

"And the king sent letters by messengers to Jerusalem and the towns of Judah; he directed them to follow customs strange to the land, to forbid burnt offerings and sacrifices and drink offerings in the sanctuary, to profane sabbaths and festivals, to defile the sanctuary and the priests, to build altars and sacred precincts and shrines for idols, to sacrifice swine and other unclean animals, and to leave their sons uncircumcised.

"They were to make themselves abominable by everything unclean and profane, so that they would forget the law and change all the ordinances. He added, 'And whoever does not obey the command of the king shall die' " (1 Maccabees 1:41-50).

We further learn from 1 Macabbees, "Now on the fifteenth day of Chislev, in the one hundred forty-fifth year [167], they erected a desolating sacrilege on the altar of burnt offering. They also built altars in the surrounding towns of Judah, and offered incense at the doors of the houses and in the streets.

"The books of the law that they found they tore to pieces and burned with fire. Anyone found possessing the book of the covenant, or anyone who adhered to the law, was condemned to death by decree of the king....

"On the twenty-fifth day of the month they offered sacrifice on the altar that was on top of the altar of burnt offering. According to the decree, they put to death the women who had their children circumcised, and their families and those who circumcised them; and they hung the infants from their mothers' necks (1 Maccabees 1:54-61).

The Maccabees (167–142 BC)

Unfortunately, many of the leaders in Israel, especially from the upper class, embraced Hellenism. However, the lovers of *Torah* rebelled. The revolt started in 167 BC in the little town of Modein (Modiin). One of the king's officers erected a pagan altar and commanded the people to sacrifice a pig on the altar as a show of loyalty to Antiochus Epiphanes.

The king's officers ordered an aged priest named Mattathias to be the first to obey in order to set an example for the rest of the town. Mattathias refused, at which time a local Jew stepped forward to make the sacrifice.

Mattathias killed the apostate as well as the king's officer and tore down the altar. He fled with his five sons into the hills and were soon joined by the *Hasidim* and the common people who were zealous for the *Torah*.

First Maccabees gives the following account, "The king's officers who were enforcing the apostasy came to the town of Modein to make them offer sacrifice. Many from Israel came to them; and Mattathias and his sons were assembled.

"Then the king's officers spoke to Mattathias as follows: 'You are a leader, honored and great in this town, and supported by sons and brothers. Now be the first to come and do what the king commands, as all the Gentiles and the people of Judah and those that are left in Jerusalem have done. Then you and your sons will be numbered among the Friends of the king, and you and your sons will be honored with silver and gold and many gifts.'

"But Mattathias answered and said in a loud voice; 'Even if all the nations that live under the rule of the king obey him, and have chosen to obey his commandments, everyone of them abandoning the religion of their ancestors, I and my sons and my brothers will continue to live by the covenant of our ancestors. Far be it from us to desert the law and the ordinances. We will not obey the king's words by turning aside from our religion to the right hand or to the left.'

"When he had finished speaking these words, a Jew came forward in the sight of all to offer sacrifice on the altar in Modein, according to the king's command. When Mattthias saw it, he burned with zeal and his heart was stirred. He gave vent to righteous anger; he ran and killed him on the altar. At the same time he killed the king's officer who was forcing them to sacrifice, and he tore down the altar....

"Then Mattathias cried out in the town with a loud voice, saying, 'Let every one who is zealous for the law and supports the covenant come out with me!' Then he and his sons fled to the hills and left all that they had in the town" (1 Maccabees 2:15-25, 27-28).

The family which led the revolt was given the name "Maccabees." We are not sure how this name originated. Some say it is an acrostic created by combining the first letter of the Hebrew words which means, "Who among the mighty is like You?" A second view is that the word "Maccabee" is derived from the Hebrew word for "hammer," which is a picture of great strength. Judah, the leader, was therefore called the Maccabee because of his great strength.

Rededicating the Temple

Mattathias died shortly after the beginning of the revolt, but three of his sons, of whom Judah(s) Maccabees was the leader, carried on the guerrilla struggle against the forces of Hellenism. The army of Antiochus Epiphanes was much larger and more powerful than the righteous remnant of Israel. Yet, God was with His covenant people and helped Judah defeat the forces of Antiochus Epiphanes.

In 164 BC, exactly three years after the altar to Zeus had been set up, the Temple in Jerusalem was cleansed, and the daily sacrifices and religious ceremonies resumed. That rededication of the Temple is still commemorated each December as Hanukkah, the Feast of Lights.

First Maccabees reads, "Early in the morning on the twenty-fifth day of the ninth month, which is the month of Chislev, in the one hundred forty-eighth year, [164 BC] they rose and offered sacrifice, as the law directs, on the new offering of burnt offering that they had built.

"At the very season and on the very day that the Gentiles had profaned it, it was dedicated with songs and harps and lutes and cymbals. All the people fell on their faces and worshipped and blessed Heaven, who had prospered them. So they celebrated the dedication of the altar for eight days....

"Then Judas and his brothers and all the assembly of Israel determined that every year at that season the days of dedication of the altar should be observed with joy and gladness for eight days, beginning with the twenty-fifth day of the month of Chislev" (1 Maccabees 4:52-56, 59).

Judah(s) Maccabees (164–160 BC)

As previously mentioned, when Mattathias died, Judah was chosen to carry on the revolt against Hellenization. Judah was one of the most extraordinary military leaders in ancient history. Although greatly outnumbered by the Syrians, Judah won victory after victory against the superior forces of Antiochus Epiphanes.

With help from the Almighty, Judah succeeded in defeating the Syrians and won the struggle for religious freedom. But religious freedom only whetted his appetite for political freedom.

Judah wanted political independence as well as religious freedom. He embarked on further military campaigns against the Syrians. Antiochus Epiphanes had died in 164 BC, but the Syrians were still a powerful force.

While the LORD used Judah to destroy the "abomination of desolation," Judah's time was over. He was killed in 160 BC while fighting against a much larger and more powerful Syrian army.

The *Hasidim* were content with their religious freedom. They had no political interest nor did they care about territorial conquests. When Judah continued to fight the Syrians, the *Hasidim* withdrew their support. As the Maccabbean dynasty became more secular, some of the more zealous *Hasidim* apparently went to Qumran where they established a community generally thought to be the Essenes.[20] Scholars believe the more moderate *Hasidim* were the forerunners to the Pharisees.

Jonathan (160–143 BC)

When Judah died, his brother Jonathan became the new leader of the Maccabees and their followers. Jonathan was not a great military leader like his brother. He was more of a politician, and he used his political skills to play his enemies against one another. In this way, Jonathan was able to gain favorable concessions from his enemies who were competing for his support. Through his leadership, Israel was able to gain territory and more political freedom from the Syrians.

The most significant event during his time happened in 152 BC, when Jonathan secured for himself the office of high priest. While many welcomed this appointment, some of the *Hasidim* opposed it. This was because the Maccabees were not from the line of Zadok, although they were from a priestly family. Jonathan now had both political and religious authority. This would be bad for

---

20. Robert L. Cate, *A History of the New Testament and Its Times* (Nashville, TN: Broadman Press, 1991), 80.

the future of the Jewish people, as it is dangerous for one person to hold both political and religious offices.

While Jonathan made significant progress towards Jewish independence, historians believe his personal ambition and lust for power led him away from the ideals that began the revolt in Modein years earlier. He was murdered in 143 BC in a betrayal by Trypho, a Syrian ruler who felt threatened by Jonathan's power.

Simon (143–134 BC)

Simon succeeded his brother as the new leader of the revolution. Judah paved the way militarily while Jonathan paved the way politically. Simon was the beneficiary. In 142 BC, Simon negotiated a treaty with Syria which gave the Jews real independence. Simon was also successful in driving out the Syrian garrison which had been stationed in Jerusalem.

Simon became the military, political, and religious leader of Israel. He was for all practical purposes, the king of the Jews. He brought peace and prosperity to the people and appears to have been a wise ruler. Although he was of the line of Aaron, he was not of the Zadok family. Furthermore, he was not of the house of David, which deeply troubled the *Hasidim*. It is believed that at this time many *Hasidim* went to Qumran.

In 141 BC, the people, including the priests, acknowledged Simon as both their civil leader and high priest forever and the two offices were made hereditary in Simon's family.

First Maccabees reads, "The Jews and their priests have resolved that Simon should be their leader and high priest forever, until a trustworthy prophet should arise, and that he should be governor over them and that he should take charge of the sanctuary and appoint officials over its tasks and over the country and the weapons and the strongholds, and that he should take charge of the sanctuary, and that he should be obeyed by all…" (1 Maccabees 14:41-43).

Simon was assassinated in 134 BC by a member of his own family. This would set the stage for a new generation of leaders.

The Hasmonean Successors

Simon was the last of the sons of Mattathias. While they had their faults, Judah, Jonathan, and Simon were great heroes who helped stay the hand of Hellenism and gained independence for their people.

Their rule would pass to Simon's descendants who did not serve the people as well as the Maccabean brothers. They wanted more power and wealth and lost their zeal for the *Torah*. While they would have the support of the wealthy Sadducees, the Pharisees and common people would no longer support them. They were in the line of Aaron, but they were not of the family of Zadok. Furthermore, they functioned as kings even though they were not of the house of David.

John Hyrcanus (134–104 BC)

John Hyrcanus succeeded Simon as ruler of Israel. Like his father, he was the political, military, and religious leader functioning as high priest. He desired to establish Israel as an independent kingdom with borders approximating those in the time of David and Solomon. He had Hellenistic tendencies and acted like a king over the people.

Hyrcanus conquered Samaria and destroyed the Samaritan temple on Mount Gerizim in 107 BC. This ended any possibility of reconciliation between the Jews and Samaritans and fanned the fires of hatred between the two groups.

Hyrcanus conquered Idumaea and forced the inhabitants to accept Judaism, requiring that all the males be circumcised. This had terrible consequences for the Jews as Daniel Fuchs and Harold Sevener write, "This terrible act was to have a terrifying result, for among the Idumeans 'converted' to Judaism was the grandfather of

Herod the Great....When Hyrcanus forcibly circumcised Herod's grandfather, he gave legitimacy to Herod's claim as king of the Jews."[21]

By the early part of John's rule, Judaism had formed the two parties called the Pharisees and the Sadducees. At first, John Hyrcanus sided with the Pharisees. However, when a member of the Pharisees demanded that he relinquish his office as high priest, Hyrcanus broke with them and joined forces with the Sadducees.[22]

Aristobulus I (104–103 BC)

Aristobulus I succeeded his father as the new ruler of Israel. He was the first Hasmonean ruler to actually take the title of king. He was afraid of his mother and brothers, so he put them all in jail except for one brother whom he later killed. He had his mother starved to death while she was in prison so there would be no competition for his throne.

Aristobulus's name was Judah in Hebrew. But he was so Hellenized, he changed it to his Greek name and acted as badly as the pagan kings around him. He did conquer much of Galilee and compelled the Galileans to accept Judaism. This set the stage for the Galilean ministry of Jesus in the New Testament. Much to the relief of the people, Aristobulus I died of a terrible sickness one year after becoming king.

Alexander Jannaeus (103–76 BC)

Aristobulus died without an heir to succeed him. His widow was a very capable woman named Salome Alexandra. She released Aristobulus' brothers from prison and married one of them, Alexander Jannaeus. Through his marriage to Salome Alexandra, Alexander Jannaeus became both king and high priest.

---

21. Fuchs and Sevener, 120.
22. D.S. Russell, *Between the Testaments* (Philadelphia: Fortress Press, 1968), 33.

Alexander Jannaeus followed the policies of John Hyrcanus in conquering and Judaizing surrounding territories. He was a ruthless dictator who alienated the Pharisees and the common people. He was only able to maintain his power by force.

On one occasion, during the Feast of Tabernacles, Alexander Jannaeus purposefully poured water on the ground rather than on the altar as was the custom. This action so infuriated the Pharisees and worshippers who were in the Temple that they pelted him with citron fruit. Alexander responded by having his soldiers kill six thousand worshippers.[23]

The relationship between Alexander Jannaeus and his subjects got so bad that a civil war broke out that lasted for six years. Alexander crushed the revolt by arresting eight hundred of the rebel leaders and crucifying them in Jerusalem. Before the victims died, Alexander had their families brought before them and executed them before their eyes.[24]

For Alexander, this was after-dinner entertainment for his palace guests in Jerusalem.

Alexander realized that his successor would need the help of the Pharisees to rule the country. So just prior to his death, he appointed Salome as queen and advised her to make peace with the Pharisees. This would have a great impact on Jewish life in the New Testament period.

Salome Alexandra (76–67 BC)

Salome was a widow for the second time. She would now rule in her own name as queen. She was a wise and able ruler, having observed the failure of two husbands who preceded her as king. Salome took the advice of Alexander Jannaeus and made the Pharisees her political advisors. They grew very powerful under her rule and dominated the Sadducees.

---

23. Cate, *A History of the Bible Lands in the Interbiblical Period*, 100.
24. Ibid.

When Salome died, a civil war started between her two sons, John Hyrcanus II who was supported by the Pharisees and Aristobulus II, who was supported by the Sadducees.

Aristobulus II (67–63 BC) Versus Hyrcanus II

Since Salome, being a woman, could not serve as high priest, she appointed Hyrcanus II to this office. Hyrcanus was a rather mild man who lacked ambition. He was controlled by his mother and the Pharisees. Aristobulus II was the opposite of Hyrcanus II. Aristobulus II was ambitious and wanted to be king. The Sadducees saw Aristobulus II as a champion for their cause.

Soon a civil war broke out between the two brothers and their supporters. Aristobulus defeated Hyrcanus and appointed himself as king. Since Hyrcanus had no real ambition to rule, Aristobulus allowed his brother to retire in peace. However, another person with ambition came on the scene who would cause the downfall of Aristobulus. His name was Herod Antipater.

Jerusalem Falls to Pompey (63 BC)

Herod Antipater was an influential Idumean (Edomite) living in Jerusalem. He was ambitious and saw an opportunity to use the defeat of Hyrcanus II to further his own plans to gain power. He persuaded Hyrcanus to fight against Aristobulus and convinced the Nabatean ruler, Aretas III, to assist Hyrcanus in the struggle.

Both Hyrcanus and Aristobulus pleaded to the Roman general Pompey for help. At first, Pompey sided with Aristobulus but then switched to Hyrcanus. Aristobulus fled to Jerusalem to take refuge. Pompey saw this as an opportunity to establish Roman presence in Judea and Jerusalem.

It was on the Sabbath in the Hebrew month of Sivan (June), 63 BC, when Pompey's soldiers broke through the walls of Jerusalem and Pompey entered the Holy of Holies in the Temple.

Jerusalem came under Roman control, and the Jews hated the Romans for violating their Temple.

Herod Antipater and John Hyrcanus II (63–40 BC)

The Romans appointed Hyrcanus as high priest and made him a figurehead ruler. But Herod Antipater was the real power in Judea. Antipater was totally loyal to Rome, which used Antipater to control Hyrcanus. Eventually, Antipater was given governing authority of Judea which would pass to one of his sons, Herod the Great. Antipater was poisoned in 43 BC.

Aristobulus II had a son named Antigonus. At that time the remnant of the old Persian empire was called Parthia. The Parthians temporarily drove the Romans out of Syria and placed Antigonus on the throne of Judea. They took Hyrcanus captive and had his ears cut off to prevent him from ever serving as high priest (Leviticus 21:17-21).[25]

Antigonus (40–37 BC)

Antigonus ruled for three brief years in Judea as a puppet king-priest for the Parthians. Before his death, Antipater had his son Herod named as governor of Galilee. Herod had to flee for his life. He took his family south to Masada where they would be safe. Herod then went to Egypt where Cleopatra helped him make a safe journey to Rome. While in Rome, Herod secured the support of the Romans to rule Judea.

The Romans defeated the Parthians in 38 BC. Herod defeated Antigonus in 37 BC at Mount Arbel. This ended the rule of the Hasmoneans. Herod then took control of Jerusalem and began his reign. He secured the release of Hyrcanus II and brought him to Jerusalem where Hyrcanus lived in comfort. Herod was paranoid

---
25. Ibid., 113.

and suspicious of everyone. He executed Hyrcanus seven years later in 30 BC.

Herod (37–4 BC) and the Romans

Let's now look back a few years to put Herodian rule into context. In 55 BC, the Roman empire was ruled by three powerful men: 1) Pompey, 2) Crassus, and 3) Julius Caesar. Crassus was killed in 51 BC while fighting the Parthians. With Crassus dead, Julius Caesar and Pompey fought for control of the empire. Caesar defeated Pompey who fled to Egypt and was assassinated.

Herod Antipater had the good sense to support Julius Caesar in his war with Pompey. As a result, Caesar appointed Antipater as governor of Judea. At this time, Antipater gave Herod the command of Galilee. With no rivals, Caesar ruled Rome as a virtual dictator. This caused great alarm among many in the Roman Senate. Led by Brutus and Cassius, Caesar was assassinated on March 15 in 44 BC.

This led to another triumvirate in Rome comprised of Mark Antony, Lepidus, and Octavian (Julius Caesar's nephew and adopted son). They defeated Brutus and Cassius but then fought among themselves for control of the empire. In order to make peace, Octavian gave his sister, Octavia, in marriage to Antony who confirmed Herod's position as governor of Galilee. With Antony's backing, the Roman Senate and Octavian agreed to make Herod king of Judea.

Herod took the throne in 37 BC, bringing an end to the Hasmonean dynasty. Meanwhile, Antony fell in love with Cleopatra and married her. This was a great insult to Octavian and his family. War was inevitable. Octavian defeated the forces of Antony and Cleopatra in 31 BC. He returned to Rome in triumph as the sole ruler of the Roman empire. Octavian was the first Roman ruler with the title "Augustus." He was then called Augustus Caesar and ruled Rome from 31 BC to AD 14.

Herod's Reign

From all that we know about Herod, we can best describe him as a charming, clever, cruel, paranoid, evil genius. His father, Antipater, as previously mentioned, was an Idumean (Edomite). His mother (Cypros), was an Arabian.[26]

As we've learned, the Romans appointed Herod as king of Judea. Upon his election in Rome, Herod sacrificed to Jupiter, the Roman high god. This clearly showed that Herod had no religious convictions and would do whatever was necessary to further his career.

While Herod tried hard to win the favor and respect of the people, they hated him because he was a Hellenistic, Roman puppet as well as being an Edomite. The only way Herod could maintain his rule was by cruel force.

When Herod became king, he sought to establish his legitimacy to the throne by marrying Mariamne, the beautiful granddaughter of Hyrcanus. Herod had ten wives and numerous children who all competed for his throne. He killed so many of his family members that Augustus Caesar observed, "It is better to be Herod's pig than his son."[27]

Herod was an able administrator who was totally loyal to Rome. He built numerous monuments to Caesar and held festivals throughout the land which he dedicated to Caesar. He is best known for rebuilding the Temple in Jerusalem. This was a major project that began in 20 BC and was not finished until AD 64, long after his death. It was a magnificent structure and one of the wonders of the ancient world.

Herod used his authority to appoint the high priest regardless of their ancestry or character. They served only as long as they pleased him. Initially, Herod appointed a Babylonian Jew named Hananel as high priest, but Hananel was not of the high-priestly

---

26. Fuchs and Sevener, 138.
27. Cate, *A History of the New Testament and Its Times*, 91.

line.[28] This appointment angered his mother-in-law, who wanted her son, Aristobulus, to be high priest. Aristobulus was very popular with the people. Herod saw this as a threat and drowned Aristobulus in a supposed swimming accident in his palace.

In a jealous rage, Herod killed Mariamne in 29 BC as well as two of his sons, Alexander and Aristobulus, whom he suspected of plotting to overthrow him in 7 BC. Herod later killed another son, Antipater, for the same reason, just before his own death in 4 BC.

In the latter years of his reign, Herod placed a Roman eagle over the gate of the Temple. This was an abomination to the Pharisees. When Herod was on his deathbed, the Pharisees heard a rumor that Herod was dead. Two leading rabbis, Judas and Matthias, pulled down the Roman eagle. However, the rumor was false. When Herod was told what happened, he killed numerous Pharisees and burned the two rabbis at the stake.

Herod knew that the people hated him and would not mourn his death. Just before Herod died, he made his sister, Salome, promise that she would execute thousands of Jewish leaders he had imprisoned to make sure there would be mourning at his death. Fortunately, she did not carry out his decree.

When Herod died in 4 BC, his family gave him an elaborate funeral with much pomp and ceremony. The procession began in Jericho and proceeded to the Herodium where Herod was buried.

Before he died, Herod divided his kingdom among three of his sons. But the real King of the Jews would not come from Herod. He had been born several years earlier in Bethlehem of the house of David.

---

28. Fuchs and Sevener, 151.

Chapter 4—Personal Study Guide

1. Describe the Greek period under Alexander.

2. Explain what happened after Alexander died.

3. Tell the story of Antiochus IV (Epiphanes).

4. Who were the Maccabees?

5. Explain the significance of the following people:
   A. Judah Maccabees

   B. Jonathan Maccabees

   C. Simon Maccabees

5. Tell the story of Herod including his relationship with the Romans and the character of his reign.

Chapter 5
The Jewish People in the New Testament Era

As we have learned, Herod was not a Jew. He was an Idumean. He was not a legitimate king of the Jews. He was appointed king by the Romans. Regardless of what the Romans decreed, the God of Heaven appointed the descendants of David to be the kings of Israel (2 Samuel 7:12-16; 1 Chronicles 17:11-14).

According to the prophet Micah, there would be a King-Messiah who would be born in Bethlehem (Micah 5:2). He would not only be King of the Jews but King of kings and Lord of lords.

Jesus of Nazareth—King of the Jews

The Gospel of Matthew tells us that Jesus was born in Bethlehem when Herod was ruling as king of the Jews. Matthew writes, "Now after Jesus was born in Bethlehem of Judea in the days of Herod the king, behold, wise men from the East came to Jerusalem, saying, 'Where is He who has been born King of the Jews? For we have seen His star in the East and have come to worship Him'" (Matthew 2:1-2).

These "wise men" from the East were actually astronomers who saw an unexplained phenomenon in the heavens, which they somehow interpreted as a sign from God that the true King of the Jews had been born. They had journeyed to Judea to worship Him.

When Herod heard that a future king of the Jews had been born he asked the Jewish religious leaders in Jerusalem where this king was to be born, under pretense that he wanted to go and worship him. Of course he really wanted to kill him.

The religious leaders answered, "...In Bethlehem of Judea, for thus it is written by the prophet: 'But you, Bethlehem, in the land of Judah, are not the least among the rulers of Judah; for out of you shall come a Ruler who will shepherd My people Israel'"* (Matthew 2:5-6).

Herod then sent for the wise men to learn when they had seen the star (Matthew 2:7) and to report the whereabouts of the child. Apparently it was two years earlier because Herod had all the male babies in Bethlehem two years old and under killed. The wise men left the country without reporting to Herod.

Matthew writes, "Then Herod, when he saw that he was deceived by the wise men, was exceedingly angry; and he sent forth and put to death all the male children who were in Bethlehem and in all its districts, from two years old and under, according to the time which he had determined from the wise men (Matthew 2:16).

Matthew explains that Herod killed the male babies two years old and under based on the time when the wise men first saw the sign (His star) in the heavens. Since we know that Herod died in 4 BC, Jesus was born between 6–4 BC. This was when Caesar Augustus ruled in Rome from 27 BC to AD 14.

Luke provides further information about the birth of Jesus, explaining that He was born at the time when Augustus issued a decree to take a census for tax purposes. This was when Quirinius was governor of Syria. Quirinius had two terms as governor of Syria from 12 BC to 6 BC and again from AD 6 to AD 16.[29]

Luke explains, "And it came to pass in those days that a decree went out from Caesar Augustus that all the world should be registered. This census first took place while Quirinius was governing Syria.

"So all went to be registered, everyone to his own city. Joseph also went up from Galilee, out of the city of Nazareth, into Judea, to the city of David, which is called Bethlehem, because he was of the house and lineage of David, to be registered with Mary, his betrothed wife, who was with child.

---
29. Cate, *A History of the New Testament and Its Times*, 121.

"So it was, that while they were there, the days were completed for her to be delivered. And she brought forth her firstborn Son, and wrapped Him in swaddling clothes, and laid Him in a manger, because there was no room for them in the inn" (Luke 2:6-7).

There is good reason to believe that Jesus was born during the Jewish Feast of Tabernacles. According to Luke 1:5, Zecharias was a priest of the division of Abijah. Luke 1:8,11 tells us that Gabriel appeared to Zecharias when he was serving as a priest in the Temple. Based on rabbinic writings, the division of Abijah served as priests during the second half of the fourth month on the Jewish religious calendar. This was late June when Elizabeth conceived John the Baptist.

According to Luke 1:35-36, Mary conceived Jesus in the sixth month of Elizabeth's pregnancy. This means that Jesus was conceived during the latter part of the Jewish month of Kislev, or late December on the Gentile calendar. Jesus was born nine months later, most likely during the Feast of Tabernacles.

The Gentile "Christian" calendar is dated based on the birth of Jesus as first suggested by a Syrian monk by the name of Dionysius Exiguus in the sixth century AD. Unfortunately, Dionysius made some errors in calculating his dates, which is why Jesus was actually born earlier than the first century of the Christian era.

The years before the birth of Jesus are designated as BC while those after His birth are referred to as AD, meaning *anno Domini*, "in the year of our Lord." Since Rabbinic Judaism does not recognize Jesus as Messiah, the Jewish calendar designates time either as BCE (Before the Common Era) or CE (the Common Era).

Jesus' Mission

According to the New Testament Scriptures and Christian understanding, Jesus was the revelation of deity in human flesh. Jesus was born of a virgin (Isaiah 7:14; Matthew 1:18-23), of the

house of David (Luke 1:31-33). He was the God-Man who came to earth to:
1. Give mankind a perfect revelation of the unseen God (John 1:14; 14:7-10)
2. Be a light to the Gentiles and the glory of Israel (Luke 2:32)
3. Announce the Kingdom of God (Matthew 4:17, 23)
4. Reveal the true meaning of *Torah* (Matthew 5:17)
5. Fulfill the Hebrew Scriptures (Luke 24:44-48)
6. Give His life as atonement for sin (John 1:29)
7. Redeem us and reconcile us to God (1 Peter 1:18-21; Colossians 1:19-23)
8. Activate the new covenant (Jeremiah 31:31-34; Matthew 26:26-28)
9. Impart God's divine life to us (John 10:10; 2 Peter 1:4)
10. Call people to follow Him (Matthew 4:18-22)
11. Commission His followers to spread His message (Matthew 28:18-20)
12. Rule over Israel and the nations as King and Lord (Psalm 2; Revelation 19:11-16).

Jesus the Jew

Jesus was not a European nor a Palestinian. He was certainly not a Christian in the modern sense of the term. He did not intend to establish a new religion called Christianity. His purpose was to renew the First Covenant by breathing the life of God into it and writing it on the fleshly tablets of our hearts. We would call Jesus a revivalist.

Jesus made His intentions very clear by saying, "Do not think that I came to destroy the Law or the Prophets. I did not come to destroy but to fulfill. For assuredly, I say to you, till heaven and earth pass away, one jot or one tittle will by no means pass from the law till all is fulfilled" (Matthew 5:17-18).

Jesus was a Jew born into a Jewish family in Bethlehem between 6–4 BC during the rule of Augustus Caesar in Rome and Herod in the land of Israel. Jesus was circumcised on the eighth day according to the *Torah* and was dedicated to the God of Abraham, Isaac, and Jacob at the Temple in Jerusalem (Genesis 17:12; Leviticus 12:3; Luke 2:21). His Hebrew name is *Yeshua*.

Jesus was raised in Nazareth in a very poor Jewish family (Luke 2:24). He apparently had four brothers and two sisters (Matthew 13:55-56). Jesus read the Jewish Scriptures (Luke 4:16-21), spoke Hebrew (Acts 26:14), wore Jewish clothes (Matthew 9:20), ate only Jewish food (Matthew 26:26-28), kept the Jewish Sabbath (Luke 4:16), celebrated the Jewish feasts (John 7:1-10, 37-39), followed Jewish customs (Matthew 8:1-4), and lived His entire life as a *Torah* observant Jew (Matthew 2:22-23; Luke 2:39-40).

Jesus' Ministry

Jesus most likely began His ministry in AD 28–29 when He was announced by John the Baptist. We learn this from Luke, who tells us that John the Baptist began his ministry in the fifteenth year of the reign of Tiberius (Luke 3:1-3). Tiberius was emperor from AD 14–37. The fifteenth year of his reign would be AD 28.

Jesus ministered as an itinerant rabbi to the poor and needy (Isaiah 61:1-2; Luke 4:16-21) and performed many miracles (Isaiah 35:4-6; Matthew 11:1-6). He clearly presented Himself as the Jewish Messiah (John 10:22-30). He was rejected as Messiah by a small handful of powerful Jewish leaders (Matthew 27:1,20; Luke 22:2), but the masses gladly followed Him (Matthew 4:23-25).

We sometimes think that Jesus had only a small group of disciples. While there were only 5,000-6,000 Pharisees during the time of Jesus, modern scholars believe that Jesus may have had as many as 100,000 followers. His movement was not a "fringe movement." It was a populist movement with views similar to those of the moderate Pharisees of His day.

In fact, there were so many people following Jesus, His movement threatened the establishment in Jerusalem (John 11:47-50, 53).

Jesus' followers were Jewish. They worshipped on Saturday, attended the Synagogue and kept the feasts. They acknowledged Jesus as the Jewish King and Messiah and wrote the "Jewish" New Testament Scriptures. The Roman governor, Pilate, who crucified Jesus, correctly wrote on His cross, "Jesus of Nazareth, the King of the Jews" (John 19:19).

 Jesus' Crucifixion, Resurrection, and Ascension

Jesus was crucified, buried, and resurrected on Jewish feast days that were spiritual pictures of the redemptive work of the Messiah. In fact, Jesus has and will accomplish all His redemptive activities on Jewish feast days.

Jesus was crucified as the ultimate fulfillment of the sacrificial "Lamb of God" who died to atone for and redeem us from our sins. The Feast of Passover was celebrated on the fourteenth day of the Hebrew month of Nisan. Jesus was crucified on the fourteenth day at the exact time when the Passover lambs were being sacrificed (Matthew 26:2; 1 Corinthians 5:7-8).

Jesus was buried on the Feast of Unleavened Bread. The Feast of Unleavened Bread was celebrated on the fifteenth to the twenty-first of Nisan. The Jewish day begins in the evening at roughly 6:00 p.m. Jesus was buried at the close of the day on the fourteenth at six clock in the evening (which begins the fifteenth).

This feast day is called a high Sabbath in the Bible (John 19:31). For that reason, Gentile scholars not connected to their Hebraic roots have mistakenly thought Jesus was crucified on Friday and buried on Saturday.

However, when we study the Hebraic background of the events in the life of Jesus, it seems that Jesus was crucified on Wednesday the fourteenth in the year AD 31 or AD 32. He was buried at the close of the day, approximately 6:00 p.m. in the

Jewish reckoning of time. Jesus stayed in the tomb for three days and nights and was resurrected at 6:00 p.m. at the close of the Sabbath and the beginning of the first day of the week. This was on the seventeenth/eighteenth, which was the Feast of Firstfruits (Matthew 28:1-6; John 20:1; 1 Corinthians 15:20-23).

Jesus appeared to His followers for forty days and then ascended to Heaven. Ten days later He sent the Holy Spirit upon His disciples on the Jewish Feast of Pentecost (Acts 2:1-8).

Furthermore, Jesus promised to return to earth and establish the kingdom of David and the Kingdom of God, when He will rule as King of Israel and King of kings and Lord of lords.

According to God's redemptive calendar, Jesus will return during the Jewish Feast season of Tabernacles which includes Trumpets, Atonement, and Tabernacles. All nations will go to Jerusalem to worship Jesus and acknowledge His kingship over Israel and the nations of the world (Zechariah 14:16). All the world will enjoy a Sabbath rest under the righteous rule of Jesus, the rightful King of the Jews.

The Spread of Christianity

The movement Jesus began was a Jewish movement to renew the covenant God made with the Jewish people. However, as we've learned, the leaders who were in control of political and religious affairs rejected His movement. As the followers of Jesus shared their message, it was accepted by the Gentiles and eventually evolved into a Gentile brand of Christianity, called the Church.

Many of the early church fathers were Greek philosophers who were anti-Semitic. They established church doctrines and practices that severed Christianity from its Jewish roots. This laid the foundation for centuries of misinterpreting much of the New Testament, and for hate and persecution of the Jewish people. When Christianity became the official religion of Rome in the fourth century, the Jesus movement of the New Testament and Hellenistic-Roman Christianity went their separate ways.

Herod's Divided Kingdom

As mentioned at the close of the last chapter, when Herod died he divided his kingdom, with Roman approval, among three of his sons. It is sometimes confusing to know about which Herod the New Testament is speaking.

Augustus approved Herod's will and gave Archelaus rule over Judea, Samaria, and Idumea. Herod Antipas was made ruler over Galilee and Perea, while Herod Philip was given governing responsibility over the area northeast of the Sea of Galilee. While Augustus agreed to let the sons rule, he had enough sense not to make them kings until they could prove themselves.

Herod Philip (4 BC–AD 34)

Herod Philip was the best ruler of the three sons. It also seems that his disposition was different from his brothers' in that he sought to govern with some sense of justice. The area he ruled was predominately Gentile. As a result, the region was generally peaceful and not so sensitive to Jewish religious matters that might cause rioting in Judea or Galilee. It was a perfect retreat for Jesus and the disciples when they needed to get away from the crowds and pressures of ministering in Judea and Galilee.[30]

Philip is credited with rebuilding the ancient town of Panias, which he made his capital. He named it after Caesar and called it Caesarea Philippi. Caesarea Philippi is best known in the New Testament as the place where Peter acknowledged that Jesus was the Messiah, the Son of the living God (Matthew 16:13-20).

Because Philip was a good ruler, he was mourned at his death in AD 34. At that time, his territory was made a province of Syria.

---

30. Ibid., 141.

Three years later, the new Roman Caesar, Caligula, gave Philip's territory to Herod Agrippa I, the grandson of Herod the Great, and made him king.

There is some confusion as to the wife of Herod Philip, because he had a half-brother who was also named Herod Philip.[31] One brother was married to Herodias and the other to Salome.

Herodias is the wicked woman who demanded the head of John the Baptist as the price for having her daughter, Salome, dance for Herod Antipas, the brother of Herod Philip. (See Matthew 14:1-12; Mark 6:14-29).

Herod Antipas (4 BC–AD 39)

Herod Antipas ruled during the entire life of Jesus and was certainly aware of Jesus' ministry (Luke 9:7-9). His political savvy enabled him to rule for such a long time. In fact, Jesus referred to Herod Antipas as "that fox" (Luke 13:32). Since he ruled during the lifetime of Jesus, it is no wonder they had an occasion to meet as recorded in Luke 23:6-12.

Jesus was taken to Pilate to be examined. When Pilate learned that Jesus was from Galilee, he sent Jesus to Herod Antipas for cross-examination. Herod Antipas had naturally heard many things about Jesus, but had not met Him. He hoped Jesus would do a miracle, but when He refused, Herod Antipas mocked Jesus and sent Him back to Pilate.

Before this occasion, Antipas and Pilate were enemies. This is probably because when Pilate placed his shields in the Temple in Jerusalem bearing the image of the emperor, Antipas appealed to Tiberius to have them removed.[32] Isn't it interesting how hatred of Jesus can unite enemies?

Herod Antipas is the man who married Herodias, the wife of his half-brother, Philip. He was a weak, immoral man who beheaded

---

31. *The International Standard Bible Encylcopedia*, 1978 ed., s.v. "Herodias."
32. Cate, *A History of the New Testament and Its Times*, 139.

John the Baptist when John preached against Herod taking his brother's wife, as noted in the previous discussion.

Herod's most significant accomplishment was building the city of Tiberius, located on the northwest shores of the Sea of Galilee. He showed his political savvy by naming the town after Tiberius, the Roman Caesar who succeeded Augustus. Antipas built the city over a graveyard in violation of Jewish law (Numbers 19:11-16).[33] Naturally, this made the Jews angry, and they refused to live in the new city. Antipas was forced to populate Tiberius with Gentiles and the poor by offering them bribes.

When Herod Philip died, Herodias wanted her husband appointed as king over Galilee. She was filled with envy when Caligula appointed a rival, Herod Agrippa I, as king. She appealed to Caligula to make Antipas king.

Agrippa heard of her scheme and convinced Caligula, who was his close friend, that Antipas was plotting an insurrection. Caligula sided with Agrippa and, in AD 39, he banished Antipas to Gaul (modern France). Caligula gave Herodias the opportunity to live in Rome. Much to her credit, she chose to accompany her husband in exile.[34]

Archelaus (4 BC–AD 6)

Archelaus was given the most important rule in that it included Judea and Samaria, as well as Idumea. This means he had to administer Jerusalem, the heart and soul of the people and the center of the Jewish religion. Unfortunately, he was not up to the task. He was the worst of the three brothers.

Archelaus was an incompetent, unwise man who sought to rule by cruel force. It was divine providence that Joseph and Mary were from Nazareth (Matthew 2:19-23) and went there when they

---

33. Cate, *A History of the Bible Lands*, 140.
34. Ibid., 139.

returned from Egypt. Jesus would be in danger if His family lived in the territory governed by Archelaus.

Archelaus was so bad that two bitter enemies, the Jews and the Samaritans, joined forces and appealed to Augustus to have him removed. When Augustus saw how much they hated Archelaus, he knew this son of Herod could never keep the peace. He banished Archelaus to Gaul in AD 6 and established direct Roman rule over his territory in the form of Roman procurators (governors).

Herod Agrippa I (AD 37–44)

Herod Agrippa I was a grandson of Herod the Great and Mariamne. He was four years old when Herod the Great killed his father, Aristobulus, in AD 7. At that time, he was sent to Rome where he was educated with the aristocracy of Rome, including members of the imperial family. This was during the reign of Tiberius. Agrippa was a boyhood friend of Caligula, who would succeed Tiberius as Caesar.

In his youth, Agrippa was very extravagant and burdened with much debt. He was forced to leave Rome due to his financial problems but returned in AD 37 at the age of 34. Back in Rome, he continued his friendship with Caligula. He was a very charming and clever person who knew how to get along with both friends and foes.

While in Rome, Agrippa made a comment that almost cost him his life. He was overheard saying that he wished Caligula was emperor instead of Tiberius.[35] Tiberius thought Agrippa was conspiring against him and put him in prison to be executed. However, his fortunes changed because Tiberius died and Caligula became emperor in AD 37.

Caligula released Agrippa from prison and made him king over the territory that was given to Herod Philip. As mentioned,

---
35. Ibid., 141.

when Herod Antipas appealed to Caligula to be made king, Caligula banished him and gave his territory to Agrippa in AD 39.

Agrippa was in Rome in AD 41 when Caligula was assassinated. He supported Claudius as the new emperor, who rewarded Agrippa in the same year by giving him the rule of Judea and Samaria. Thus, Agrippa reigned as king over the same territory as his grandfather, Herod the Great.

King Agrippa I was a very astute politician. He got along with most factions by simply being what they wanted him to be and doing what they wanted him to do when it was in his power. Outside the land of Israel, he was a Hellenistic-Roman, but among his Jewish subjects, he was a pious devotee to Judaism. He gained the favor of the Pharisees by committing himself to Jewish causes.

Caligula went mad and ordered that a statue of himself be erected in the Temple at Jerusalem. Agrippa convinced Caligula to temporarily rescind his order.[36] Fortunately, Caligula died in AD 41 before the decree could be carried out. Agrippa further pleased the Pharisees by persecuting the Jewish followers of Jesus.

We learn in the Book of Acts that Agrippa I killed James, the brother of John, with the sword. When he saw how this pleased the Jews, he had Peter arrested and was going to kill him, but an angel of the Lord set Peter free (Acts 12:1-19).

Herod Agrippa I died a sudden, violent death in Caesarea at the young age of 41. Because he accepted praise as a god, the true God of Abraham, Isaac, and Jacob sent an angel to strike him dead (Acts 12:20-24).

Herod Agrippa I left a seventeen-year-old son, Agrippa II, and three daughters, including Bernice and Drusilla. All three are mentioned in the Book of Acts (Acts 24:24; 25–26). Herod Agrippa II would eventually become king. Bernice would become known for her immorality, and, according to tradition, Drusilla, who was married to Felix, perished in Pompeii in AD 79 at the eruption of Vesuvius.[37]

36. Ibid.
37. *The International Standard Bible Encyclopedia*, 1978 ed., s.v. "Herod Agrippa I."

Herod Agrippa II (AD 49–70)

When Herod Agrippa I died, Claudius thought his son was too young to be king. Claudius appointed Roman governors to administer his father's kingdom. However, in AD 49, at the age of 22, Claudius did give Herod Agrippa II rule over a small kingdom in what today would be Lebanon.[38]

Four years later in AD 52, he was given rule over the territory that had belonged to Philip. In AD 55, he was given the territory that had belonged to Antipas. He was also given the authority to appoint the high priest in Jerusalem, whose appointment had been made by the Romans.

Herod Agrippa II is mentioned in the New Testament in the Book of Acts along with his sister Drusilla, the wife of Felix, and his sister Bernice, with whom he had an incestuous relationship (Acts 24–26).[39] The apostle Paul defended himself to Felix, and then to Festus.

Paul spoke to Felix and Drusilla about "righteousness, self-control, and the judgment to come" (Acts 24:24-25). This is most interesting, seeing that Felix had persuaded Drusilla to leave her previous husband shortly after their wedding to marry him.[40]

Paul then defended himself to Festus in the company of Herod Agrippa II and Bernice (Acts 25:13; 26:32).

In the First Jewish Revolt (AD 66–70), Herod Agrippa II appealed to the Jews to forsake their revolution. He knew they could never win against the Romans. However, they would not listen. When the revolt broke out in Galilee, Herod Agrippa II fought on the side of the Romans.

At the end of the war, Agrippa II, along with Bernice, went to Rome where they lived out the rest of their years. Agrippa II lived

---

38. *The International Standard Bible Encyclopedia*, 1978 ed., s.v. "Herod Agrippa II."
39. Scott, 101.
40. Ibid.

another thirty years and died in the year AD 100 at the age of 73. Bernice became mistress to the emperor Titus.[41]

---

41. Ibid.

Chapter 5—Personal Study Guide

1. Describe the background of the birth of Jesus.

2. Describe the "Jewishness" of Jesus' life and ministry.

3. Describe Jesus' crucifixion, resurrection, and ascension in light of the Feast of the Lord.

4. Who was:
   A. Herod Philip

   B. Herod Antipas

   C. Archelaus

   D. Herod Agrippa I

   E. Herod Agrippa II

Chapter 6
The Jewish People and Rome

We don't know the origin of Rome. Tradition tells us it was founded by Romulus on April 21, 753 BC. For the first 240 years, (753–509), Rome was governed by seven kings. In 509, the last king was overthrown by the army and Rome was established as a republic governed by consuls and the Senate, made up of the upper class patricians. These were the elite of Rome.

These leading families governed Rome for the next 450 years. During this period of time, Rome defeated its rivals and eventually ruled all the Mediterranean. By the time of the first century of the Christian era, Rome had emerged as an empire that would change the course of history.

From Republic to Emperor

In 60 BC, three powerful men formed the first triumvirate. These were Julius Caesar, Pompey, and Crassus. They fought for control of the empire. In 53 BC, Crassus was defeated by the Parthians, at which time a civil war began between Julius Caesar and Pompey. Caesar defeated Pompey, who fled to Egypt where he was assassinated.

With no rivals, Caesar was appointed dictator for life. He constantly fought with the Senate for control of the empire. Finally, two leading members of the Senate, Cassius and Brutus, murdered Caesar in a conspiracy on March 15, 44 BC. The conspirators were forced to flee from Rome and were defeated in battle. Brutus and Cassius committed suicide.

Octavian, Julius Caesar's nephew and adopted son, was appointed as the new Caesar. However, he was not strong enough to establish himself as sole ruler. Therefore a second triumvirate was formed consisting of Octavian, Mark Antony, and Aemilius

Lepidus. Antony and Octavian split up the empire. Octavian settled in Rome while Mark Antony established his base of power in Alexandria, Egypt, where he married Cleopatra in 36 BC.

Antony and Octavian threatened to fight each other for control of the empire. Octavian gave his sister in marriage to Antony to make peace between them. But as you can imagine, hostilities arose when Antony later married Cleopatra.

These two powerful enemies soon went to war. Octavian defeated Antony in the battle of Anzion in 31 BC. Antony and Cleopatra committed suicide.

Octavian was given the title of "Augustus" by the Roman Senate. Although Augustus appeared to favor preserving the form of a republic, through charm and astute political savvy, he gradually got all the power into his own hands.

From this time forward, Rome passed from a republic to an imperial system ruled over by the Caesars. Jesus of Nazareth was born during the reign of Augustus.

The Roman Caesars

The world of the first century Jew in the New Testament era was a Roman world ruled over by Caesars. They issued decrees, made political appointments, fought wars, collected taxes, sentenced people to death, etc., and influenced the lives of millions of people, including the Jews.

Three of the Caesars are mentioned in the Bible. For this reason, it is important to know something about those who ruled the Roman empire and the impact they had on the Jewish people who lived in Israel.

Augustus (27 BC–AD 14)

Augustus had a long and successful rule. He was the most successful of all the emperors because of his natural charisma, political savvy, common sense, and relative moral restraint.

Augustus established what came to be known as the *pax Romana*, the peace of Rome. Because Rome ruled without rival, the Augustan period was one of relative peace and prosperity. The Roman government was able to allocate a large share of its resources for domestic purposes such as building roads. The Romans built many roads that enabled the people to travel from one end of the empire to the other. Roman legions also marched on these roads to maintain the peace.

It was very costly to support the Roman military that was scattered throughout the empire. As a result, Rome levied heavy taxes on subject nations, including Judea. The Romans used local people from the subject nations to collect these taxes. These forerunners to the IRS were called "tax farmers."[42] As we can imagine, the people hated them and considered them traitors. In the New Testament, the tax collectors were called publicans.

The Roman world under Augustus was not only connected by roads, it was also united by the common Greek language and culture that had been adopted by the Romans. The followers of Jesus could travel throughout the empire on Roman roads with a Hebrew Scripture in Greek explaining the nature of the one true God and His plan of redemption in Jesus, the Jewish Messiah and Savior to the world.

Luke tells us that Jesus was born into this Roman world, when Augustus issued a decree to take a census for the purposes of taxation (Luke 2:1-7). Quirinius, the Syrian administrator, conducted this census sometime between 6 BC and AD 6.

The census caused an uprising that would eventually lead to the First Jewish Revolt, which took place from AD 66–73. The Romans crushed this revolt, which ended tragically when they burned the Temple and devastated Jerusalem. This would change the world, as the Jews would be scattered among the nations for centuries.

There were two prominent Galilean leaders who led the revolt. They were Judas of Galilee (Gamala) and Saddok, a

---

42. Cate, *A History of the New Testament and Its Times*, 108.

Pharisee. They were not just angry about the census, which they knew would lead to a heavy tax increase, but more importantly, they resisted it from a religious view.

These two zealots remembered that God severely judged King David when he counted the people as recorded in 2 Samuel 24. To Judas and Saddok, God was the only one who had the right to take a census. Quirinius's act called for a "holy war" against the Romans.

The descendants of Judas carried on the fight against the Romans from the time of the census until the destruction of Masada in AD 73.

Two of his sons, Jacob and Simon, were crucified in later struggles with the Roman authorities. One of his descendants, Eleazar, led the last stand of the freedom fighters at Masada.[43]

Judas is mentioned in the New Testament in the Book of Acts. The great Pharisee, Gamaliel, referred to Judas when giving his advice regarding the Jewish believers in Jesus. Gamaliel said, "...Judas of Galilee rose up in the days of the census, and drew away many people after him. He also perished, and all who obeyed him were dispersed" (Acts 5:37).

Augustus divided the empire into provinces. He placed legates (regional rulers) over the larger provinces. They supervised the administration of specific areas in their province through the procurators (governors).[44] The legate of Syria had administrative responsibility for Judea.

We noted in the previous chapter that Augustus approved Herod's will and allowed his three sons to rule in Israel. However, when Archelaus proved to be incompetent, Augustus replaced him with direct Roman rule through Roman procurators.

The first procurator Augustus appointed was Coponius (AD 6–9). He was governor during the tax revolt, which made his job

---

43. Steve Mason, *Josephus and the New Testament* (Peabody, MA: Hendrickson Publishers, 1992), 205-209.
44. Scott, 90.

extremely difficult since the zealots were calling for the overthrow of the Romans.

Steve Mason quotes Josephus regarding this situation and writes that "Coponius came with full powers, including that of capital punishment."[45] This would set the stage for Pontius Pilate who would later give the death sentence to Jesus.

Augustus also appointed the next two procurators. These were Ambibulus (AD 6–12) and Rufus (AD 12–15). We don't have any significant information about them except to note that they both governed during the time when Jews were still angry about the tax census and Jesus was still in his teens.

After a long and successful rule, Augustus died, apparently of natural causes, in AD 14 at the age of seventy-six. Fortunately, he had made provision for a successor in the person of his adopted son, Tiberius.[46]

Tiberius (AD 14–37)

Augustus was married to Livia, who was Tiberius' mother by a pervious marriage. When Augustus realized he would not have a son or grandson to succeed him, he adopted Tiberius. Augustus gave Tiberius important responsibilities which allowed for a peaceful transition of power to Tiberius when Augustus died.

Tiberius is mentioned in the New Testament where we learn that John the Baptist began his ministry in the fifteenth year of the reign of Tiberius (Luke 3:1). He was emperor during the entire adult life and ministry of Jesus. As previously mentioned, Herod Antipas built and named the city of Tiberius after this emperor. Tiberius also imprisoned Agrippa I.

The emperors were constantly on the watch for plots, conspiracies and supposed conspiracies. Tiberius was no exception. He grew paranoid. He trusted no one but was suspicious of everyone.

---

45. Mason, 103.
46. Michael Grant, *The Twelve Caesars* (New York: Barnes and Noble, 1996), 54.

Because of his suspicions, Tiberius became a recluse. He placed much of the day-to-day operations of the government in the hands of a man named Lucius Sejanus.

Sejanus was the head of the imperial guard, which had the responsibility of protecting the emperor. Unknown to Tiberius, Sejanus wanted more power for himself.

Sejanus falsely accused many powerful adversaries of plotting against Tiberius. He even convinced Tiberius to move to the Isle of Capri in AD 26 for his own safety. Tiberius would never return to Rome.[47]

With Tiberius ruling from Capri, Sejanus became the real power in Rome. Because of his charges of treason against anyone who stood in his way, it became very important to be known as a "friend of Caesar."

Sejanus hated Jews.[48] One of his protégés was Pontius Pilate. We learn in the New Testament that when Pilate decided to release Jesus against their wishes, the small group of powerful Jewish leaders threatened Pilate with these words, "…if you let this Man go, you are not Caesar's friend…" (John 19:12).

Pilate understood clearly the political implications of the accusation, even though it was false. He quickly changed his mind and had Jesus crucified.

Tiberius finally discovered the truth about Sejanus and had him executed in AD 31. This was a year or less before Jesus was also executed by Sejanus's political ally and friend.

Tiberius approved the appointment of three procurators over Judea. The first was Valerius Gratus (AD 15–26), who had a significant role in events recorded in the New Testament.

Earlier, Coponius had appointed Annas as high priest in Jerusalem. Annas is mentioned in the New Testament (Luke 3:2; John 18:13,24; Acts 4:6). He and his family had a major role in the first century, in that five of his sons followed him in the office of

---

47. Ibid., 84.
48. Cate, *A History of the New Testament and Its Times*, 224.

high priest.[49] Annas served as high priest from AD 6–15, but he exerted his influence over his sons who succeeded him.

Gratus appointed four high priests during his administration. The first three were: Ishmael, Eleazer, and Simon. Each served only a short period of time from AD 15–18. Finally, Gratus appointed Caiaphas as high priest. He was the son-in-law of Annas and functioned as high priest from AD 18–37.

Caiaphas was the wicked high priest mentioned in the New Testament during the trials of Jesus (Matthew 26:3, 57; Luke 3:2; John 11:49; 18:13,14,24,28; Acts 4:6). Amazingly, the stone box containing his bones, with his name inscribed on it, was found in recent times in Jerusalem.

Gratus was succeeded by Pontius Pilate, who was governor of Judea from AD 26–36. The Jews hated Pilate and for good reason. On one occasion, Pilate brought the shields of his troops into Jerusalem during the night. The shields bore the image of the emperor, which to the Jews was idolatry, based on Exodus 20:4. The Jews reacted with such violence that Pilate had the shields withdrawn.

At another time, Pilate built an aqueduct to bring water to Jerusalem. This seemed like a good deed. However, Pilate robbed the Temple treasury to pay for the project. Naturally, the Jews rioted. Pilate crushed the protest but not the hate the Jews felt towards him.

Pilate is represented in history as a cruel tyrant. He was finally recalled to Rome and replaced by Marcellus in AD 36. Marcellus was procurator for one year only, at which time Caligula was made emperor.

Caligula (AD 37–41)

Caligula was Tiberius's nephew. His actual name was Gaius. His father was a great Roman military leader. As a result, Caligula

---

49. Mason, 127.

grew up in military camps. When Caligula was an infant, he was given miniature military boots to wear. The soldiers gave him the nickname, Caligula, meaning "Little Boots."

When Caligula was seven, his father was poisoned. At the age of seventeen, his mother and two brothers were arrested and later killed. As we can appreciate, these family tragedies left Caligula with a very warped personality.

At a later date, Caligula was taken to Tiberius on the Isle of Capri. This was the signal that Tiberius had chosen Caligula to succeed him. When Tiberius died in AD 37, the Praetorian Guard acclaimed Caligula as the new emperor. Caligula was twenty-five at the time.

Shortly after becoming emperor, Caligula became very ill, which left him mentally disturbed. He became totally irrational. Today, we would say he was insane and/or demon possessed.

As part of his twisted humor, Caligula made his favorite horse a Roman Senator. He had a sadistic, evil mind. He both lived in incest with his sisters and prostituted them to his friends. Yet, he deified his favorite sister, Drusilla, after he killed her in AD 38.[50]

Caligula allowed the Jews to be persecuted, which resulted in a violent action against the Jewish community in Alexandria, Egypt.

Caligula declared himself to be a god. In AD 40, he ordered his statue to be placed in the Temple in Jerusalem. This would be the worst abomination of desolation to the Jewish people. They could not ignore such an idolatrous act.

The government officer overseeing Judea at this time was a man named Petronius. Petronius realized that if he carried out this order, the entire populace would riot. He begged Caligula to rescind his order.

At the same time, Agrippa I convinced Caligula to delay the order. Caligula agreed, but wrote Petronius a letter demanding that Petronius kill himself for not obeying the order. Fortunately for

---

50. Grant, 118.

Petronius and the Jews, Caligula died. The Praetorian Guard could only tolerate four years of Caligula. They assassinated him on January 21, AD 41.[51]

While not mentioned in the New Testament, Caligula had a major impact on the Jewish people. He appointed Agrippa I as king, giving him the territory formerly belonging to Herod Philip and Herod Antipas. He allowed acts of violence against the Jews which further fanned the flames of rebellion and Jewish hatred of the Romans. Caligula appointed Marullus (AD 37–41) as procurator in Judea.

Claudius (AD 41–54)

Claudius was Caligula's uncle, the least likely candidate to be the next emperor. He had numerous physical disorders, including stuttering and uncontrolled jerking of his head. He was very unsightly. He was an embarrassment to his family, who excluded him from public life. Claudius turned to study and became one of the leading scholars and historians of his day.[52]

Against all reason, the Praetorian Guard acclaimed Claudius as the new Caesar. They did so, almost as a joke, thinking they could control him. The Senate had no choice but to accept the wishes of the Praetorian Guard. Claudius was fifty years of age at the time.

Claudius was full of self-doubt and hesitated to accept the invitation. But as we learned earlier, Agrippa I was in Rome when Caligula was assassinated. He encouraged Claudius to agree to be emperor.

Claudius suprised everyone including himself by becoming one of the more able administrators of the empire. He brought into his government the freed slaves of the empire who were known for their administrative abilities. He successfully managed the affairs

---

51. Ibid., 109.
52. Ibid., 126.

of the empire through these capable, professional bureaucrats. Although he had no military experience, Claudius expanded the empire by adding several provinces, including Britain.

Claudius is mentioned twice in the New Testament. The first instance is when Paul and Barnabas were in Antioch. A prophet warned them about a famine that was coming similar to the one that had happened during the rule of Claudius.

Acts reads, "Then one of them, named Agabus, stood up and showed by the Spirit that there was going to be a great famine throughout all the world, which also happened in the days of Claudius Caesar" (Acts 11:28). This famine was in AD 46.

The second reference is in Acts 18 where we learn that Claudius expelled the Jews from Rome. This was in AD 49. Acts reads, "And he [Paul] found a certain Jew named Aquila, born in Pontus, who had recently come from Italy with his wife Priscilla (because Claudius had commanded all the Jews to depart from Rome); and he came to them" (Acts 18:2).

As mentioned previously, Claudius appointed his friend, Agrippa I, as king over all the former territory of his grandfather, Herod the Great. After Agrippa I died, Claudius appointed four procurators. The first was Fadus (AD 44–46). He was replaced by T. J. Alexander (AD 46–48).

Both Fadus and Alexander had to deal with some uprisings, but their administrations of Judea were relatively peaceful, because they did not overtly violate Jewish customs.[53]

Alexander is the man who crucified the two sons of Judas the Galilean. There was also a famine during his time, which seems to be the one where Paul and Barnabas took aid to the believers in Jerusalem as mentioned in Acts 11:28-30.[54]

The next procurator was Cumanus (AD 48–52). His administration was not so peaceful. During Passover, a Roman soldier on duty at the Temple made an indecent gesture to the crowd of

---

53. Mason, 106.
54. Cate, *A History of the Bible Lands*, 143.

devout worshippers. This caused a riot which resulted in the death of thousands of Jews.

On another occasion, some Samaritans killed Galilean Jews who were traveling through Samaria to Jerusalem. Instead of punishing the Samaritans, Cumanus took a bribe. This touched off another round of violence, resulting in many Jews and Samaritans being killed. Because of continuing trouble, Cumanus was finally summoned to Rome where Claudius relieved him of his position.[55]

Claudius appointed Antonius Felix as the next procurator. Felix was governor from AD 52–60. We previously mentioned Felix in his meeting with the apostle Paul as described in the Book of Acts (Acts 23:23;24:27).

Felix was one of the freedmen who governed during the administration of Claudius. Cate described his administration as "practicing every kind of cruelty and lust, he wielded royal power with the instincts of a slave."[56] Felix's administration was a disaster. He was a cruel, unjust governor who cared little for Jewish sensitivities. He showed no mercy in dealing with rebels. Because he was so severe, many joined the cause of the zealots.

During this time, an extremist group of assassins was organized. They were called the *sicarii* because they used daggers called *sica* to murder their enemies. The *sicarii* hid their daggers in their clothes and then mingled with the crowds. They would assassinate anyone they considered an enemy and then disappear into the crowd.

It was also during the administration of Felix that an Egyptian (AD 56) came to Jerusalem claiming to be a prophet who would overthrow the Romans. He convinced a large crowd to accompany him to the Mount of Olives where he promised the walls of Jerusalem would fall at his command. When this did not happen, Felix killed the rebels, but the Egyptian himself escaped.[57]

---

55. Mason, 107.
56. Cate, *A History of the Bible Lands*, 144.
57. Craig Evans, *Noncanonical Writings and New Testament Interpretation* (Peabody, MA: Hendrickson Publishers, 1992), 250.

Sometime later, a Roman soldier mistakenly thought the apostle Paul was the Egyptian who had returned to Jerusalem to cause more trouble (Acts 21:38). Because Felix could not maintain peace and order, Nero, who was now emperor, relieved him of his duties.

Back in Rome, Claudius married a fourth time, to a woman named Agrippina. Agrippina had her son, Nero, by a former marriage. She convinced Claudius to adopt Nero with the intention that Nero would succeed Claudius.

Four years later, Agrippina murdered Claudius by feeding him poisoned mushrooms. Claudius was sixty-three when he died.

Nero (AD 54–68)

Nero was only seventeen when he succeeded Claudius. Since he was technically too young to be emperor, Agrippina was the real power in Rome. Five years later, Nero murdered his mother, his sister, and his wife in order to eliminate all rivals to his throne.

Nero was an egomaniac who fancied himself to be an accomplished musician, singer, and actor. He neglected his official duties and spent time performing for his "adoring" public. He entered many contests and naturally won all of them.

Nero desired to build a great new palace, which he called the Golden House. However, Rome was already overbuilt. In AD 64, a fire of curious origin burned a major part of Rome. The people blamed Nero for the fire. Nero shifted the blame by accusing the Christians of starting the fire.

Nero inflicted horrible sufferings on the believers. He covered them with skins of wild beasts so dogs would tear them to pieces. He used them as human torches in his garden at night by fastening them to crosses and setting them on fire. He subjected them to many other cruel and inhuman deaths. The citizens of Rome realized the Christians were innocent and pitied them.[58]

---

58. *The Zondervan Pictorial Bible Dictionary*, 1963, s.v. "Nero."

The Roman Senate finally issued a decree that Nero must be killed. Nero retaliated by putting many of them to death. Nero died by a forced suicide in the summer of AD 68.

During his rule, Nero appointed three procurators to administer Judea. The first was Porcius Festus (AD 60–62). The apostle Paul was still in jail in Caesarea when Festus replaced Felix (Acts 24:27). Paul defended himself to Festus and Agrippa II as recorded in the Book of Acts (Acts 25–26). When Paul believed he would not get justice, he demanded to be tried before Caesar.

Hostilities between the Jews and occupying Romans only got worse under Festus, who died unexpectedly in office. Before Nero could replace Festus, the high priest in Jerusalem, who was Annas II, took advantage of the change in administration and killed some of his enemies, including James, the brother of Jesus.[59]

Nero appointed Albinus (AD 62–64) as the next procurator. Albinus was worse than his predecessors. He allowed terror to go unchecked and took bribes from all sides.

Cate writes that, "Anarchy became the rule of the day. No longer was any room left in Jerusalem for moderates or middle-of-the-roaders. People were forced to take a side. The anti-Roman forces grew in numbers and strength. The situation was totally out of control."[60]

Nero recalled Albinus and replaced him with Gessius Florus (AD 64–66). Cate explains, "Florus was so greedy and so willing to accept bribes that his predecessor appeared like a saint in comparison. He was clearly the worst of a bad lot. He plundered villages and cities and allowed any thief to practice his trade as long as the procurator got his share. His rule was the last straw....War was inevitable. No other outcome was possible."[61]

---

59. Scott, 101.
60. Cate, *A History of the Bible Lands*, 146.
61. Ibid.

Galba/Otho/Vitellius (AD 68–69)

Nero died without a clear successor to the throne. This led to a civil war resulting in four different generals declaring themselves emperor in AD 69, which became known as the "year of the four emperors."

The first was Galba (AD 68–69). Galba was in Spain with his legions when he learned that the Praetorian Guard had declared him as the new Caesar. This was in the summer of AD 68.

Galba was about seventy years of age at the time. His reign lasted only about seven months when he was murdered on January 15 by Otho, who succeeded him.[62]

Otho (AD 69) was thirty-seven when he was declared emperor. At the same time, other legions declared his rival, Vitellius, as emperor. The two armies met in battle with Vitellius defeating Otho. After reigning for only three months, Otho committed suicide on April 16.[63]

Vitellius (AD 69) was declared emperor, but other legions recognized Vespasian as emperor. A battle between the two armies took place in Rome with Vespasian's legions winning the fight. This was December 19.[64] Vitellius was emperor for only eight months.

Vespasian (AD 69–79)

After the First Jewish Revolt began in AD 66, Nero sent Vespasian to stop the uprising. By the summer of AD 68, Vespasian had successfully subdued the revolt with the exception of Jerusalem.[65]

---

62. Grant, 178.
63. Ibid., 189.
64. Ibid., 198.
65. Ibid., 212.

When word reached Vespasian of Nero's death, he stopped his campaign to wait further orders from Nero's successor. Little did he know there would be three successors and that he would be the fourth.

Before Vespasian left for Rome, he commissioned his son, Titus, to complete the job of ending the Jewish revolt. He then went to Rome where he had the difficult job of rebuilding the empire after the civil wars.

Vespasian was a military man, not a politician. Even so, he was a hard worker and got along well with the army and the Senate. As a result, he brought a decade of much needed peace and stability to the empire. This allowed him to build the Coliseum in Rome. He died of natural causes at the age of seventy-nine and was succeeded by his son Titus.[66]

Titus (AD 79–81)

As mentioned, when Vespasian went to Rome to become emperor, he left Titus in charge of the war against the Jews. Titus made history as the general who conquered Jerusalem and burned the Temple in AD 70. The famous "Arch of Titus" still stands today in Rome as a monument to his triumph.

Titus was forty years of age when he became emperor. As mentioned previously, he took Bernice, sister of Agrippa II, as his mistress. Mount Vesuvius destroyed Pompeii during his reign in AD 79. Titus reigned only for two years and died of an unknown cause at the age of forty-two. The Jews attrbuted his early death to divine retribution.[67]

---

66. Ibid., 212-213.
67. Ibid., 229.

Domitian (AD 81–96)

Domitian was Titus's younger brother who succeeded him as emperor at the age of thirty. Because he was raised in the shadow of his more celebrated father and brother, Domitian was possessed by a sense of inadequacy. He compensated for this by exalting himself as a god.

In the latter years of his reign, Domitian terrorized the Senate and other leaders whom Domitian suspected of threatening his insecurities. He also persecuted Jews and Christians. The persecutions were so bad that there was talk Domitian was Nero come back to life. Domitian was finally murdered by the Praetorian Guard on September 18, AD 96.

Nerva (AD 96–98)

Nerva only ruled for two years. His major accomplishment was adopting a son to be his heir so there would be a peaceful succession of power. The man he adopted was a very popular military man by the name of Trajan.

Trajan (AD 98–117)

Trajan had a very successful military career. He extended the Roman empire to its widest extent. He was an able administrator with an aggressive building program.

Under his rule, the empire flourished and was at its peak. In leading his legions to war, Trajan massacred many Jewish communities, particularly the large community in Alexandria, Egypt.

Hadrian (AD 117–138)

Trajan was succeeded by his nephew Hadrian. Hadrian had a long and successful rule. He is best know for being the emperor who reigned during the Second Jewish Revolt from AD 132–135. He crushed the revolt and destroyed 50 camps and 985 villages, while killing over 500,000 in a merciless slaughter of the Jews.[68]

The First Jewish Revolt

To Rome, Judea was a small, insignificant province. The procurators sent there were not the most able administrators nor were they of great character. They were greedy, petty bureaucrats. Each seemed to be worse than his predecessor.

It was difficult enough for the Jews to have to live under Roman rule, but the caliber of the procurators made life intolerable. Finally, Jewish Zealots initiated a revolt in AD 66. It ended in AD 73 with the fall of Masada, where 967 Zealots took their own lives rather than allow themselves to be taken by the Romans.

The Zealots were nationalistic-minded Jews who hated the Romans and wanted to drive them out of Israel. They had considerable influence among the common people and were waiting for an opportune moment to rally them against the Romans.

The Roman governor, Florus, gave them that opportunity. On one occasion, he robbed the Temple treasury. The Jews mocked him by taking up a public offering on his behalf. Florus became so angry that he turned his troops loose on the people.

In response, Elazar, the high priest at the time, stopped offering the daily sacrifice on behalf of the emperor's health. This was the moment for which the Zealots had been waiting. The revolt quickly spread throughout the land.

Vespasian marched his legions into Galilee and easily smashed the resistance. But as mentioned previously, he was called to Rome at the death of Nero and made emperor. Titus took command and marched on Jerusalem. He had 80,000 well-seasoned Roman soldiers at his command.

---

68. Robert Grant, *Augustus to Constantine* (New York: Barnes and Noble, 1996), 84.

The siege lasted six months and ended on the 9th of Av (July–August), the same day Nebuchadnezzar destroyed Solomon's Temple in 586 BC.

Jerusalem was well-fortified and could have held out much longer, but there were factions within the city that fought one another as much as they fought the Romans. A leader of one of the factions was John of Gischala. He fled to Jerusalem and took refuge when Galilee fell to Vespasian. The leader of another faction was Simon of Gerasa.

These factions, along with others, fought each other for control of the city. They killed thousands of their own people inside the city. It was said that the city never suffered any worse from the Romans than it suffered from John and Simon.[69]

The famine inside the city was so bad that people cannibalized their own children. This was prophesied in the Hebrew Scriptures (Leviticus 26:29; Deuteronomy 28:53-57; Jeremiah 19:9; Ezekiel 5:10).

We read of one woman named Mary who killed her infant son, roasted him, and ate half of his body while hiding the rest.

Hungry gangs smelled the meat burning and came to her house demanding it from her. When Mary offered them the other half of her son's body for food, they were repulsed. She ridiculed them for being weaklings because they could not do what a woman had done.[70]

Because the siege took place at Passover, there was a large number of pilgrims who were trapped inside the city. Hundreds of thousands perished. John of Gischala was taken captive and sentenced to life imprisonment. Simon was taken to Rome and strangled in the parade of triumph.

---

69. A Barbour Book, *Josephus Thrones of Blood* (Uhrichville, OH: Barbour and Company, 1988), 203.
70. Ibid., 223.

The Second Jewish Revolt

A generation later a new hope for freedom arose in the person of Simon Bar Kochba. He was a military leader who claimed to be the deliverer who would overthrow the Romans. He led the Jews in another great war of revolt in AD 132.

Bar Kochba was aided in his quest by the honored rabbi Akiba, who convinced the desperate Zealots that Bar Kochba was the Messiah. Rabbi Akiba gave Simon the name "Bar Kochba" which means "Son of a Star." This is a messianic title from the Book of Numbers (Numbers 24:17).

The revolt lasted three years and was crushed by Hadrian. Hadrian showed no mercy and slaughtered more than half a million people in his ruthless conquest. He completely destroyed Jerusalem and constructed a temple to Jupiter on the site of the Jewish Temple. The last stronghold was Beitar, which also fell on the ninth of Av.

Jews were forbidden to enter Jerusalem. As a further insult, Hadrian renamed the land of Israel after their ancient enemy the Philistines. He called it Palestine! He renamed Jerusalem in honor of himself (Hadrian Aelius) and the temple of Jupiter at Rome on Capitoline Hill. He called Jerusalem "Aelia Capitalina."

The Romans captured Rabbi Akiba and tortured him by raking his body with hot combs. As he was about to die, Rabbi Akiba said the Shema with great joy. When his students asked him how he could be happy in the midst of such suffering, he said, "All my life I taught that one must love God even at the price of one's life. Now that I am able to perform this mitzvah myself, shouldn't I be glad?"[71]

Rabbinic Judaism

During the siege of Jerusalem by Titus, the Zealots forbade anyone to leave the city, except in a coffin. If you were alive, you

---

71. Yaffa Ganz, *Sand and Stars* (Brooklyn, NY: Shaar Press, 1994), 38.

couldn't leave. You fought to the death. They did agree, however, that the dead could be taken outside the city for burial.

Rabbi Johanan ben Zakkai arranged to sneak out of the city in a coffin. He met the Roman general and asked him to spare the sages and allow them to establish a religious academy at Yavneh, a small village near the modern city of Joppa. The Roman general granted his request.[72]

The religious leaders assembled at Yavneh for the purpose of restructuring Judaism so that it could survive without the Temple, sacrifices, and priesthood. The strategy for survival was to form a theological center where the rabbis would develop and teach their restructured Judaism.[73]

Rabbi Johanan ben Zakkai became the head of the academy. While Rabbi Zakkai laid the foundation for rabbinic Judaism, Rabban Gamaliel II (AD 90–115) provided the necessary leadership that caused the people to accept it as authoritative. He is called "Rabban" rather than rabbi due to the honor given to him.

During his time of leadership the boundaries of rabbinic Judasim were set and a prayer of condemnation was given excluding any Jews who did not conform to the norm established by the rabbis at Yavneh.

Up until this time, the Jewish followers of Jesus were an accepted part of the Jewish community. The prayer of condemnation excluded them.

There were two famous schools of Pharisees during this period of time, and they competed against each other. The school of Shammai was more strict than the school of Hillel. The rabbis decided that the teachings of the school of Hillel would form the basic foundation on which to rebuild their restructured Judaism.

When it came to the holiness of God, Jesus would have sided with the school of Shammai. However, when needing to show

---

72. Ibid., 24–25.
73. Richard Booker, *How the Cross Became a Sword* (Houston, TX: Sounds of the Trumpet, 1994), 6–7.

compassion to people, He would have gone along with the teachings of Hillel. In many ways, Jesus was a moderate Pharisee whose teachings were similar to those of the school of Hillel.

Later in the second century, the center of rabbinic Judaism was relocated to Tiberias. At that time, Rabbi Judah the Prince collected the Jewish oral *Torah* (Law) and began to put it in written form. This compilation of writings was finally assembled in AD 220. It is a book of laws that became the foundational document for rabbinic Judaism from the time it was written until now.

The rabbis taught that when God gave Moses the written *Torah*, He also gave an Oral *Torah*, or tradition, to guide the people in living by the written *Torah*. For example, the written *Torah* says to keep the Sabbath, but it doesn't say exactly how to do so.

As a result, the rabbis believed that God gave oral instructions which they still consider to be sacred Scriptures along with the written *Torah*. The oral *Torah* was committed to memory and passed from rabbi to student. However, with the Jews being dispersed among the nations, it became important to document the oral *Torah*.

The written documentation containing the oral *Torah* is called the *Talmud*, which means "learning." The *Talmud* is made up of many volumes of rabbinic writings. It is divided into two major sections.

The first section is called the "Mishna." The *Mishna* is the rabbinic commentary on the written *Torah*, the Word of God. It was the first written documentation of the oral *Torah* and goes into great detail explaining how to apply the written *Torah* to everyday life.

For the next four hundred years, between 200–600 AD, societies changed, which required further clarification regarding how to apply the *Mishna* to a different world. As a result, the rabbis wrote a commentary on the *Mishna*, called the "Gemara." The *Gemara* is a commentary on a commentary. It contains Jewish laws (*halachah*) as well as Jewish stories and legends (*Haggadah*) that seek to interpret and apply the *Mishna* to different times and circumstances than existed earlier.

Unfortunately, over the centuries, Judaism has applied more study to the oral *Torah* (the *Talmud*) than to the written Word of God. Historic Christian denominations have made the same mistake by emphasizing their traditions as the rule of life rather than the Bible.

The Jewish People and Rome

Chronology and Relationship of Rulers

Emperors	Governors in Judea/Samaria	Rulers in Galilee/Perea
Augustus (27 BC–AD 14)	Herod the Great (37–4 BC) Archelaus (4 BC–AD 6) Coponius (AD 6–9) Ambibulus (AD 9–12) Rufus (AD 12–15)	Herod the Great (37–4 BC) Herod Antipas (4 BC–AD 39)
Tiberius (AD 14–37)	Gratus (AD 15–26) Pontius Pilate (AD 26–36) Marcellus (AD 36)	
Caligula (AD 37–41)	Marullus (AD 37–41)	King Agrippa I (AD 39–41)
Claudius (AD 41–54)	King Agrippa (AD 41–44) Fadus (AD 44–46) T. J. Alexander (AD 46–48) Cumanus (AD 48–52) Felix (AD 52–59)	King Agrippa I (AD 41–44) Fadus (AD 44–46) T. J. Alexander (AD 46–48) Cumanus (AD 48–52) Felix (AD 52–59)
Nero (AD 54–68)	Festus (AD 60–62) Albinus (AD 62–64) Florus (AD 64–66)	King Agrippa II (AD 59–70)

Galba/Otho/Vitellius (AD 68–69)
Vespasian (AD 69–79)
Titus (AD 79–81)
Domitian (AD 81–96)
Nerva (AD 96–98)
Trajan (AD 98–117)
Hadrian (AD 117–138)

Chapter 6—Personal Study Guide

1. Discuss Augustus and his rule.

2. Discuss Tiberius and his rule.

3. Discuss Caligula and his rule.

4. Discuss Claudius and his rule.

5. What relationship did the following emperors have to Israel:
   A. Vespasian

   B. Titus

   C. Hadrian

6. Discuss the First Jewish Revolt.

7. Discuss the Second Jewish Revolt.

8. Discuss rabbinic Judaism.

Chapter 7
Christian Anti-Semitism

One of the greatest Jewish scholars of all time was Rabbi Moshe ben Nachman, better known as the Ramban. He was the rabbi of Barcelona who led a Jewish delegation in a debate against church leaders in AD 1263. The Ramban made the following statement in defense of Judaism:

"The Church comes as the Prince of Peace, but more blood has been spilled by Christians than all the rest of humanity together. You have come on behalf of the poor, but no one has exploited the poor more than the church. The proof of the eternal truth of Judaism is that a people like the Jewish people exists in this world. The proof of the falsehood of Christianity is that there are people who act and behave like the Christians."[74]

The words of the Ramban should pierce the heart of every true Christian. Christians should get on their knees, repent, and cry out to God for forgiveness for the tragic history of Christian persecution of the Jews. Even though we are not personally responsible for the past, we are part of it because it is our history.

While Jesus said that love was the true mark of His follower-disciples (John 13:34-35), organized Christianity early developed a theology and practice of hate towards the Jews.

How did the movement that began as a sect of Judaism with a Jewish Savior establish such a legacy of hatred towards the Jewish people? How did Christianity become so anti-Semitic? Why did it exchange the cross for a sword? We will seek to answer these questions in this chapter.

I have written on this subject in another publication, entitled *How the Cross Became A Sword*. Much of the following information is taken from that publication. While both early Christianity

---

74. Yaffa Ganz, 137.

and Rabbinic Judaism contributed to this tragic past, the focus of this chapter is on the failings of Christianity.

The Jewish Revolts

Prior to the First Jewish Revolt, Jerusalem was the center of worship for traditional Judaism as well as the followers of Jesus who were almost all Jewish. They were known as Nazarenes and "The Way" (Acts 22:4). They were first called Christians in Antioch (Acts 11:26) by their enemies who used the name in a derogatory sense. As mentioned in a previous chapter, Jesus and His followers worshipped on Saturday in the synagogue and celebrated the feasts.

The Jewish apostle Paul, who was reinterpreted by later church leaders, made every effort to keep the feasts (Acts 20:16). He, too, worshipped in the Synagogue on the Sabbath (Acts 17:2).

Paul had his Gentile missionary partner circumcised (Acts 16:3). He kept a Nazirite vow according to the *Torah*. This apostle of grace sacrificed and purified himself in the Temple (Acts 21:26). He was proud of his Jewish heritage (Philippians 3:5).

In other words, Jesus and his disciples, including the apostle Paul, were *Torah* observant Jews. What set them apart was the fact that Jesus claimed to be the Jewish Messiah and his followers believed Him.

Jesus prophesied the destruction of Jerusalem and warned His followers to flee the city before it was destroyed. Jesus said, "But when you see Jerusalem surrounded by armies, then know that its desolation is near.

"Then let those who are in Judea flee to the mountains, let those who are in the midst of her depart, and let not those who are in the country enter her" (Luke 21:20-21).

Jesus' followers remembered His words. When they realized the Romans were going to attack Jerusalem, many of them fled the city and took refuge in Pella. Pella was located about 60 miles northeast of Jerusalem in what would today be Jordan.

The believers either stayed behind or returned to Jerusalem, because Eusebius wrote that fifteen bishops guided the church from the time of James (Acts 15) to the Second Jewish Revolt.[75] These bishops were *Torah* observant Jews who kept their faith connected to its Jewish roots.

Because the believers did not support the revolt, the surviving Jewish community considered them to be traitors. Since many of them were no longer in Jerusalem, the Jesus movement, which would become known as Christianity, was not as clearly perceived as a sect of Judaism. With the destruction of Jerusalem, Gentile cities would become the center of Christianity. Jerusalem would no longer be its "Mother City."

The Second Jewish Revolt also contributed to the separation of Christianity from its roots and was a major cause of anti-Semitism entering the church. The Jewish believers refused to fight because they could not support the messianic claims of Simon Bar Kochba. They were considered traitors. By this time, the Jewish leadership in Jerusalem were either all dead or scattered among the Gentiles. The Jesus movement which sought to renew Judaism would be taken over by the Gentiles.

The Gentile Church Fathers

Some of the most influential of the Gentile leaders of the early church had little regard for or understanding of Jews. They were Greek philosophers who attempted to merge Greek philosophy with the Hebrew Scriptures and the New Testament. Due to the Greek influence in their lives and the lack of a Hebraic perspective of the Bible, many of the new Christian leaders were anti-Semitic.[76] They interpreted the Bible through the eyes of Plato more than through the eyes of Moses and Jesus.

---

75. Eusebius, *The History of the Church* (New York: Barnes and Noble, 1965), 156.
76. Booker, 11.

These "Christian Fathers" expressed their hatred of the Jews through their speeches and writings, which laid the foundation for anti-Semitic policies at the very beginning of the Gentile-led, Christian church.

Ignatius was the bishop of the church at Antioch in the second century. He wrote a letter called the *Epistle to the Philippians*. He said that anyone who celebrated the Passover with the Jews, or received emblems of the Jewish feast, was a partaker with those who killed the Lord and His apostles. This is just the opposite of Paul's instructions to the Gentile believers in Corinth to "keep the feast" (1 Corinthians 5:7-8).

An influential letter written in the same time period was the *Epistle of Barnabas*. The writer said that the Jews no longer had a covenant with God and that it was a sin to say they did. This is totally contradictory to the Bible, which says God's covenant with Abraham is everlasting (Genesis 17:7-8).

Justin Martyr, in the second century, claimed that God's covenant with the Jews was no longer valid and that the Church had replaced the Jews in God's redemptive plan. This is contrary to Romans 11.

Irenaeus was the bishop of Lyon in the second century. He wrote that the Jews were disinherited from the grace of God. But the apostle Paul wrote that the gifts and calling of God are irrevocable (Romans 11:29).

Clement of Alexandria in the second century emphasized Greek philosophy rather than the Hebrew Scriptures as the means God gave the Gentiles to lead them to Jesus.

Origen, in the second and third centuries accused the Jews of plotting to kill Christians.

Hippolytus was a bishop in Rome in the second and third centuries. He said that the Jews were condemned to perpetual slavery because they killed the Son of God.

Tertullian was another important Christian teacher and writer in the second and third centuries. He blamed the entire Jewish race for the death of Jesus. This is interesting, since most of the Jews were scattered among the Gentiles when Jesus was crucified. They had not even heard of Jesus. Furthermore, as we earlier learned, many thousands of Jews acknowledged Jesus as Messiah.

Cyprian was the bishop of Carthage in the third century. He demanded that all Jews leave his region or die.

Eusebius lived in the third and fourth centuries. He wrote the history of the church for the first three centuries. He taught that the promises of God in the Hebrew Scriptures were for the Christians and the curses were for the Jews. He declared that the Church was the "true Israel of God" that had replaced literal Israel in God's covenants.

The Christian leader who expressed his hate for the Jews more than any other was John Chrysostom. He was the bishop of the church at Antioch in the fourth century. He said there could never be forgiveness for the Jews and that God had always hated them. He taught it was the "Christian duty" to hate the Jew. He said the Jews were the assassins of Christ and worshippers of the devil.

In one of his milder sermons, Chrysostom declared, "The synagogue is worse than a brothel…It is the den of scoundrels…the temple of demons devoted to idolatrous cults…a place of meeting for the assassins of Christ…a house worse than a drinking shop…a den of thieves; a house of ill fame, a dwelling of iniquity, the refuge of devils, a gulf and abyss of perdition…As for me, I hate the synagogue…I hate the Jews for the same reason."[77]

Jerome lived in the fourth and fifth centuries. His great contribution was to translate the Scriptures into Latin. He claimed that the Jews were incapable of understanding the Bible and that they should be severely punished unless they confess the "true faith." It is hard to image such statements coming from Christian leaders. May God forgive us for such hatred.

---

77. Malcolm Hay, *The Roots of Christian Anti-Semitism* (New York: Liberty` Press, 1981), 27-28.

The basic concept behind all these statements was that the Jews as an entire race of people killed Christ. Therefore, they lost their place in God's covenant and have since been replaced by the Church. The Church should persecute the Jews to show the superiority of Christianity over Judaism.

However, Christendom should not totally destroy the Jews because some need to be left alive as a witness that they are suffering because they rejected Christ. This is a long way from Jesus' statement on the cross, "Father, forgive them, for they do not know what they do" (Luke 23:34).

The "Christ-Killers"

The early church fathers blamed the entire Jewish race for the death of Jesus. They did not understand there was no "one Jewish voice" which spoke for all the Jewish people any more than there is one Christian voice that speaks for the entire Church.

In the first century, there were five basic Jewish sects. First were the Sadducees. They were the priests who controlled and administered the sacrificial worship at the Temple. While small in number, they were the powerful, aristocratic, Hellenistic group who wanted to keep the status quo in order not to upset their arrangement with the Romans. The Sadducees perished as a group with the destruction of the Temple in AD 70.

The next major sect was the Pharisees. Whereas the Sadducees were politicians, the Pharisees were "people of the Book." They were the Bible teachers of their day who were highly respected by the people. We might think of them as the "fundamentalist branch" of Judaism.

The Pharisees have been negatively stereotyped by the Christian world. While there were certainly those who lacked compassion, just as with some Christian ministers, the Pharisees were God-fearing religious leaders. Although much of their zeal was misguided, they genuinely wanted to please God.

Because of their emphasis on the Bible, tradition, and the synagogue, they survived the destruction by the Romans and established the rabbinic form of Judaism which became the foundation for Jewish faith and practice for Orthodox Judaism.

Another sect, which we have previously mentioned, was the Zealots. They wanted to overthrow the Romans and establish Israel as an independent kingdom. The Zealots perished in the two Jewish wars with the Romans.

A fourth sect was the Essenes. We mentioned in an earlier chapter that the pious Jews became disillusioned with the Maccabean leaders who lost their focus and were not of the line of Zadok. The best we can understand is that some of the pious established a religious community at Qumran where they wrote the *Dead Sea Scrolls*. The Romans destroyed this community in AD 68.

The last major sect were the Jewish believers in Jesus. They survived the Jewish wars. However, they were scattered among the Gentiles, and were rejected by the Jews as well as by the Gentile Christians. When they died, their movement died with them.

God Himself, with full cooperation and participation by Jesus, planned and carried out the death of Jesus as atonement for the sins of the world (Isaiah 53). The ethnic people God used to actually put Jesus to death were the Romans and Jews.

But it wasn't all the Jews nor all the Romans that "killed Christ." We have already seen that tens of thousands of Jews acknowledged Jesus as Messiah while most Romans had never even heard of Jesus. If we blame all the Jews for crucifying Jesus we should also blame all the Italians (Romans).

Several times in the New Testament we are told that "the Jews sought to kill Christ" (John 5:18; 7:1). Once again, the Gentile church fathers generalized these statements to mean the Jews as a race of people killed Christ. They did not understand the use of the word "Jews" in these statements.

In the New Testament period, the Jewish people who lived in the north were called Galileans. Those who lived in Judea were called Jews. Jesus and His followers were from Galilee. When the Galilean followers of Jesus said the Jews killed Christ, they did not mean "all Jews." They were referring only to the political and religious leaders in Jerusalem. They meant a small group of leaders in Jerusalem who were jealous of Jesus' fame and afraid He would upset their comfortable relationship with the Romans.

This is substantiated many times in the New Testament where we learn it was the aristocratic, Saduccean priests, not the average Jew, who plotted to kill Jesus (John 11:47-50, 53; Mark 15:9-10). His blood was on their hands (Matthew 27:25).

Those of us who live in America can understand this situation clearly. Although we are all Americans, people who live in New England are often called "Yankees." People who live in the South are called "Southerners." Not all Yankees are "carpetbaggers" who exploited the South at the end of the Civil War; not all Southerners belong to the Ku Klux Klan; and not all Jews killed Christ.

A modern example of blaming an entire group of people for the actions of a few is seen in the Western ignorance of the Middle East, particularly the Arab people.

The violence in the Middle East, which is spreading to the West, is not caused by the "Arab people." It is caused by a small group of Islamic fundamentalists who hate Jews and Christians and want to establish Islamic rule in all the nations.

This relatively small group of terrorists are able to intimidate and excite their followers to acts of violence just as the "Jews" did in Jerusalem when they gathered a small crowd of hoodlums to demand the release of Barabbas and the death of Jesus (Matthew 27:15-26).

While there is a huge cultural difference between those who live in the Middle East and those who live in the West, the average Arab is like the average American, a normal person struggling to care for his family, raise his kids, pay his bills, improve his quality of life, get along with his spouse, etc.

Humans have a tendency to stereotype others. However, it is not correct to "blame the Arabs" for the violence in the Middle East any more than it is correct to "blame the Jews" for the death of Jesus.

The Allegorical Interpretation of Scripture

Instead of reading the Bible for its natural, literal meaning, the church fathers allegorized much of what they read, particularly the Scriptures relating to the relationship between Israel and the Church and the end-time prophecies. This contributed significantly to the development of a theology of anti-Semitism in the early church.

Since many of the early leaders of the new Christian church were Greek philosophers, they used the allegorical method for interpreting the deep mysteries of life.

The first Christian seminary was established in Alexandria, Egypt. Because Alexandria was a Greek city, the leaders, whom we would call seminary professors, sought to merge Greek philosophy with Christianity by using the allegorical method of interpreting the Bible.[78]

The first head of the school in Alexandria was a man named Pantaenus. He became the head professor around the year AD 180. His most famous student was Clement, who succeeded Pantaenus as the head professor.

Clement played a major role in blending Greek philosophy with Christianity for the purpose of making Christianity acceptable to the Greeks who were embracing the new Christian faith. He taught that God gave philosophy to the Greeks to lead them to Christ in the same way that He gave the Hebrew Scriptures to Moses to lead the Jews to Jesus as their Messiah.

Clement placed greater emphasis on Greek philosophy than he did on the Hebrew Scriptures. As we shall see, this would have

---
78. Booker, 24.

a devastating impact on relationships between the Christians and the Jews.

Clement had a student named Origen who succeeded Clement as the head professor at the seminary. Origen was the greatest scholar of his time. Naturally, he taught the allegorical interpretation of the Scriptures. Instead of accepting and understanding the words in the Bible for their natural meaning, Origen looked for hidden meanings behind the words in the Bible.

He developed an elaborate method of interpreting the words which led him to many false conclusions about the meaning of the text. He was excommunicated on more than one occasion because his views were so unorthodox.[79]

Even though the new bishops and scholars of the church rejected many of Origen's views, they did accept his allegorical method of interpreting the Scriptures as the standard for the Church.

This allegorical approach to Scripture resulted in the teaching that the Church was the "New Israel" of God that had replaced literal Israel and the Jewish people in God's plan of redemption.[80]

Origen literally interpreted the Scriptures that spoke of curses on the Jews, but allegorized those that spoke of blessings for the Jews and applied them to the Church. In this way, Origin "stole" the Hebrew Scriptures from the Jews and made them acceptable to the Gentile Christian Church.

Origen established a school of theology and a library at Caesarea where he taught many students who would later become the leading theologians of the early church. They used Origen's allegorical method of interpreting the Scriptures from that time forward. This would lay the foundation for anti-Semitism in the Church that was taught by successive generations until the Puritan revival in the 1600s.[81]

---

79. Ibid., 26.
80. Ibid.
81. Ibid., 27.

Because of this method of interpreting the Scriptures, the historic Christian denominations have taught and practiced an anti-Semitic view known as Replacement Theology.

Origin was succeeded by a man named Pamphilus who was successful in teaching Origen's views to his students. Pamphilus financed the establishment of the school and library at Caesarea in order for Origen to teach there. His most important student was Eusebius (AD 263–339).

Eusebius was greatly influenced by Origen and the allegorical method of interpreting the Scriptures. His great contribution to church history was his book entitled *Ecclesiastical History*. This book is the only surviving account of the Church during the first 300 years to the time of the Roman emperor Constantine.

Eusebius became the theological advisor and friend of Constantine, who embraced Christianity as the official religion of Rome. He taught Constantine Origen's allegorical interpretation of the Scriptures which resulted in anti-Semitism being formalized as official church doctrine and practice down through the ages.

Constantine

Constantine has had a great impact on the history of Christianity. He was born into an important Roman family around the year AD 280. At that time, the Roman empire was divided into numerous regions which were ruled by Caesars.

Constantine's father, Constantius, ruled the region that included Gaul (France) and Britain. When Constantius died in AD 306, his army acclaimed Constantine as the new Caesar of his father's region.

In AD 310, Constantine was forced to fight a rival Caesar named Maxentius for control of the empire. Their famous battle took place outside Rome at the Milvian Bridge. Constantine won the battle and became sole emperor of the empire.

Before going into battle, Constantine had a dream in which he saw a symbol in the sky. Under the symbol was a banner which read, "In this sign conquer." Constantine credited his victory to the sign. He even had the sign put on the armament of his soldiers when they went into battle.

While we don't know exactly what the sign looked like, nor what it represented, church tradition has taught that Constantine saw the sign of the Christian cross. Other historians believe the sign Constantine saw was the ancient oriental representation of the sun.[82] Constantine said the vision was given to him by God, but he did not say which god.

Constantine, either for political or spiritual reasons, stopped the persecution of the Christians and issued the Edict of Milan in AD 313. This edict granted the Christians freedom of worship. He also showed great favor to Christianity by building churches, providing funds for Christian causes, and advancing Christians in the empire.

For Eusebius and other leaders of the persecuted Church, this dramatic turn of events must have seemed like direct intervention by God on their behalf. They believed that Constantine had converted to Christianity. As emperor of Rome and now head of the church, Constantine and the Roman state church represented the visible manifestation of the Kingdom of God on the earth.

But the emperor's favor would come at a very great price. For Constantine would merge Roman sun worship and Christianity into a new state religion whose decrees he dictated and enforced with the sword. With Eusebius at his side, Constantine issued formal decrees against the Jews in the name of Christianity. He would enforce these with the sword, thus formalizing institutional Christianity's hatred and persecution of the Jews.

---

82. David Hargis, *The Constantine Conspiracy* (Virginia Beach, VA: Zadok Scroll Works, 1994), 8-10.

The Council of Nicea

Constantine unified the Roman empire by converting it to a pagan brand of Christianity. However, Christianity itself was not united. At this time, there were several major controversies that threatened to tear it, and the empire, apart. Constantine could not allow this to continue. He called for a church council to settle the issues. The Council of Nicea met in AD 325 to settle the controversy regarding the true nature of Jesus and the proper date to celebrate Jesus' resurrection. Constantine assembled 318 bishops for the council.

David Hargis writes, "All rose when Constantine made his appearance. He came into their presence as a celestial messenger of God. The glittering of his purple robe dazzled the eyes of all the bishops. His robe appeared to be flaming with fire from the sunbeams that danced off the gold and precious stones of his attire. A low chair, made of gold, was placed before Constantine. After the Emperor was seated, all the rest seated themselves."[83]

It doesn't take much imagination to realize the impact Constantine's appearance would have had on the bishops.

Constantine addressed the bishops and encouraged, although some might say threatened, them to settle their controversies. The date to celebrate Jesus' resurrection was particularly embarrassing, because the biblical date is on the Jewish feast of First Fruits. However, Eusebius wanted to separate Christianity from anything that was Jewish.

Constantine, with Eusebius at his side, decreed that the Church would celebrate the resurrection of Jesus on the Sunday following the first full moon after the vernal equinox (March 21) rather than on the biblical date. The Roman pagan calendar replaced the Jewish calendar, and the Jewish feast of First Fruits (the resurrection feast) became Easter, the spring festival when the pagans worshipped Ishtar.

---

83. Ibid., 25.

When the Council was over, Constantine held a great banquet in which he required the bishops to pass through a circle of guards and soldiers stationed at the entrance of the palace with drawn swords as a way of making sure the bishops understood his decrees would be carried out by the power of the state.[84]

Constantine sent a letter to all the churches concerning the decision of the Council. His letter changed the nature of the Church and the course of history. Part of his letter reads as follows. I have added italics for emphasis.

"Constantine Augustus, to the churches:

"Having experienced, in the flourishing state of public affairs, the greatness of divine goodness, I thought it especially incumbent upon me to endeavor that the happy multitudes of the Catholic Church should preserve one faith....

"When the question arose concerning the most holy day of Easter, it was decreed by common consent to be expedient, that this festival should be celebrated on the same day by all, in every place. For what can be more beautiful, what more venerable and becoming, than that this festival...be observed by all in one and the same order, and by a certain rule.

"And truly, in the first place, it seemed to everyone *a most unworthy thing that we should follow the custom of the Jews* in the celebration of this most holy solemnity, who, *polluted wretches! having stained their hands with a nefarious crime, are justly blinded in their minds.*

"It is fit therefore, that *rejecting the practice of this people*, we should perpetuate to all ages the celebration of this rite, in a more lawful order, which we have kept from the first day of our Lord's passion even to the present times.

"*Let us then have nothing in common with the most hostile rabble of the Jews. We have received another method from the Savior.*

---

84. Daniel Gruber, *The Church and the Jews* (Springfield, MO: General Council of the Assemblies of God, 1991), 31-32.

"A more lawful and proper course is open to our most holy religion. In pursuing this course with unanimous consent, let us *withdraw ourselves*, my much honored brethren, *from that most odious fellowship*.

"It is indeed in the highest degree preposterous, that they should superciliously *vaunt themselves, that truly, without their instruction, we cannot properly observe this rite. For what can they rightly understand...being carried away by an unrestrained impulse wherever their inborn madness may impel them....Why then should we follow those who are acknowledged to labor under a grievous error?*

"But if what I have said should not be thought sufficient...use every means, that the purity of your mind may not be affected by a conformity in any thing with the *customs of the vilest of mankind*. Besides, it should be considered that any dissension in a business of such importance, and a religious institution of so great solemnity, would be *highly criminal*....

"Wherefore, that a suitable reformation should take place in this respect [substituting Easter in the place of Passover], and that one rule should be followed, is the will of divine providence, as all, I think, must perceive. As it is necessary that this fault be so amended that we have *nothing in common with the usage of these parricides and murderers of our Lord;...and to have no fellowship with the perjury of the Jews.*

"And to sum up the whole in a few words, it was agreeable to the common judgment of all, that the most holy feast of Easter should be celebrated on one and the same day. Nor is it becoming, that in so sacred an observance there should be any diversity; and it is better to follow that decision, in which all participation in the sin and error of others is avoided.

"This being the case, receive with cheerfulness the heavenly and truly divine command. For whatever is transacted in the holy councils of the bishops, is to be referred to the divine will...."[85]

---
85. Ibid., 28-30.

The Day of the Sun

The Romans worshipped many gods, but their high god was the sun. Constantine minted coins which had an image of *Mithra*, the sun-god, on one side and the letters IHS (In This Sign) on the other side.[86] When told that Jesus was the Sun of Righteousness according to Malachi 4:2, Constantine may have thought Him to be an incarnation of *Mithra*.[87]

The great winter festival dedicated to the worship of *Mithra* was on December 25, which the pagans considered to be the birthday of the sun. In AD 440, the Romanized church arbitrarily assigned this date as the birthday of Jesus to accommodate the heathens. Instead of celebrating the birth of Jesus at the Jewish Feast of Tabernacles, the most likely time of His birth, the Church chose to paganize the date.

The Romans set aside a special day each week to worship the sun. They called it the "Day of the Sun." We know it as Sunday. The state decreed that Sunday would be set aside as a holiday to worship the Christian God. Thus, the special day of worship was changed from Saturday to Sunday.

A triumphant Constantine enforced these new decrees by the sword of the state. He established anti-Semitic policies and declared that contempt for the Jews and separation from them was the only proper Christian attitude. By AD 339, it was considered a crime to convert to Judaism.

Renouncing One's Identity

Furthermore, Jews who acknowledged Jesus as Messiah had to renounce their Jewishness and convert to the Gentile brand of Christianity. This is how the perception began that Jews who accepted Jesus as Messiah were no longer Jewish.

---

86. Hargis, 14.
87. Ibid.

David Stern notes that the church of Constantine required the following profession of Jews who accepted Jesus as Messiah.

"I renounce all customs, rites, legalisms, unleavened breads and sacrifices of lambs of the Hebrews, and all the other feasts of the Hebrews, sacrifices, prayers, aspersions, purifications, sanctifications and propitiations, and fasts, and new moons, and Sabbaths, and superstitions, and hymns and chants and observances and synagogues, and the food and drink of the Hebrews.

"In one word, I renounce absolutely everything Jewish, every law, rite and custom—and if afterwards I shall wish to deny and return to Jewish superstition, or shall be found eating with Jews, or feasting with them, or secretly conversing and condemning the Christian religion instead of openly confuting them and condemning their vain faith, then let the trembling of Cain and the leprosy of Gehazi cleave to me, as well as the legal punishments to which I acknowledge myself liable.

"And may I be anathema in the world to come, and may my soul be set down with Satan and the devils."[88]

Every true Christian should weep after reading this statement. The institutional church merged with the state and tragically became the bride of Constantine. The Roman state/church considered itself to be the Kingdom of God on the earth, combining the political and military might of Constantine with Origen's allegorical interpretation of Scripture. Anyone who has visited Rome and Vatican City can clearly see the imperialistic nature of this state/church wedding.[89]

Theodosius became emperor in AD 379. He was a zealous Christian who hated Jews. He made Christianity the only legal religion of the Roman empire.[90]

---

88. David Stern, *Restoring the Jewishness of the Gospel* (Jerusalem: Jewish New Testament Publications, 1988), 8.
89. Booker, 31.
90. Ganz, 73-74.

A Flood of Pagans

The church was soon flooded with pagans who embraced the new Christian religion but never experienced a personal relationship with Jesus as Lord and Savior. They outwardly professed to be Christians in order to advance in the Roman world. This changed the nature and character of the church.

These baptized pagans brought their hate of the Jews with them into the Christian church. Hatred of the Jews was manifested by anti-Semitic declarations and actions from the Roman church and government which were essentially one and the same.

Relations between the church and the Jews rapidly deteriorated. They finally broke in the fifth century with the Roman state/church viewing Jews, as second class citizens who were to be forever branded as outcasts from the normal order and decencies of society.

This early anti-Semitic policy of the powerful Roman state/church laid the foundation for the future of the Jews, as they would experience unbelievable suffering and persecution for the next fifteen hundred years.

As Christianity spread, more and more countries came under the influence of the Roman state/church. Many peoples in these countries accepted Christianity without having a personal relationship with Jesus. Their hearts never changed. All they did was change religions. All the so-called "Christian" nations would adopt the anti-Jewish policies and attitudes of the Origen-Eusebius-Constantine church.

Augustine (AD 354–430)

Augustine was a great scholar who wrote a monumental work called *The City of God*. In this work, Augustine explained the Hellenistic-Roman understanding of Scripture to the Church and the world.

He was not a violent anti-Semite as were his predecessors. However, because Augustine used Origen's allegorical method of interpreting the Scriptures, he spiritualized the relationship between the Church, the Jews and events in the Bible that relate to the end times and the Kingdom of God.

Augustine wrote that the millennial kingdom of God was not literal but spiritual. He taught that the Kingdom of God was present and not future and existed only in the spiritual sense in the hearts of believers.

The idea of a Jewish Jesus returning to Jerusalem to establish a literal kingdom of David over a restored Israel just did not fit into the new Roman-Christian theology.

The triumphant Roman state/church was proclaimed to be the visible manifestation of the Kingdom of God on the earth. As proof of this, Augustine wrote that the Church was to dominate the Jews, who were to be forever humiliated and disgraced by Christendom.

Roman Christianity taught that the Church replaced Israel in God's redemptive plans and purposes. The Jews were judged by God for "killing Christ." Yet, the Jews survived two Roman wars.

Augustine needed some explanation for their continued existence. He wrote that, while the Jews deserved death, God would keep a remnant alive to wander the earth as a witness to their punishment and the victory of the church over the synagogue. The greater their humiliation, the greater the triumph of the church. It has been said that his attitude towards the Jews was that they should survive but not thrive.

Augustine's writings became the theological textbook for the Church down through the centuries. His views are still taught today by much of the Christian world.

When we learn the history of anti-Semitic Roman theology and practice, we can begin to understand the great gulf that exists between the Jewish world and the Christian world. Only the Almighty can heal the hurts caused by the tragic history between Christendom and the Jews.

The Crusades

The Crusades were military expeditions conducted under the authority and with the blessings of the Church. Their purpose was to recover the Holy Land from the Moslems and stop the spread of Islam.

The Crusades took place during the eleventh, twelfth, and thirteenth centuries. While Hollywood has romanticized these "Christian" adventures, the truth is that they were carried out by evil-hearted men who saw the Crusades as an opportunity to kill and plunder with impunity in the name of God while having their sins forgiven by the Pope.

While I'm sure some of the Crusaders had noble intentions, many were the rabble of Europe who hated not only the Moslems but also the Jews. Unfortunately, the religious leaders were just as bad in their hatred of the Jews. During their conquest of the Holy Land, which turned out to be a failure, the Crusaders savagely butchered thousands of Jews. This was all done under the banner of the cross and in the name of Christ.

Fred Wright explains, "A Crusade led by the popular French preacher, Peter the Hermit, composed mostly of rabble departed from Cologne in 1096 happily raping, looting and pillaging their way throughout Europe. If any Jews could be found to burn, crucify or kill on the way, that was seen as being profitable service to God. 'Kill the Christ Killers' was their cry. To kill a Jew was considered both meritorious and profitable."[91]

Wright tells us that Peter the Hermit's Crusaders "suddenly attacked a small band of Jews, they decapitated many and inflicted serious wounds, they destroyed their homes and synagogues, and divided a very great sum of looted money among themselves."[92]

---

91. Fred Wright, *Words from the Scroll of Fire* (Jerusalem: Four Corners Publishing, 1994), 124.
92. Ibid., 125.

Wright reports another massacre led by Count Emich de Leisingen; "Count Emich was an enemy of the Jews....He was known as a man who had no mercy on the old, or on young women, who took no pity on babies or sucklings or the sick, who pulverized God's people like the dust in threshing, who slew their young men with the sword and cut open their pregnant women."[93]

A Crusader monk named Radulf inflamed the mobs against the Jews with the cry, "First avenge Christ, the crucified one, upon his enemies [the Jews] who stand before you; and then, only go to fight against the Muslims."[94]

A leader of the first Crusade was a man named Godfrey Bouilon. He exhorted the mobs with these words, "Avenge the blood of Christ on Israel, and leave no single member of the Jewish race alive."[95]

When the Crusaders finally arrived in Jerusalem, their swords were already drenched in the blood of the Jews. They killed the Moslems, rounded up all the Jews, and herded them into the synagogue. These "Christian" Crusaders then nailed the door shut and set fire to the synagogue. As they burned the Jews alive inside the synagogue, the Crusaders sang, "O Christ We Adore Thee."[96]

Anti-Semitic Hysteria

In the twelfth century, a new charge was leveled against the Jews. This was the charge of ritual murder. It was said that each year at Passover, the Jews killed a Christian boy and used his blood in the Passover ritual. This was a totally irrational charge since the Jews are forbidden to eat blood. Yet, it always enflamed the angry mobs to attack the Jews. Of course this was all done in the name of Christ.

---

93. Ibid.
94. Ibid., 126.
95. Ibid.
96. Booker, 33-34.

The Jews were also accused of stealing the communion wafer (bread) which the Catholic Church taught literally became the body of Christ. The Christians accused the Jews of sticking pins in the wafer as a means of torturing Christ. This too caused violent mob action against the Jews.

To further humiliate the Jews, from time to time, the Christian nations expelled them from their countries. At other times, they forced the Jews to wear distinctive clothing or badges to readily identify themselves as Jews.

In some countries the badge was a yellow "O" similar to the yellow star which Nazi Germany would use to mark its Jews. As shocking as it may be to the reader, Nazi Germany got many of its ideas for the Holocaust from the Church.

The Jews were also blamed for the plague that devastated Europe in 1347–1350. This plague, known as the black death, killed approximately one-fourth of Europe's population. Many millions died. This terrible plague was transmitted by fleas and carried by rats. Because the Jews practiced better hygiene than the Gentiles, they were not as susceptible to the plague.

When people suffer, they need someone to blame for their misery. As usual, "Christian" Europe turned their wrath against the Jews. They accused the Jews of poisoning the wells.

Unruly mobs attacked the Jews and killed them unmercifully. Before the plague ended, thousands of Jews were slaughtered and hundreds of entire Jewish communities were annihilated. If you think these accusations are a thing of the past, think again. The PLO makes the same accusations against the Israelis today.

The Inquisition

The Inquisition in the fifteenth and sixteenth centuries was one of the worst periods in all of Church history. The Church tortured and murdered many thousands of true believers who were falsely accused of being heretics. In their heartless passion for blood, they also killed thousands of Jews.

The Inquisition was especially perilous for the Jews living in Spain and Portugal. Ferdinand and Isabella, at the insistence of the Church, began a systematic action that brought great suffering on the Jews. Thomas de Torquemada was put in charge of the Inquisition. He gave the Jews the choice of forced baptism or exile. If they accepted baptism, the Jews had to renounce their Jewishness. Those who converted were called "conversos" or "marranos," which means pigs. They were constantly interrogated to make sure they were not secretly practicing Judaism. If they refused to be baptized, they were tortured and murdered.

Finally, in 1492, at the very time when Columbus sailed to discover the new world, the Jews were expelled from Spain. Many Jews fled to Portugal. However, this did not prove to be a safe haven. The Church initiated an Inquisition in Portugal that eventually led to the Jews being expelled.

The Reformation

The Protestant Reformation was certainly a needed blessing for Christendom. Yet, it brought further disaster on the Jews. While the reformers read the Bible in its literal sense, they continued to use the allegorical method of interpreting the Scriptures regarding the relationship of the Church to the Jews and the prophetic Scriptures concerning Israel and end-time events.[97]

Erasmus is known by Christian historians as the greatest scholar of the Reformation. His contribution to the Reformation was translating the New Testament based on fresh scholarly research. This is a man greatly respected by Christianity. Yet Erasmus hated the Jews. He wrote, "Who is there amongst us that does not hate this race of men…If it is Christian to hate the Jews, here we are all Christians in profusion."[98]

---
97. Ibid., 36-37.
98. Wright, 135.

Martin Luther is revered by all Protestants as the man who sparked the Reformation. Tragically, his anti-Semitic writings were used by Nazi Germany against the Jews. Luther considered the evils of Catholicism as the biggest stumbling block to the Jews accepting Jesus as Messiah.

In 1523, he wrote a paper entitled, *Jesus Christ Was Born a Jew*. He hoped this positive, sympathetic approach to the Jews would cause them to convert to his new, "purer" form of Christianity.

Luther wrote, "If I were a Jew, I would suffer the rack ten times before I would go over to the Pope...The papists have so deemed themselves that a good Christian would rather be a Jew than be one of them, and a Jew would rather be a sow than a Christian...

"Fools, papists, Bishops, sophists, monks, the rude asinine heads, have behaved badly towards the Jews in such a way to turn good Christians away....They have been treated as though they were dogs.

"Yet Jews are our kinsmen and brethren of our Lord...God granted the Holy Scriptures to them....How can they improve when they are excluded from human society and driven to usury?

"We should apply the laws of love to them. They should be enabled to work and earn a livelihood together with us. That would convince them of the teaching and good life of Christians."[99]

These comments by Luther were considered radical and gave Jews hope for better days ahead. However, when the Jews did not embrace Luther's brand of Christianity, he turned on them.

His pamphlet entitled *On Jews and Their Lies* contains some of the most hateful words that have ever been written against the Jews. His ideas and writings would later be used by Hitler for "Christian" justification of the Holocaust.

---

99. Ibid., 135-136.

Luther wrote, "We are at fault for not slaying them. Rather we allow them to live freely in our midst despite all of their murdering, cursing, blaspheming, lying and defaming....

"What shall we Christians do with this rejected and condemned people, the Jews? Since they live amongst us we dare not tolerate their conduct...

"Firstly, their synagogues should be set on fire, and whatever does not burn up should be covered or spread over with dirt so that no one may ever be able to see a cinder or stone of it. And this ought to be done for the honor of God and Christianity in order that God may see that we are Christians, and that we have not wittingly tolerated or approved of such public lying, cursing and blaspheming His Son and His Christians.

"Secondly, their homes should likewise be broken down and destroyed. For they perpetrate the same things there that they do in their synagogues....Thirdly, they should be deprived of their prayer books and Talmuds in which such idolatry, lies, cursing and blasphemy are taught.

"Fourthly, their Rabbis must be forbidden under threat of death to teach any more....

"Fifthly, passports and traveling privileges should be absolutely forbidden to the Jews....Sixthly, they ought to be stopped from usury....Seventhly, let the young and the strong Jews and Jewesses be given the flail, the axe, the hoe, the spade, the distaff, and the spindle and let them earn their bread by the sweat of their noses."[100]

Luther further wrote, "I advise you [Christians] not to enter their [Jews] synagogues: all devils might dismember and devour you there....For he who cannot hear or bear to hear God's word is not of God's people. And if they are not of God's people, then they are of the devil's people."

"I cannot understand it except by admitting that they have transformed God into the devil, or rather the servant of the devil,

---

100. Ibid., 135-136.

accomplishing all the evil the devil desires, corrupting unhappy souls and raging against himself. In short the Jews are worse than devils....

"They are real liars and bloodhounds. Their heart is set on the day on which they can deal with us Gentiles as they did with the Gentiles in Persia at the time of Esther....The sun has never shone on a more bloodthirsty and vengeful people than they who imagine that they are God's people who have been commissioned and commanded to murder and slay the Gentiles. In fact the most important thing that they expect of their Messiah is that he will murder and kill the entire world with their sword."[101]

As hard as it is to accept, we see from Luther's writings that his solution to the "Jewish problem" was the same as the Nazis. Thank God that some leaders in the Evangelical Lutheran church have issued public statements repudiating Luther's words and apologizing to the Jews for their past anti-Semitism.

The Russian "Pogroms"

In the latter part of the nineteenth century, Russia began to flex her muscles and conquer border states where there were large Jewish communities. These included parts of Poland, Romania, and other Eastern European countries. Russia suddenly found herself with a large unwanted Jewish population.

Following the example of nations in the past, Russian leaders pointed to the Jews as the cause for many of their internal problems. Their solution to the "Jewish problem" was forced conversion for one-third of the Jews, emigration for another third, and starvation for the last third.

The Russian word "pogrom," which means destruction, was the name given to this formal persecution of the Jews which took place between 1881–1921 with the tacit approval of the Russian Orthodox Church.

---

101. Ibid., 136-137.

The following description is given of one of the pogroms which took place in 1903. "…some Jews had nails driven into their heads. Some had their eyes put out. Children were thrown from garret windows, dashed to pieces on the street below.

"Women were raped, after which their stomachs were ripped open, their breasts cut off. Still the police did nothing, nor did the city officials, nor the so called intelligentsia. They walked leisurely along the streets watching the show."[102]

Protocols of the Learned Elders of Zion

It was also during this period of time that a spurious manuscript was published called the "Protocols of the Learned Elders of Zion." This document, which has been proved to be a forgery, is supposed to expose an international plot by the Jews to take over the world. It seems that the original document was a novel written in 1868 by a man named Hermann Goedsche who wrote under the pen name of Sir John Retcliffe.[103]

In his novel, the author tells of a secret meeting of the leaders of international Jewry who gathered in the Jewish cemetery in Prague to conduct a black Sabbath. The devil presided over the meeting and devised a plan by which he could rule the world through the Jews.

In 1864 another man named Maurice Joly wrote a pamphlet about the attempts of Napoleon to rule the world. These two documents were combined to produce the "Protocols" which was forged in the 1890s in Paris by the Russian secret police. It was distributed worldwide in 1917 by Russians who fled Russia during the revolution.[104]

Anti-Semitics quickly began to use the "Protocols" to attack the Jews. Henry Ford gave wide credibility to the "Protocols" by publishing excerpts from it in a book entitled *The International*

---
102. Ibid., 64.
103. Ibid., 75-76.
104. Ibid., 76.

Jew. Although he later apologized when he learned it was a forgery, his support of the document gave cause for anti-Semites to speak evil against the Jews.

As to be expected, the Nazis made great use of the "Protocols" as did other hate groups in Europe and America. The "Protocols" is standard reading today in Arab countries who use it to justify their hatred of Israel and the Jews.

The Holocaust

There are no human words to describe the horrors of the Holocaust in which six million Jews and five million non-Jews perished. How could such a thing happen in "civilized" Europe?

Unfortunately, as we have seen, the anti-Semitic policies of Christianity provided the theological justification that allowed Hitler to go forward with his "final solution" to the Jewish problem. He knew he could implement his plan to exterminate the Jews because European Christendom was anti-Semitic to the core.

Hitler's Youth

Much of the following information about Hitler is taken from *A Legacy of Hatred*, by David A. Rausch (Moody Press).

Adolf Hitler was born in Austria in 1889 to a middle-to-upper class family. His father (Alois) was an illegitimate child who fathered Hitler in his third marriage. In his youth, Hitler was a poor student who transferred from one school to another. He seemed to be lazy and, from the author's view, had an inferiority complex. When his father died, Adolf was too lazy to work but sponged off his mother, who had been left a pension at the death of Adolf's father.

Hitler fancied himself as an artist. In 1907 he enrolled in the Academy of Fine Arts in Vienna, but failed the entrance examination.

When his mother died, Adolf lived off her savings and his deceased father's pension. He stayed on in Vienna where he developed his hatred for the Jews.

It seems that Hitler failed at everything until World War I gave him an opportunity to express his intense German nationalism. He enlisted in the army and proved himself to be brave in battle, being wounded twice. He received the Iron Cross, but never rose above the rank of a lowly corporal.

Germany's Humiliation

Archduke Franz Ferdinand, the heir to the Austrian throne, was assassinated on June 28 by a Serbian nationalist. This triggered World War I in which Russia, France and Great Britain allied themselves against Austria-Hungry and Germany. The outcome of the war was decided against Germany when the American forces entered the war.

In 1919, the victorious nations forced Germany to sign the Treaty of Versailles, which humiliated Germany by blaming Germany alone for the war and making impossible demands on a nation already devasted by the war. This "treaty without mercy" would pave the way for the Nazis, who would restore German pride and blame the Jews for Germany's subsequent humiliation and later economic collapse.

Hitler's Defeat and Rise to Power

After the war, Hitler joined the newly formed National Socialist German Workers' Party. The party changed its name to the Nazi Party and Hitler became its leader in 1921.

Hitler declared his intentions from the very beginning of his rise to prominence. In an early speech, Hitler said, "None but members of the nation may be citizens of the State. None but those of German blood, whatever their creed, may be members of the nation."

Hitler then concluded, "No Jew, therefore, may be a member of the nation."[105] In the same speech, Hitler said, "The Party, as such, stands for positive Christianity."[106]

In 1924, Hitler failed in his attempt to overthrow the government in Munich. He served less than one year of a five year prison sentence. During his year in prison, Hitler wrote *Mein Kampf* in which he expressed his racial theories of the superiority of the German Aryan race and his hatred for Jews and other non-Aryans.

When Hitler was released from prison, his movement seemed to be over. His party was banned and a strong economic recovery for the next four years brought stability and hope to the average German. Yet Hitler never gave up. He reorganized his party and kept circulating his propaganda.

The stock market crash in 1929 led to a worldwide economic depression. As the economy in Germany worsened, membership in the Nazi Party increased. The existing government was not powerful enough to help relieve the misery of its citizens.

Hitler appealed to the masses with simplistic slogans and solutions to their woes. Finally, on January 30, 1933, the president of Germany reluctantly appointed Hitler chancellor of Germany.

Hitler soon consolidated his power and began to persecute the Jews and any other group he thought would hinder his plans to impose Nazi doctrine and practice on Germany. He passed laws barring Jews from many occupations, public schools, the military, etc. On September 15, 1935, Hitler enacted the Nuremberg Laws, which denied German citizenship to Jews based on racial purity.

The Night of Broken Glass

While the Nazis were expelling the Jews from Germany, few countries offered to give them refuge. An international conference

---
105. David Rausch, *A Legacy of Hatred* (Chicago: Moody Press, 1984), 59.
106. Ibid.

was convened in Evian, France in July 1938 to discuss the problem, but the countries refused to adjust their immigration quotas to help the Jews.

In October of the same year, the Nazis expelled thousands of Polish Jews who were living in Germany. However, Poland did not accept them, so the people were stranded in a no-man's land. They were barely surviving under the harshest of conditions in a Polish camp called Zbaszyn.

A 17-year-old German-born Polish Jew, named Herschell Grynszpan, was in Paris at the time and learned that his parents were in the camp.

The young man became very angry and went to the German Embassy in Paris with the intention of killing the German ambassador. But instead of killing the ambassador, he killed Ernst Von Rath, who was the Third Secretary to the ambassador. This was on November 7, 1938. The secretary died two days later on November 9.

The Nazis were waiting for an incident like this to justify an action against the Jews. Hitler, the preacher of positive Christianity, gave his storm troopers a free hand against the Jews. When Ernst Von Rath died on November 9, they went on a rampage of terror and destruction.

Approximately 250 synagogues were set on fire, 815 Jewish shops destroyed, several hundred houses destroyed, and 30,000 Jewish men rounded up and sent to concentration camps. Of this number, thirty-six were murdered on the way to the camps.[107]

This action against the Jews came to be known as *Kristallnacht*, meaning the "Night of Broken Glass" because the streets were filled with broken glass from the shops and synagogues destroyed by the Nazis.[108] It was the official beginning of the Holocaust.

---

107. Wright, 175-176.
108. Rausch, 84.

Hitler's Death Camps

Hitler invaded Poland in 1939 and quickly extended his victories throughout Europe. With every victory, Hitler set out to destroy the Jews. In addition to mobile killing units, forced death marches, ghettos, and every other evil imaginable, the Nazis shipped trainloads of Jews from their homelands to concentration camps. The Jews were told they were going to work camps. In reality they were death camps that could mass murder 25,000 human beings every day.

Upon arrival, the Jews were separated according to those who would live and those who would die. They were stripped of their clothes and herded like cattle into gas chambers which they believed to be showers. When the room was full, the doors were shut and the people were gassed to death.

When it was safe, workers entered the chambers and the bodies were retained long enough to extract gold teeth and wedding rings to be melted down into gold bars. Women's hair was cut and used in the manufacture of cloth and mattresses. Body fat was used to make inexpensive soap. Afterwards, the bodies were cremated and their ashes used for fertilizer.

The Jewish population in Europe in 1939 was about nine million. Hitler reduced it to three million. The horror of the Holocaust awakened the Jews to the fact they would never be safe living in the Gentile nations.

Hitler's plan to destroy the Jews almost succeeded, but God had other plans. Hitler committed suicide on April 30, 1945. Israel was born on May 15, 1948.

Christians and the Holocaust

While no one would seriously believe that Hitler and his murdering thugs were Christians, it is still true that European Christendom, both Protestant and Catholic, refused to stand with the Jews.

There were true Christian people who risked their lives to help the Jews but these were the exception. Where were the Christians during the Holocaust? They had centuries of anti-Semitism in their own church doctrines and practices that enabled them to embrace the Nazi propaganda of hate against the Jews.

We Christians must examine our hearts and ask the Lord to reveal and remove any hatred we may have towards Jews. We must repent of the past sins of the Church and then go to the Jewish community in our neighborhoods and ask for forgiveness. We must determine to take our stand with the Jewish people and bless, comfort, love, and support them with our prayers and deeds of kindness.

We Christians must say to our Jewish friends, "Never Again" will we stand on the sidelines when you are persecuted for the mere fact that you are Jews. Only then will the curse of Abraham be lifted off the Church and the fullness of God's blessing be given to the people of God.

Chapter 7—Personal Study Guide

1. Discuss the major contributing factors to the church separating from its Jewish roots.

2. Explain who killed Jesus.

3. Discuss the allegorical interpretation of Scripture and the role of Clement, Origen, and Eusebius.

4. Discuss the person of Constantine and the impact he had on Christianity.

5. Discuss the Council of Nicea and the impact it had on Christianity.

6. Discuss the person of Augustine and the impact he had on Christianity.

7. Describe the following:
   A. Russian *Pogroms*

   B. Protocols of Learned Elders of Zion

8. Describe the Holocaust

9. How should Christians relate to the Jewish people in light of the Holocaust?

Chapter 8
Judaism and Christianity

For centuries, the Church has taught that Judaism is a religion of law and works while Christianity is a religion of grace and faith. In fact, anytime Christians speak about the Jewish roots of their faith, they are accused of trying to put Christians "under the Law." This is a false teaching that developed early in the Christian era by the same Greek philosophers mentioned in the previous chapter. They despised the Jews, had no connection to the Hebraic background of the New Testament, and sought to sever Christianity from its Hebraic/Jewish roots.

Because of their background and education, the early church fathers misunderstood and misinterpreted many of Paul's sayings, which they used to establish differences in Christianity and Judaism that cannot be supported in the Bible.

D. Amiel Amos has noted the following similarities between Judaism and Christianity:

1. Both affirm a living God; the God of Abraham, Isaac and Jacob; the God of Israel as both Creator and King, Judge and Redeemer.
2. Both understand that Abraham was called from a pagan land to follow "El Shaddai" and that Abraham would be established as the covenant father of many nations.
3. Both see God as revealing Himself through acts in human history, and the Bible is seen as both the means and source for this revelation.
4. Both see man as in need of redemption; responsible to God on his own volition. Both see man as rebelling against God and that man's only hope for salvation is through repentance and a restoration of his relationship with God in total love and obedience.

5. Both see that this restoration is only possible through the grace and lovingkindness of a merciful God.
6. Both understand that ethical obedience is an essential requirement of the faith and that God demands a moral righteousness in our life and actions towards others.
7. Both are eschatological in that they see and expect a culmination of history that will have both judgment and fulfillment. Then the full meaning of life and history will be revealed.
8. Both are historical religions in that faith is enacted in history and in historical events. Neither Judaism nor Christianity can be understood apart from history. This is represented by Sinai for the Jew and the resurrection for the Christian since both are events in history."[109]

While it is clear that there are differences between rabbinic Judaism and Constantine Christianity, it is the author's belief that biblical Judaism and biblical Christianity are the same. Both require grace and faith that leads to works of lovingkindness as evidence of one's relationship to the Lord.

The place of grace and faith in Christianity is well known. But most are not aware that grace and faith are also an important part of Judaism.

The Place of Grace in Judaism and Christianity

The Hebrew word that best expresses the concept of grace is *hesed*. The word means to show favor, mercy, and kindness to one who has no right to claim something from you. In the Hebrew Scriptures it is translated into English by the words "grace," "mercy," and "lovingkindness." It is God's unfailing love and goodness to bless those who do not deserve His blessings.

---

109. D. Amiel Amos, *"Halacha" Jewish Lifestyle*, (Plano, TX: A Beth El Shaddai Publication, 1993), 2-3.

The English word "grace" is found in the Hebrew Scriptures 38 times. We learn in Genesis, "But Noah found grace in the eyes of the LORD" (Genesis 6:8). Our English word "lovingkindness" is mentioned 26 times. Psalm 36:7 reads, "How precious is Your lovingkindness, O God! Therefore the children of men put their trust under the shadow of Your wings."

Hesed is most often translated by the English word "mercy," which is used 205 times in the Hebrew Scriptures. The Psalmist writes, "Oh, give thanks to the LORD, for He is good! for His mercy endures forever" (Psalm 106:1).

This means that the Christian meaning of grace is better understood as mercy. Grace has more of the meaning of beauty, attractiveness, charm, etc. Mercy is understood as God's unmerited favor towards those who don't deserve it.

When the LORD appeared to Moses He revealed Himself to be a God of grace and mercy. We read in Exodus, "Now the LORD descended in the cloud and stood with him [Moses] there, and proclaimed the name of the LORD. And the LORD passed before him and proclaimed, 'The LORD, the LORD God, merciful and gracious, longsuffering, and abounding in goodness and truth.' " (Exodus 34:5-7).

The prophet Daniel offered the following prayer that any "good Christian" could pray, "O my God, incline Your ear and hear; open Your eyes and see our desolations, and the city which is called by Your name; for we do not present our supplications before You because of our righteous deeds, but because of Your great mercies" (Daniel 9:18).

Rabbi David Blumenthal writes that God's grace can be seen in His creation, in His covenant with the Jewish people, and in His forgiveness.[110] He points out that Psalm 136, which begins with the worshipper thanking God for His mercy, continues for the next

---

110. David R. Blumenthal, *The Place of Grace and Faith in Judaism* (Dayton, OH: Center for Judaic-Christian Studies, 1985), 12-15.

eight verses praising God for His mighty acts in creation which are attributed to God's grace or mercy.

Rabbi Blumenthal also notices the clear connection between God's covenant and His grace in Deuteronomy 7:9 which reads as follows, "Therefore know that the LORD your God, He is God, the faithful God who keeps covenant and mercy (grace) for a thousand generations with those who love Him and keep His commandments."

God's grace, mercy, and lovingkindness is clearly evident in His granting forgiveness. King David prayed, "Have mercy upon me, O God, according to Your lovingkindness; according to the multitude of Your tender mercies, blot out my transgressions. Wash me thoroughly from my iniquity, and cleanse me from my sin" (Psalm 51:1-2).

Rabbi Blumenthal shares the following prayer to the LORD from rabbinic Judaism, "Deal with your servant according to Your grace —You really do have pleasure in our good works! But, if we have no merit or good works, act toward us in our *hesed*. As You redeemed those of old, not through their works but through Your grace, so may You act toward us."[111]

The apostle Paul picks up the theme of grace and mercy from the Hebrew Scriptures and carries it into the New Testament. He writes, "For by grace you have been saved through faith, and that not of yourselves, it is the gift of God, not of works, lest anyone should boast"(Ephesians 2:8-9).

Paul further explains, "But when the kindness and the love of God our Savior toward man appeared, not by works of righteousness which we have done, but according to His mercy He saved us..." (Titus 3:4-5).

The Place of Faith in Judaism and Christianity

Judaism and Christianity are both religions of faith. Both claim Abraham as their father, and Abraham was a man of faith.

---
111. Ibid., 15.

We learn from the Book of Genesis, "And he [Abraham] believed in the LORD, and He accounted it to him for righteousness" (Genesis 15:6).

In the New Testament Paul uses Abraham as the great example of the necessity of faith in the life of both Jews and Gentile believers. He explains, "For if Abraham was justified [declared righteous] by works, he has something to boast about, but not before God. For what does the Scripture say? 'Abraham believed God, and it was accounted to him for righteousness' " (Romans 4:2-3).

The Hebrew Scriptures also tell us, "…But the just shall live by his faith" (Habakkuk 2:4). Paul refers to this Scripture and connects it to the gospel message concerning faith in Jesus of Nazareth as Redeemer, Savior, and Lord.

Paul writes, "For I am not ashamed of the gospel of Christ [Messiah], for it is the power of God to salvation for everyone who believes, for the Jew first and also for the Greek. For in it the righteousness of God is revealed from faith to faith; as it is written, 'The just shall live by faith' " (Romans 1:16-17).

Faith and Works in Judaism and Christianity

Biblical Judaism and biblical Christianity include works of lovingkindness as necessary acts of faith without which there is no genuine faith.

We learn from the prophet Micah, "He has shown you, O man, what is good; and what does the LORD require of you but to do justly, to love mercy, and to walk humbly with your God?" (Micah 6:8)

According to the prophet, God expects those who know Him to live a life that reflects His own goodness, justice, and grace (mercy). These characteristics in a person's life are the true evidence that the person has experienced the grace of God in his or her life.

God's grace and mercy operate through faith which is manifested by works of lovingkindness. While we certainly are not saved by works, there is no saving faith without Spirit-inspired-and-empowered works.

The LORD further declares through the prophet Hosea, "For I desire mercy and not sacrifice, and the knowledge of God more than burnt offerings" (Hosea 6:6).

The teaching that genuine, redemptive faith leads to works of lovingkindness is also found in the New Testament.

On one occasion, a certain sect of Pharisee that held to a strict, legalistic keeping of the Sabbath, criticized Jesus for violating their traditions. They accused His disciples of working on the Sabbath by plucking heads of grain when they were hungry.

Jesus answered them with the words from the prophet Hosea. He said, "If you had known what this means, 'I desire mercy and not sacrifice,' you would not have condemned the guiltless" (Matthew 12:7).

James writes these words, "What does it profit, my brethren, if someone says he has faith but does not have works? Can faith save him? If a brother or sister is naked or destitute of daily food, and one of you says to them, 'Depart in peace, be warmed and filled,' but you do not give them the things which are needed for the body, what does it profit? Thus also faith by itself, if it does not have works, is dead" (James 2:14-17).

Christian scholars usually emphasize Paul's statements on grace and faith and totally ignore his statements on works as if grace and faith were opposed to works. Biblically speaking, nothing could be further from the truth. While works of lovingkindness do not produce grace and faith, they are a result of grace and faith.

In his writings, Paul speaks of different kinds of works. One is works of self-righteousness. These are good deeds we do out of our own righteousness in order to gain favor with God. But Daniel (9:18), Isaiah (64:6-7), and Paul (Titus 3:5) agree that our own righteous acts are not the fruit of grace and faith.

Paul also writes of works of lovingkindness that are produced by grace and faith. They are the true evidence of a person's relationship to God. Regarding evil men, he wrote, "They profess to

Judaism and Christianity

know God, but in works they deny Him..."(Titus 1:16). He then writes to the believers, "in all things showing yourself to be a pattern of good works..." (Titus 2:7).

Paul writes of Jesus "who gave Himself for us, that He might redeem us from every lawless deed and purify for Himself His own special people, zealous for good works" (Titus 2:14).

Paul continues, "This is a faithful saying, and these things I want you to affirm constantly, that those who have believed in God should be careful to maintain good works...And let our people also learn to maintain good works, to meet urgent needs, that they may not be unfruitful" (Titus 3:8,14).

Creed or Deed?

While divine grace and faith is a necessary part of Judaism and Christianity, there is a major difference between the two religions in the emphasis they give to faith and works of lovingkindness.

Judaism is more interested in deeds while Christianity stresses creeds. Christianity is more focused on what a person believes than on what a person does. Though Judaism does care about what a person believes, it is much more concerned with what a person does.

During the First Testament era, Jewish religious life centered around the Temple, the sacrificial system, and the duties of the High Priest. The focus was on the offering of the innocent substitutionary sacrifice for atonement for sin. The LORD said to His people, "For the life of the flesh is in the blood, and I have given it to you upon the altar to make atonement for your souls; for it is the blood that makes atonement for the soul" (Leviticus 17:11).

We might say that "Hear O Israel: the LORD our God, the LORD is one" (Deuteronomy 6:4) and "It is the blood that makes atonement for the soul" (Leviticus 17:11) were the two basic creeds of biblical Judaism.

Biblical Judaism emphasized grace, faith, and good works as the fruit of a person's covenant relationship with God. These spiritual qualities did not originate with the New Testament.

When the Babylonians conquered Judea, they burned Jerusalem and the Temple and took the people captive, where they stayed in Babylon for seventy years. During this time of captivity, the Jews did not have a Temple where they could worship God through the sacrifices which God ordained. As a result, the focus of Judaism began to change from Temple worship through sacrifice to the study of *Torah* and good works. This was a major development that would forever change Judaism.

Prior to the captivity, Jews were constantly aware of their covenant with God through Temple worship. Because they were in covenant with God, they studied *Torah* and did good works (*mitzvot*).

These deeds were not done in order to gain God's favor but as evidence of their covenant relationship with God. They already had His favor through covenant. They had been redeemed from Egypt through the blood of the lamb and showed their gratitude by worshipping at the Temple through sacrifices and by doing works of lovingkindness.

When the Jews were in exile and without their Temple, study and deeds became the means to secure God's favor rather than acts of gratitude for already having God's favor.

By the time of the first century of the Christian era, Judaism had shifted from an emphasis on Temple worship as an expression of covenant relationship with God to an emphasis on study and deeds in order to have a covenant relationship with God. What Jews did was more important than what they believed. The emphasis on deeds rather than creeds evolved over the centuries and is a major difference in Judaism and Christianity today.

It is obvious that New Testament Christianity also emphasized grace and faith as well as works of lovingkindness as evidence of true faith. However, as with Judaism, this would soon change.

When Constantine decided to made Christianity the official religion of Rome, it was necessary that he settle several major controversies concerning the nature of Jesus and other issues. He called a church council which met at Nicea in AD 325. At that time, the church council issued a creed for the purpose of defining what Christianity believed.

Later, when other controversies surfaced, more councils met and more creeds were issued. The most famous of the early creeds came to be known as the "Apostles' Creed." The result was that Christianity became a religion of creeds rather than deeds. What a person believed became more important than how a person lived. Christianity would focus on belief in Jesus as the atonement for sin rather than following Jesus as a way of life.

Of course, what a person believes is important. However, the emphasis on creed rather than deed has misled millions of people throughout Christendom to think they could be right with God just because they agreed to a confession of faith without any evidence of grace and faith in their lives producing works of lovingkindness.

It is the author's opinion that both Judaism and Christianity need a better balance of creed and deed. Judaism needs to give more concern to what Jews believe (creed) while Christianity needs more emphasis on lifestyle (deeds). It is important what we believe, and it is important how we live.

Law and Grace

The subject of Law and grace is one of the most difficult to understand and explain because of centuries of wrong teaching in the Christian church. The basic Christian teaching is that "the Jews were saved by the Law (which is bad) while Christians are saved by grace (which is good). Now that Jesus has come, the Law has been done away with and Christians are free to live as they choose."

Once again, this was due to the fact that some of the early Christian fathers and scholars were Greek philosophers who did not have the necessary Hebraic understanding of the teachings of Jesus and the writings of the apostle Paul. The confusion began with a misunderstanding of the word "Law."

The Meaning of *Torah*

The Hebrew word for Law is *Torah*. Strictly speaking, *Torah* refers to the first five books of the Bible including the instructions they contain. In the wider use of the word, *Torah* is often used to refer to the whole of the Hebrew Scriptures, what Christians call the Old Testament.

The more proper name for the Hebrew Scriptures is *Tanakh*. *Tanakh* is an acronym for the three main divisions of the Hebrew Scriptures which are *Torah* (Law or Instructions), *Nevi'im* (Prophets), and *K'tuvim* (Writings).

The root word for *Torah* is another Hebrew word, *yarah*. It was a term used in archery and meant "to take aim," "to shoot," "to hit the mark" as in the shooting of an arrow. *Yarah* meant to "point out," "to teach," "to instruct," "to guide" so that the archer would hit the target with his arrow.

Torah, or Law, in the biblical sense means instructions, guidance, teachings, and directions for walking with God. It does not mean a legalistic set of rules one must follow in order to be saved. The Western view of *Torah* is legalism, but it is not the biblical view, nor was it the view that Jesus and Paul understood.

In the Hebrew Scriptures, *Torah* expressed the will of God in positive and negative commandments (*mitzvot*) that enabled the Jews to "hit the mark" in their walk with God. The rabbis calculated that there were 613 of these commandments or instruction. Of the 613 commandments, 248 are positive commands while 365 are negative.

Torah told the Jews the kind of life that pleased God. *Torah* instructed, guided, and directed the people in their walk with God. They were to keep *Torah* because they loved God and wanted to please Him. A Jew who obeyed the *Torah* would have a full life while one who refused to live by *Torah* would miss God's blessings. Therefore, "To walk in the *Torah*" meant to live a life that pleased God with the result being that the person would enjoy a full, fruitful life.

Paul had this exact idea in mind when he wrote the believers in Galatia to "walk in the Spirit" (Galatians 5:25). Paul meant that the believers should allow the Holy Spirit to control their lives so that they could live a life that pleased God. The Holy Spirit would live out the *Torah* which was written on their hearts. He would enable us to live the true spritual meaning of the *Torah*. This is not legalism, as many would suggest.

The Purpose of the *Torah*

In his excellent booklet, *The Spirit of the Law*, Ron Moseley gives the following nine-fold purpose of the *Torah*:

1. To teach the believer how to serve, worship, and please God (Psalm 19:7-9; Acts 18:13-14)
2. To instruct the believer how to treat his fellow man and have healthy relationships with him (Leviticus 19:18; Galatians 5:14; 6:2)
3. To teach believers how to be happy and prosper here on earth by manifesting the power and authority of God's reign in their lives (Joshua 1:8; Psalm 1:1-3; Luke 12:32)
4. To measure man's deeds both toward God and his fellow man, and straighten out all matters contrary to sound doctrine (1 Timothy 1:8-10; 2 Timothy 2:5; 1 Corinthians 3:13; 6:1-12; Romans 2:12; Revelation 20:12-13)
5. To be a schoolmaster showing that we are guilty of sin and then leading us to Jesus as our means of justification (Galatians 3:21-24; Romans 3:19)
6. To give us both the knowledge and depth of our sin (Romans 3:20; 4:15; 7:7; 8; Luke 20:47)

7. To reveal the good, holy, just and perfect nature of God and serve as the visible standard for God's will (Romans 2:17-18; 7:12; 2 Peter 1:4)
8. To be established or accomplished by faith, therefore, it is called the Law of faith (Romans 3:27, 31)
9. To be written on our hearts, and through God's Spirit, we can delight and serve the Law of God (Romans 7:6-25)."[112]

The Essence and Blessings of *Torah*

We discover the essence of *Torah* in the following Scripture, "And now, Israel, what does the LORD your God require of you, but to fear the LORD your God, to walk in all His ways and to love Him, to serve the LORD your God with all your heart and with all your soul, and to keep the commandments of the LORD and His statutes which I command you this day for your good?" (Deuteronomy 10:12-13)

The *Tanakh* uses various words to refer to the LORD'S instructions for His people. The most commonly used words are: 1) laws, 2) commands, 3) decrees, 4) judgments, 5) ordinances, 6) statutes, 7) testimonies, etc.

While these words have different meanings, they all relate to the way of life God expected of His people. Those who loved the LORD delighted in His instructions and sought to please Him by obeying His word. The New Testament teaches this same view of love towards God.

Psalm 119 gives the following statements about God's *Torah*:

"Blessed are the undefiled in the way, who walk in the law of the LORD! Blessed are those who keep His testimonies, who seek Him with the whole heart" (Psalm 119:1-2)

"With my whole heart I have sought You; Oh, let me not wander from Your commandments!" (Psalm 119:10)

---

112. Ron Moseley, *The Spirit of the Law* (Sherwood, AR: Mozark Research Foundation, 1993), 22-24.

"I have rejoiced in the way of Your testimonies,...I will meditate on Your precepts, and contemplate Your ways. I will delight myself in Your statutes; I will not forget Your word" (Psalm 119:14-16).

"...But Your servant meditates on Your statutes. Your testimonies also are my delight and my counselors" (Psalm 119:23-24).

"Teach me, O LORD, the way of Your statutes, and I shall keep it to the end. Give me understanding, and I shall keep Your law; indeed, I shall observe it with my whole heart. Make me walk in the path of Your commandments, for I delight in it" (Psalm 119:33-35).

"Unless Your law had been my delight, I would then have perished in my affliction. I will never forget Your precepts, for by them You have given me life" (Psalm 119:92-93).

"Oh, how I love Your law! It is my meditation all the day. You, through Your commandments, make me wiser than my enemies; for they are ever with me.

"I have more understanding than all my teachers, for Your testimonies are my meditation. I understand more than the ancients, because I keep your precepts" (Psalm 119:97-100).

Psalm 1:1-2 reads, "Blessed is the man who walks not in the counsel of the ungodly, nor stands in the path of sinners, nor sits in the seat of the scornful; but his delight is in the law of the LORD, and in His law he meditates day and night."

Psalm 19:7 says, "The law of the LORD is perfect, converting the soul...."

Jeremiah tells us that God will put His *Torah* in our minds and write it on our hearts (Jeremiah 31:33).

Torah in the New Testament

We noted in an earlier chapter that Jesus perfectly kept the *Torah*. He said, "Do not think that I came to destroy the Law or the Prophets. I did not come to destroy but to fulfill. For assuredly, I say to you, till heaven and earth pass away, one jot or one tittle will by no means pass from the law till all is fulfilled" (Matthew 5:17-18).

The word "fulfill" does not mean to abolish but to give the correct interpretation. From a Christian view, Jesus was the embodiment of the *Torah*. He was the living *Torah* in human flesh whose life and teachings exemplified the true meaning and interpretation of the *Torah*. When understood biblically, Jesus embodies the grace or beauty of the *Torah* because He lived the true meaning of *Torah*.

Jesus certainly did not view *Torah* as a burdensome, legalistic system of laws which the Jews had to keep to be saved. Jesus understood *Torah* as the expression of God's will for right living. He lived it perfectly.

The Book of Acts informs us that many thousands of Jews were followers of Jesus and were also zealous for the *Torah* (Acts 21:20).

Because of the misunderstanding of the meaning of *Torah* and its role in the life of the Jews, Paul is accused of being anti-*Torah*. Yet Paul wrote, "Therefore the law is holy, and the commandment holy and just and good" (Romans 7:12). He said, "For we know that the law is spiritual..." (vrs.14). "For I delight in the law of God according to the inward man" (vrs. 22).

Paul was a *Torah*-observant Jew. He circumcised Timothy (Acts 16:3), regularly attended synagogue (17:2), took a Jewish vow (18:18), hurried to Jerusalem to keep the Feast of Pentecost [*Shavu'ot*], paid for other Jews to offer sacrifices at the Temple (21:23-27), and claimed to have kept the laws and customs of his people (25:8; 28:17).

Jewish followers of Jesus in the New Testament era kept the *Torah*, not in order to be saved, but because they were saved. They accepted Jesus as the true interpretation of *Torah* and sought to live their faith within the context of their culture and customs. We need to understand very clearly that God never "did away" with the *Torah*.

Rabbi Wayne Dosick explains that approximately 200 of the 613 *Torah* instructions cannot be kept at this time because they relate to Temple worship and/or living in the land.[113]

This means that about 413 *Torah* instructions can still be kept. When the Jews rebuild the Temple and return to the land, all 613 *Torah* instructions will be applicable.

The *Torah* and Gentiles

In the New Testament period, many Gentiles embraced Jesus as their Lord and Savior. The question arose about their responsibility to the *Torah*. A special council was called to resolve the problem. James headed the council and gave the final verdict.

James recognized that the Gentiles were saved by grace through faith in Jesus (Acts 15:9-10), but for purposes of fellowship with their Jewish brethren, the Gentile converts should: 1) abstain from things polluted by idols, 2) from sexual immorality, 3) from things strangled, and, 4) from blood.

Although the Jerusalem Council gave only these four requirements, the Gentile believers were encouraged to learn the *Torah* and keep as much of it as they desired, particularly the elements of *Torah* that so clearly pointed to Jesus. The purpose was not to be saved but to relate to their Jewish brothers and sisters.

The *Torah* Misinterpreted

How did something so wonderful as the *Torah* become a "despised legalistic system of rules" that Jesus and Paul supposedly declared to be null and void? How did Western Christianity come to so misunderstand this critical subject? It came about when the Hebrew Scriptures were translated into Greek in the Septuagint in approximately 250 BC.

---

113. Dosick, 33.

The Greeks did not have a word that was the equivalent of *Torah* (instructions). They used the closest Greek word which was *nomos*. *Nomos* means "law."

When the Bible was translated into English, *Torah* was interpreted by the Western concept of law—not as instructions for righteous living as the Jews understood the term, but as a burdensome, legalistic set of rules and regulations no longer in force.

This misunderstanding of the meaning of *Torah*, combined with the anti-Semitism of the early church fathers, resulted in misinterpretation of the sayings of Jesus, the gospel writers, and especially Paul, when they spoke about the Law.

The Greek-speaking church fathers erroneously concluded that the Jews were saved by keeping the Law. But now through Jesus we are saved by grace, so there is no longer any need for the Law.

But as we have just learned, both biblical Judaism and biblical Christianity teach that salvation is by grace through faith in the blood of the innocent subsitutionary sacrifice given for sin. The New Testament presents Jesus as that innocent substitutionary sacrifice. The unfortunate result of this misunderstanding is that Christianity became a "lawless" religion in which people believed they could simply confess a creed and live any way they desired.

Problem Passages

When Paul appears to be speaking against the *Torah*, he is actually speaking against the misuse of the *Torah* as a legalistic system of rules to be kept for salvation.

Paul also speaks against a certain group of Jewish believers called Judaizers who taught that the Gentiles had to keep the *Torah* as a requirement for salvation.

Paul also speaks of different kinds of laws but this is hard to distinguish because the same Greek *nomos* is used for each reference and translated into English as law without any distinction.

In fact, the Greek word *nomos* is used 190 times in the New Testament. It is variously translated into English and referred to as "another law," "the law of sin," "the law of God," "law of the Spirit of life in Christ," "law of sin and death," "law of righteousness," "works of law," "under the law," "end of the law," "book of the law," and "curse of the law."

Since Paul's writings do not make a clear distinction between the holy "Law of God" and the "law of sin and death," it is easy to get confused and think that Paul was writing negatively about the *Torah*.

C.E.B. Cranfield explains, "…the Greek language of Paul's day possessed no word group corresponding to our 'legalism,' 'legalist,' and 'legalistic.' This means that he lacked a convenient terminology for expressing a vital distinction, and so was surely seriously hampered in the work of clarifying the Christian position with regard to the law.

"In view of this, we should always, we think, be ready to reckon with the possibility that Pauline statements, which at first seem to disparage the law, were really directed not against the law itself but against the misunderstanding and misuse of it for which we now have a convenient terminology. In this very difficult terrain Paul was pioneering."[114]

As mentioned, when Paul seems to be writing negatively about the *Torah*, he is writing against the misuse of the *Torah* as a legalistic system of rules and regulations one must keep in order to be saved. Phrases such as "under the law," "works of the law," "curse of the law," etc., refer to this perversion of the law.

Paul clearly seems to say that the Law has been terminated in Romans 10:4. He writes, "For Christ is the end of the law for righteousness to everyone who believes."

The Greek word translated as end is *telos*. The meaning of *telos* is "goal" or "purpose." Paul is simply saying that the *Torah*

---

114. David Stern, 47.

pointed people to Jesus as the ultimate goal and reality of the *Torah*.

This is the same thought Jesus was presenting when He said He did not come to destroy the Law or the Prophets but to fulfill them (Matthew 5:17).

New Testament Statements About the *Torah*

Ron Moseley identifies the following 12 statements the New Testament makes about the Torah:
1. The hearers of the Law are not justified before the Lord, but the doers of the Law will be justified (Romans 2:23)
2. Paul taught the Ephesians that the promises of God come out of the Law and they were to obey them so things could be well with them and that they may live long on this earth (Ephesians 6:2-3; Exodus 20:12; Deuteronomy 5:16)
3. The writer of the Book of Hebrews confirms that this is the same covenant of God's Law that He promised to renew by writing it on our hearts and minds (Hebrews 10:16)
4. James reminds us that if we commit sin, we are actually transgressing the Law (James 2:11; 2:8-26)
5. By keeping the Lord's commandments we know that we know Him (1 John 2:3-4)
6. We have our prayers answered because we keep the Lord's commandments and do those things pleasing in His sight (1 John 3:22)
7. As we keep the commandments, God will dwell in us and we will have assurance through His Spirit (1 John 3:24)
8. By the keeping of God's commandments we know that our love for God and His children is real (1 John 5:2-3)
9. The definition of biblical love is to walk after God's commandments (2 John 6)

10. Only those who keep the Lord's commandments will have the right to the Tree of Life (Revelation 22:14)
11. Referring to the Old Testament (Hebrew Scriptures), the only Law available, James says, whosoever looks into the perfect Law of Liberty, and continues therein, being not a forgetful hearer, but a doer of the work, shall be blessed in his deed (James 1:25)
12. The man who says he knows the Lord, but does not keep His commandments is a liar and the truth is not in him (1 John 2:4).[115]

The *Torah* and Christians

The Jews in the First Testament era were redeemed from Egypt by the blood of the lamb. The LORD then gave them the *Torah* to show His covenant people how to walk with Him.

While the people were not perfect, and often failed God, those who loved God lived according to the *Torah* as an expression of the grace and faith they had in Him. To "walk in the *Torah*" meant to walk with God, not in order to be saved (redeemed), but because they already were saved.

The rabbis determined that the *Torah* had 613 instructions, 248 positive commands and 365 negative commands. These instructions guided the people in their walk with God.

During the intertestamental period, there was a gradual change in the thinking regarding the role of the *Torah*. Many rabbis taught that "keeping the *Torah*" was necessary for redemption rather than the result of redemption.

In was during this time that, for some, *Torah* became a legalistic system of rules and regulations people were required to keep in order to gain God's favor rather than an expression of grace and faith in their hearts. Judaism was becoming more of a religion than a company of people in covenant reationship with God.

---

115. Moseley, 48-50.

To summarize, Jewish followers of Jesus in the New Testament were zealous to keep the *Torah* (Acts 20:21) and most of the *Torah* is still applicable for Jews in our modern times.

While the Gentile believers (Christians) were given only four instructions for the purpose of fellowship with their Jewish brethren, they were encouraged to learn the *Torah* and keep as much as they desired (Acts 15:9-10).

Because of the misunderstanding of the relationship between grace, faith, and law, the Church has taught that grace means that Christians are free from any *Torah* in their lives and can live as they please. Nothing could be further from the truth.

While there are only 613 commandments in the *Torah* for the Jews, the New Testament contains approximately 1050 commandments to the followers of Jesus, be they Jew or Gentile.[116]

In fact, the entire New Testament is *Torah*. Jesus said to His followers, "Go therefore and make disciples of all the nations, baptizing them in the name of the Father and of the Son and of the Holy Spirit, teaching them to observe all things that I have commanded you; and lo, I am with you always, even to the end of the age" (Matthew 28:19-20).

John further wrote these words of Jesus, "If you love Me, keep My commandments. And I will pray the Father, and He will give you another Helper, that He may abide with you forever—the Spirit of truth, whom the world cannot receive, because it neither sees Him nor knows Him; but you know Him, for He dwells with you and will be in you" (John 14:15-17).

Paul exhorts Christians to "walk in the Spirit" (Galatians 5:25). This is simply another way of saying, "walk in the *Torah* of the New Testament." We walk in the Spirit by allowing the Holy Spirit to empower us so we can keep the 1050 commandments in the New Testament. This is how we present our bodies as a living sacrifice to God (Romans 12:1-2).

---

116. Stern, 58.

Christians do not keep the New Testament *Torah* in order to be saved (redeemed) but because we have been saved by the blood of the Lamb of God (1 Peter 1:18-21). We are not perfect, and often fail God, but we seek to keep His commandments as an expression of the grace and faith He has put in our hearts.

This is what it means to be saved by grace through faith. We have been set free from the powers of darkness and the law of sin and death that we might keep the New Testament *Torah* to the glory of God in our lives.

Chapter 8—Personal Study Guide

1. Explain the place of grace in Judaism and Christianity.

2. Explain the place of faith in Judaism and Christianity.

3. Explain the relationship between faith and works in Judaism and Christianity.

Chapter 9
Basic Jewish Beliefs and Christianity

In the preceding chapters, we studied the historical aspects of Jews and Judaism and the relationship between Judaism and Christianity. We learned that the Almighty chose Abraham and his descendants for certain of His divine plans and purposes on the earth.

Because of their divine calling, the LORD promised to keep alive a remnant of Jews down through the ages, even though they should have passed off the stage of world history long ago.

We learned of the call of Abraham and his descendants who formed themselves into twelve tribes that eventually became the nation of Israel. We surveyed their story in the First Testament, between the Testaments, and in the New Testament era. We learned of the relationship between the Jewish people and Rome and the tragic history of Christian anti-Semitism.

In the last chapter, we noted similarities between biblical Judaism and biblical Christianity while pointing out how Christendom has misunderstood and misinterpreted much of the New Testament to the detriment of both Jews and Christians.

In the chapters that follow, we will seek to understand Judaism from a practical standpoint by learning basic Jewish beliefs and practices, the Jewish life cycle, religious cycle, and Jewish denominations and literature.

The purpose of learning this material is not to make righteous Gentiles into Jews, nor to "put Christians under the Law." The purpose is to help Gentile believers better understand the rich Hebraic/Jewish-Christian connection in the Bible as well as in Jewish tradition.

Basic Jewish Beliefs

While Christianity in general has a core set of basic beliefs, the various denominations differ on their interpretation and practice of Bible doctrines. The same is true in Judaism.

For purposes of this chapter, we need to know that Judaism is divided by various denominations, and as with Christianity, they vary in their interpretation and practice of their faith.

Orthodox Judaism adheres more closely to the ancient traditions of the sages in both doctrine and practice. Conservative Judaism holds to the doctrinal beliefs of traditional Judaism but seeks to practice their faith in a way compatible with American culture. Reform Judaism is very liberal in both doctrine and practice.

There is also a small group called Reconstructionist, as well as secular Judaism. Perhaps the most controversial group, as well as the fastest growing, is Messianic Judaism. These are Jews who acknowledge Jesus as Messiah.

The Thirteen Principles

Moses Maimonides (AD 1138–1204) was a prolific writer and is considered to be one of the greatest of Jewish scholars. He is widely known as *Rambam* from the acronym of Rabbi Moses Ben Maimon. He wrote the *Thirteen Principles of Faith* in which he sought to codify Jewish beliefs. While not all agree with his views, the *Thirteen Principles of Faith* became a classic in Jewish literature.

In this important work, Maimonides begins each of the Thirteen Principles with the phrase, "I believe with perfect faith." His following statements give a good basic understanding of traditional Jewish beliefs.

"I believe with perfect faith…
1. …that the Creator, blessed be His Name, is the Author and Guide of everything that has been created and that He alone has made, does make, and will make all things.
2. …that the Creator, blessed be His Name, is a Unity, and that there is no Unity in any manner like unto His, and that He alone is our God who was, is, and will be.

3. …that the Creator, blessed be His Name, is not a body and that He is free from all the properties of matter, and that He has not any form whatsoever.
4. …that the Creator, blessed be His name, is the First and the Last.
5. …that unto Him alone, it is right to pray, and that it is not right to pray to any being besides Him.
6. …that all the words of the Prophets are true.
7. …that the prophecy of Moses, our teacher, peace be unto him, was true, and that he was the chief of the Prophets, both those who preceded him and those who followed him.
8. …that the whole *Torah* now in our possession is the same that was given to Moses, our teacher, peace be unto him.
9. …that this *Torah* will not be exchanged, and there will never be any other law from the Creator, blessed be His Name.
10. …that the Creator, blessed be His Name, knows every deed of the children of men, and all their thoughts, as it is said, 'It is He that fashioneth the hearts of them all, that give heed to all their works.'
11. …that the Creator, blessed be His Name, rewards those that keep His commandments, and punishes those that transgress them.
12. …in the coming of the Messiah, and though he tarry, I will wait daily for his coming.
13. …that there will be a revival of the dead at the time when it shall please the Creator, blessed be His Name and exalted be His Name forever and ever."[117]

---

117. Benjamin Blech, *Understanding Judaism* (Northvale, NJ: Jason Aronson, 1991), 227-228).

The Hebrew Scriptures

We noted in the previous chapter that Christendom refers to the first part of the Bible as the Old Testament. This is unfortunate because such a designation implies that this part of the Bible is no longer relevant and has been replaced with the New Testament.

The Hebrew Scriptures are certainly relevant to our day, and they have not been replaced with the New Testament. From a Christian perspective, we might consider the New Testament as a "Messianic Commentary" on the Hebrew Scriptures.

We also pointed out that Jewish people call the Hebrew Scriptures the *Tanakh*. This Hebrew word is an acronym formed by taking the first letter of each of the three sections of the Hebrew Bible and making them into a new word—*Tanakh*.

As previously mentioned, the three sections in the Hebrew Bible, are: 1) *Torah* (Instructions), 2) *Nevi'im* (Prophets), and last, 3) *K'tuvim* (Writings). Vowels and vowel points are added for pronunciation. These are the same books found in the first part of the Christian Bible, but they are arranged in a different order.

Torah

The word *Torah* means instruction or teaching. It does not mean a legalistic way of salvation. In the most narrow use of the word, *Torah* refers to the first five books of the Bible.

These books are often called the Five Books of Moses. The word is sometimes used to refer to the entire *Tanakh* as well as the *Talmud* (traditional Jewish writings). It may also be used to refer to the scroll containing the first five books of the Bible.

In Hebrew, these books are sometimes called the *Chumash* because this is the Hebrew word for five. The five books of the *Torah* are: 1) Genesis, 2) Exodus, 3) Leviticus, 4) Numbers, and 5) Deuteronomy.

The *Torah* is handwritten on a scroll by scribes who have been trained for such a sacred duty. The scroll is called *Sefer Torah*. This scroll is kept in an ark in the synagogue sanctuary when not in use.

For purposes of reading, the *Torah* has been divided into fifty-four portions. A portion is read every Sabbath each week of the year beginning at Genesis as well as completing the reading cycle on the Jewish holiday called *Simchat Torah* (rejoicing in the *Torah*). This is a special holiday after the last day of the Feast of Tabernacles (*Sukkot*). In this way, the entire *Torah* can be read in one year. Select portions are also read during the High Holy Days on the Jewish calendar.

Nevi'im

The second section of the Hebrew Bible is known as the Prophets. *Nevi'im* is divided into two divisions which are: 1) The Early Prophets, and 2) The Latter Prophets.

The Early Prophets consists of the following books:
1. Joshua
2. Judges
3. 1 and 2 Samuel
4. 1 and 2 Kings

The Latter Prophets is further sub-divided into the Major Prophets and the Minor Prophets. The Major Prophets are:
1. Isaiah
2. Jeremiah
3. Ezekiel

The twelve Minor Prophets are:
1. Hosea
2. Joel
3. Amos
4. Obadiah
5. Jonah
6. Micah

7. Nahum
8. Habakkuk
9. Zephaniah
10. Haggai
11. Zechariah
12. Malachi

K'tuvim

The third section in the Hebrew Scriptures is known as the Writings. It consists of the following twelve books.
The three books of poetry and wisdom:
1. Psalms
2. Proverbs
3. Job

The five *Megillot* (scrolls):
4. Song of Songs
5. Ruth
6. Lamentations
7. Ecclesiastes
8. Esther

The four books of history:
9. Daniel
10. Ezra
11. Nehemiah
12. 1 and 2 Chronicles

Jewish Views About the *Tanakh*

Jews consider the *Torah* to be the most inspired part of the *Tanakh* because the LORD gave it directly to Moses. They consider the rest of the Hebrew Scriptures inspired, but to a lesser degree than the *Torah*.

The Orthodox and Conservative Jews view the Hebrew Bible as being the literal record of God at work in history in the midst of

His creation. They accept the traditional interpretations from rabbinic writings as to the significance of these events.

Many Jews consider these traditional writings in the *Talmud*, the Oral Law, to be equally inspired as the Tanakh.

Reform Jews have a more liberal view of the Hebrew Bible. They do not understand their Scriptures to be inspired by God in the same sense as do the Orthodox and Conservative Jews. Neither do they accept the biblical writings as being a record of literal, historical events, full of the supernatural, and free of error.

Reform Jews look to the *Tanakh* as a book that teaches moral and ethical truths which do not necessarily reflect actual, historical events.

The New Testament view is that the entire Hebrew Bible is the inspired word of God. Paul was referring to the *Tanakh* when he wrote, "All Scripture is given by inspiration of God, and is profitable for doctrine, for reproof, for correction, for instruction in righteousness, that the man of God may be complete, thoroughly equipped for every good work" (2 Timothy 3:16-17).

Jesus said the *Tanakh* was pointing to Himself as the Messiah who would die for our sins but be raised from the dead.

Luke records these words from Jesus, "Then He said to them, 'These are the words which I spoke to you while I was still with you, that all things must be fulfilled which were written in the Law of Moses [*Torah*] and the Prophets [*Nevi'im*] and the Psalms [*K'tuv'im*] concerning Me.'

"And He opened their understanding, that they might comprehend the Scriptures [*Tanakh*].

"Then He said to them, 'Thus it is written, and thus it was necessary for the Christ [Messiah] to suffer and to rise from the dead the third day, and that repentance and remission of sins should be preached in His name to all nations, beginning at Jerusalem. And you are witnesses of these things'" (Luke 24:44-48).

God

Traditional Judaism teaches belief in a personal God who created mankind in His image, revealed Himself at Sinai through *Torah*, and will redeem mankind at the end of the age. Rabbi Morris Kertzer writes, "It has been said that you can sum up Jewish belief in these three words, *God, Torah, Israel.*"[118]

The Jewish declaration of faith in God is called the Shema (meaning "hear") and is based on Deuteronomy 6:4. It reads, "Hear, O Israel: The LORD our God, the LORD is one!" In Hebrew it reads, *Shema, Yisrael: Adonai Eloheynu, Adonai Echad.* This confession is repeated as a daily prayer by observant Jews along with Deuteronomy 11:13-21 and Numbers 15:37-41.

The next verse reads, "You shall love the LORD your God with all your heart, with all your soul, and with all your strength" (Deuteronomy 6:5).

Since this is the most important faith declaration in Judaism, it is helpful to learn what it really means.

Shema Yisrael

This declaration begins with the exhortation: "Hear, O Israel." This opening statement tells us that the God of the Jews is a personal God for He asks us to listen to Him, which would not be possible if God was simply a force or power without personality. It also tells us that God wants to communicate with us and that we can hear Him.

This was certainly a new revelation when God gave it centuries ago, because the pagan nations of the world at that time worshipped impersonal deities that could neither speak nor hear. The God of the Bible wants to relate to us personally and desires that we know Him intimately.

---

118. Kertzer, 109.

Adonai Eloheynu

The second part of the declaration is: "The LORD our God." This statement is important because it identifies God by His name. The word "God" is generic and can refer to any deity.

The ancient world had many gods, and the only way to know which god they worshipped was to identify the god by name.

When the God of the Bible identified Himself to Moses He revealed His name by saying, "I AM WHO I AM" (Exodus 3:13-15). This most unusual name in Hebrew is spelled *YHWH* and means "to be."

This self-disclosure by God tells us that He is the Self-Existing One who transcends time and space. He "was," "is," and "will always be." He is the same yesterday, today, and tomorrow. He is limitless, measureless, and boundless. Therefore, He is all-sufficient to meet every need of those who call upon His name.

God's name was so sacred to the Hebrews they were afraid to even pronounce it. In fact, they were not even sure how to pronounce God's name since it does not have vowels. When the Hebrews wanted to use God's name, they substituted the word Lord (*Adonai* in Hebrew).

However, the word Lord also refers to God's rule over His creation. When they wrote about God, the Hebrews had to have some way to distinguish when they were talking about His name and when they were talking about His rule. When the Bible was translated into English, the word LORD was put in all capital letters when it referred to God's name and lower case Lord when it referred to His rule.

Hebrew Bible scholars called the Massoretes added vowel points to the Hebrew Scriptures to help us pronounce the words. During the Renaissance and Reformation period, Gentile Bible scholars misunderstood these vowel points and thought God's name was *Yahweh*, pronounced as Jehovah. Ever since then, Christians have used this name when addressing the God of the Bible.

The LORD is not the "generic god of the world." His name is not Vishnu (Hindu), nor Allah (Islam). His name is YHWH. He is not the god of other religions. He is not the god of Mohammed, Komheini and Arafat. He is the covenant God of Abraham, Isaac, and Jacob. He is not the god of the Koran. He is the God of the Bible.

The Hebrew word used in the Shema for God is *Eloheynu*. This is a plural form of the word which is translated into English as God. In this self-disclosure, God is telling us something very interesting about His nature. He is informing us that He is one God but, in a way hard for us to understand, He exists as a composite unity.

Christianity has understood this to mean that God is one God who has revealed Himself as a triunity, or Trinity. Because Christianity teaches that God exists as a Trinity, this has been misunderstood to believe that Christians worship three Gods.

Christians do not worship three Gods. We worship the one God of the Bible and believe He exists as a Trinity. This understanding is further suggested by the next phrase in the Shema.

Adonai Echad

These words tell us that the "LORD is One." There is more to this statement than meets the eye because of the meaning of the word "One." There are two Hebrew words used in the Scripture that are translated into English by the word one. One word is *yachid*. This word means absolute unity as in "only one." For example, we see the use of this word in Genesis 22:2 where God says to Abraham, "…Take now your son, your only son Isaac…." Isaac was the one and only child of Abraham by Sarah.

Another Hebrew word for one is *echad*. This word means one in the sense of a composite unity. We find this word used, for example, in Genesis 2:24, which reads, "Therefore shall a man leave his father and mother and be joined to his wife, and they shall become one flesh." Adam and Eve were two different personalities but they were one in that they came together in unity as one flesh.

Another example of the use of *echad* is in Genesis 11:6 which says, "And the LORD said, 'Indeed the people are one....' " The background of this statement was the people coming together to build the Tower of Babel. There were many people but they were in unity regarding the building of a tower in order to make a name for themselves.

For one further example, we turn to the Book of Numbers which tells us about the spies carrying a cluster of grapes. It says, "Then they came to the Valley of Eshcol, and there cut down a branch with one [echad] cluster of grapes..." (Numbers 13:23). Although this was one cluster, it contained many grapes. It was a composite unity.

Several passages in the Hebrew Scriptures help us understand this aspect of God's nature. In Genesis 1:26, God says in regard to Himself, "...Let Us make man in Our image, according to Our likeness...." We read in Genesis 3:22, "Then the LORD God said, 'Behold, the man has become like one of Us....'." He is speaking of Himself as a composite unity.

The Hebrew Scriptures also speak of God having a Son. Psalm 2 tells us that God's Anointed [Messiah] and King is none other than God's Son. It reads, "I will declare the decree: the LORD has said to Me, You are My Son, today I have begotten You. Ask of Me, and I will give You the nations for Your inheritance, and the ends of the earth for Your possession....Kiss the Son, lest He be angry, and you perish in the way, when His wrath is kindled but a little. Blessed are all those who put their trust in Him" (Psalm 2:7-8,12).

We also discover in Proverbs a question regarding the name of God's Son. It reads, "...What is His [God's] name, and what is Son's name, if you know?" (Proverbs 30:4).

The prophet Isaiah refers to God as Father (*Abba*), the Messiah (*Moshiach*), and the Holy Spirit (*Ruach HaKodesh*) in his grand statements as recorded in Isaiah 63.

It's unfortunate that when Moses Maimonides wrote his *Thirteen Articles* he substituted *yachid* in place of *echad* when commenting on the *Shema*. The obvious implications of God being a composite unity were too much for him to face in light of Christian teachings on the composite nature of God.

All of this information strongly suggests to us that, while there is only one God, He exists as a collective unit which Christianity understands as a Triunity. This is not a pagan concept which the Christians made up in the New Testament.

The fact that God is a composite unity is suggested in the most fundamental statement of faith in Judaism. He is the One God of Abraham, Isaac, and Jacob who exists in more than one personality. This understanding of the nature of God is given in the Hebrew Scriptures and fully revealed in the New Testament as Father, Son, and Holy Spirit.

The New Testament presents Jesus of Nazareth as the Son of God referred to in the Hebrew Scriptures. When Jesus was baptized, both the Father and the Holy Spirit were involved.

Matthew writes, "When He had been baptized, Jesus came up immediately from the water; and behold, the heavens were opened to Him, and He saw the Spirit of God descending like a dove and alighting upon Him. And suddenly a voice came from heaven, saying, 'This is My beloved Son, in whom I am well pleased.' " (Matthew 3:16-17).

On one occasion, a religious leader among the Jews asked Jesus the following pointed question, " 'Teacher, which is the great commandment in the law?' Jesus said to him, 'You shall love the LORD your God with all your heart, with all your soul, and with all your mind.' This is the first and great commandment. And the second is like it: 'You shall love your neighbor as yourself.' On these two commandments hang all the Law and the Prophets" (Matthew 22:35-40).

Jesus would never contradict the *Torah*. He answered the question by referring the man to the *Shema* and its demands to love God as the greatest of all the commandments.

Jesus also spoke of the composite unity of God when He told His followers, "Go therefore and make disciples of all the nations, baptizing them in the name of the Father and of the Son and of the Holy Spirit, teaching them to observe all things that I have commanded you; and lo, I am with you always, even to the end of the age" (Matthew 28:19-20).

Man and Sin

The Bible tell us that Adam was created in the image of God, but that he sinned against God. The result was that Adam was separated from God by his sin. As a consequence of Adam's sin, death entered into the human race, and all of us die because all of us sin (Genesis 1:26-27; 3).

The *Tanakh* says, "The LORD looks down from heaven upon the children of men, to see if there are any who understand, who seek God. They have all turned aside, they have together become corrupt; there is none who does good, no not one" (Psalm 14:2-3). (See also Psalm 53:2-3.)

The writer of Ecclesiastes says, "For there is not a just man on earth who does good and does not sin" (Ecclesiates 7:20). King David confessed to the LORD, "Behold, I was brought forth in iniquity, and in sin my mother conceived me" (Psalm 51:5).

The apostle Paul refers to these verses when he writes, "There is none righteous, no, not one; there is none who understands; there is none who seeks after God. They have all turned aside; they have together become unprofitable; there is none who does good, no, not one....For all have sinned and fall short of the glory of God" (Romans 3:10-12,23).

While both Judaism and Christianity recognize the obvious, that human beings are sinners, they have different views on the nature of man. Unlike Christianity, Judaism does not teach the doctrine of "original sin," which means that man inherits a sin nature passed down from Adam to all his descendants.

Instead, Judaism teaches that when we are born, our soul is pure and is composed of two basic inclinations. These are the bad or evil inclination (*yetser hara*) and the good inclination (*yetser hatov*).

Judaism teaches that man has a free will and can choose good or evil through his own actions. In this view, while man has evil tendencies, he is basically good and can act in a righteous way through his own efforts without requiring divine assistance. While he may be temporarily overcome by his evil inclination which leads him to sin, man can choose to master it and do good.

This is a much more positive view of man's potential than is taught in Christianity. This view encourages mankind to do their best to follow their *yetser hatov* in order to reach their full potential for good rather than acknowledging their need for a spiritual change within.

The Jewish understanding of sin has changed much through the centuries. In Bible times, sin was thought of as falling short of the moral perfections of God. It meant to "miss the mark."

This could be witting or unwitting. It related to our falling short in our relationship with God, God's commandments, and our fellow man. The remedy was to make atonement by bringing a sin offering or trespass offering to the LORD, confessing one's sins, and making restitution.

For many Jews today, sin is seen as failing to live up to the high moral standards that are part of being Jewish. But all sense of morality originates in the moral character of God.

Most of Christianity believes the Bible teaches the concept of "original sin." As just mentioned, this means that when Adam sinned, his basic nature was changed from being righteous to being sinful, and that we have all inherited this sinful nature. King David said, "We are born in sin."

In the New Testament, Jesus seemed to be agreeing with this view when He said, "For from within, out of the heart of men, proceed evil thoughts, adulteries, fornications, murders, thefts, covetousness, wickedness, deceit, lewdness, an evil eye, blasphemy, pride, foolishness. All these evil things come from within and defile a man" (Mark 7:21-23).

Basic Jewish Beliefs and Christianity

The doctrine of original sin does not mean that humans do not have a free will and cannot show compassion to their fellow man by doing good works. This should be obvious. It means we are in bondage to this sinful nature and must have help from God to be set free. It also means that the good deeds of which we are capable are stained by this sinful nature, and therefore, they do not give us merit before God.

The *Tanakh* makes this very clear in the words of the prophet Isaiah who said, "But we are all like an unclean thing, and all our righteousnesses are like filthy rags…(Isaiah 64:6).

While Christianity obviously encourages mankind to do good, it teaches that we cannot ultimately do good without divine assistance.

Because Christianity teaches that man is born in a sinful condition, his soul must be redeemed from sin and have a spiritual rebirth. This is not a concept made up by the writers of the New Testament but is taken from the *Tanakh* as well as being found in rabbinic teachings.

Moses said that God would circumcise our hearts (Deuteronomy 30:6). The great Jewish commentator, Rashi, says of this verse, "Once you repent, God will help you by 'circumcising your heart,' meaning that He will help you overcome the hurdles that the Evil Inclination always places in the way.

"Unlike the physical foreskin, which must be removed by people, God will remove the spiritual impediment to total repentance….The 'foreskin' is the spiritual barrier that prevents goodness from dominating the Jewish heart….The circumcision of this verse is the removal from humanity of the natural desire to sin." [119]

God presented the same thought through the prophets. For example, He inspired Ezekiel to write these words, "I will give you a new heart and put a new spirit within you; I will take the heart of stone out of your flesh and give you a heart of flesh. I will put My

---

119. Rabbi Nosson Scherman and Rabbi Meir Zlotowitz, ed., *The Chumash* (Brooklyn: Mesorah Publications, Ltd, 1993), 1091.

Spirit within you and cause you to walk in My statutes, and you will keep My judgments and do them" (Ezekiel 36:26-27).

In the New Testament, Jesus spoke of this when He told the Jewish religious leader, "...unless one is born again, he cannot see the kingdom of God....unless one is born of water and the Spirit, he cannot enter the kingdom of God" (John 3:3,5).

This teaching of a new birth associated with water is perfectly compatible with Judaism. Rabbi Dosick writes concerning baptism (*mikveh*), "The waters are not used to remove any physical uncleanliness, but rather to serve as a symbolic rebirth, an emergence from the purified, cleansing waters of new beginnings.... Immersion in a *mikveh* engenders feelings of waters of new spiritual rebirth and rejuvenation."[120]

Once again, we see that Paul expressed the same thought with these words, "...Not by works of righteousness which we have done, but according to His mercy He saved us, through the washing of regeneration and renewing of the Holy Spirit" (Titus 3:5).

Salvation (Atonement)

While traditional Judaism and Christianity have different views on the subject of salvation (atonement), biblical Judaism and biblical Christianity both teach atonement for sin through blood sacrifice.

The word atonement means "covering." God chose to cover our sins through a blood covenant sacrifice. This began with Adam and Eve when God killed an animal and covered them with the animal skins as atonement for their sins. When God looked at Adam and Eve, He did not see them in their sins, He saw them covered with the skins of the innocent substitutionary sacrifice.

God told Adam and Eve that they would die if they sinned (Genesis 2:17). When Adam and Eve rebelled, God instituted the

---
120. Dosick, 269-271.

Basic Jewish Beliefs and Christianity

blood covenant principle of an innocent substitutionary sacrifice that would take their place.

In this way, God could judge sin while at the same time show mercy to the sinner. From this time forward, the concept of "one dying in the place of another" became the central focus of atonement and redemption in the Bible.

To make this principle of substitutionary death absolutely clear, God established a great Day of Atonement on the Jewish calendar. The Day of Atonement was the one day in the year when the High Priest would go behind the veil into the Holy of Holies with the blood of the sacrifice and sprinkle it on the Mercy Seat. The offering made possible the atonement for the sins of the entire nation. This dramatic procedure is described in detail in Leviticus 16.

While the Day of Atonement ritual was still fresh on the people's minds, God told them, "For the life of the flesh is in the blood, and I have given it to you upon the altar to make atonement for your souls; for it is the blood that makes atonement for the soul" (Leviticus 17:11).

The heart of the innocent substitutionary sacrifice for atonement naturally centered on the Temple, the High Priest, and the sacrificial system that God established with the Hebrews. When the second Temple was destroyed in AD 70, and the people scattered among the nations, they could no longer offer a sacrifice for their sins.

In view of this, the rabbis substituted repentance, prayers, and good deeds in place of sacrifice. In rabbinic Judaism, these three human efforts became the basis by which one could be made right with God.

One Scripture that seems to support the rabbinic view is in the Book of Hosea where God says, "For I desire mercy and not sacrifice, and the knowledge of God more than burnt offerings" (Hosea 6:6).

By this statement, the LORD did not mean that He no longer wanted sacrifices, but that the sacrifices were of no benefit unless the one offering the sacrifices truly worshipped God from his heart and loved people. Rabbinic Judaism, out of necessity, became a religion that would emphasize deeds and a works/righteousness, whereas Christianity would emphasize atonement through the sacrificial death of Jesus.

Judaism would teach that one could be made right with God through repentance, prayers, and good deeds. While these righteous acts are certainly expected by God in the life of a believer, Christianity would emphasize the shed blood of Jesus as the innocent substitutionary sacrifice for sin in fulfillment of Leviticus 17:11.

To the Christian, salvation or atonement is personal, based on one's relationship to Jesus. Jesus lived a perfectly righteous life, and His righteousness is credited to the account of those who sincerely follow Him as the "One who died in their place."

Since Judaism does not teach the concept of inherited sin, it thinks of salvation in terms of world redemption through social activism and good works. From a Christian view, one can never be right with God through works of self-righteousness, because God is morally perfect and demands the same of His creation. Only through a personal identification with Jesus and His righteousness can we have right standing with God.

Rabbi Yechiel Eckstein quotes Rabbi Heschel regarding the differences between Christianity and Judaism on the subject of salvation. He says, "Christianity starts with one idea about man; Judaism with another.

"The idea that Judaism starts with is that man is created in the likeness of God. You do not have to go far, according to Judaism, to discover that it is possible to bring forth the divine within you and the divine in other men. There is always the opportunity to do a *mitzvah* (good deed). It is with that opportunity that I begin as a Jew.

"Christianity begins with the basic assumption that man is essentially depraved and sinful—that left to himself he can do nothing. He has to be saved. He is involved in evil. The first question of Christianity is: What do you do for the salvation of your soul?

"I have never thought of salvation. It is not a Jewish problem. My problem is what *mitzvah* can I do next. Am I going to say a blessing? Am I going to be kind to another person? Am I going to study *Torah*? How am I going to honor the *Sabbath*? These are my problems."

"The central issue in Judaism is the *mitzvah*, the sacred act. And it is the greatness of man that he can do a *mitzvah*. How great we are that we can fulfill the will of God! But Christianity starts with the idea that man is never able to fulfill the will of God. All he has to do, essentially, is to wait for salvation."[121]

According to Leviticus 16, on the Day of Atonement, the High Priest was to present two goats before the LORD. He would then cast lots over the goats to determine which would be offered to the LORD and which would be led into the wilderness as the scapegoat. The goat on which the LORD's lot fell was offered as a sin offering. (See Leviticus 16:5-10.)

The religious leaders considered it a good omen if the lot marked "for the LORD" was drawn by the priest in his right hand. But according to rabbinic writings, for forty years prior to the destruction of the Temple, the lot "for the LORD" appeared in his left hand. As we can imagine, this bad omen caused great fear of impending doom among the people.

The High Priest then tied a crimson wool thread around the horns of the scapegoat and sent him off into the wilderness accompanied by a priest. The priest was then escorted for twelve miles to a designated place where he pushed the goat over a cliff bearing Israel's sins.

A portion of the crimson thread was attached to the door of the Temple before the goat was sent into the wilderness. When the

---

121. Eckstein, 66-67.

goat was pushed off the cliff and died, the thread on the door of the Temple was said to turn from red to white. This was a sign from God to the people that He had accepted their sacrifice and their sins were forgiven.

This sign was based on Isaiah 1:18 which reads, "…though your sins are like scarlet, they shall be as white as snow; though they are red like crimson, they shall be as wool." Rabbinic writings tell us that for forty years prior to the destruction of the Temple, the thread stopped turning white.

Further signs of doom were that the westernmost light on the Temple candelabra would not burn. This was a bad omen that the light of the Temple was going to be extinguished. Furthermore, the Temple doors would open by themselves.

The rabbis saw this as a sign that the Temple was going to be destroyed by fire as God's judgment for their ungodliness. This was based on their understanding of Zechariah 11:1 which says, "Open your doors, O Lebanon, that fire may devour your cedars."

To the follower of Jesus, the fact that these signs began to appear at the time Jesus was crucified were clear statements from God that Jesus was the final, and ultimate sacrifice for our sins. His death in our place provides atonement for our sins and gives us right standing with God, which will be evidenced by our love for God and works of lovingkindness towards our fellow man as genuine evidence of true saving faith.

Isaiah said of Messiah, "Surely He has born our griefs and carried our sorrows; yet we esteemed Him stricken, smitten by God, and afflicted. But He was wounded for our transgressions, He was bruised for our iniquities; the chastisement for our peace was upon Him, and by His stripes we are healed.

"All we like sheep have gone astray; we have turned, every one, to his own way; and the LORD has laid on Him the iniquity of us all" (Isaiah 53:4-6).

The Messiah

At the beginning of the chapter we cited the "Thirteen Principles" of basic Jewish beliefs stated by Moses Maimonides. The twelfth principle says, "I firmly believe in the coming of the Messiah, and although he may tarry, I wait daily for his coming."

The major theological difference between Christianity and Judaism concerns the identity of this Messiah.

The word Messiah comes from the Hebrew *Mashiach* and means "anointed." The word was first used in the Bible as a reference to Aaron and his sons who were anointed with oil while being consecrated to their priestly ministry (Exodus 28:41). The High Priest was called the "Anointed of God."

When the monarchy was established in Israel, the term was also applied to the king who was anointed with oil at his dedication. The king was called the anointed of the LORD in 1 Samuel 2:10 and other places. Thirdly, the prophet was anointed with oil when set apart for that office. We learn in 1 Kings 19:16 how Elijah anointed Elisha as his successor.

In the Hebrew Scriptures, these three anointed offices of prophet, priest, and king were best represented through Moses (prophet), Aaron (High Priest), and David (king). They foreshadowed the coming of "The Messiah" who would combine all three offices within himself. He would function as the ultimate, anointed Prophet, Priest, and King of God.

Messiah would be the perfect spokesman for God (Prophet), the perfect representative and intercessor for the people (Priest), and the perfect King who would rule with righteousness over Israel and the nations.

The Messiah as Prophet

Moses spoke of the Messiah as a Hebrew Prophet greater than himself to whom the people should listen. He said, "The LORD your God will raise up for you a Prophet like me from your midst, from your brethren. Him you shall hear" (Deuteronomy 18:15).

The LORD confirmed these words and said to Moses, "I will raise up a Prophet like you from among their brethren, and will put My words in His mouth, and He shall speak to them all that I command Him. And it shall be that whoever will not hear My words, which He speaks in My name, I will require it of him" (Deuteronomy 18:18-19).

While the Jews revered Moses as their great deliverer, they were looking for "The Prophet" who would be even greater than Moses. All the prophets pointed the people to the Messiah who would come as the ultimate spokesperson for God.

In this regard, we learn in the Book of Maccabees the dilemma the Jews faced concerning what to do with the altar which had been profaned by the Greeks. The account says, "They discussed what should be done about the altar…which had been profaned and very properly decided to pull it down…and deposited the stones in a suitable place on the Temple hill to await the appearance of the Prophet who should give a ruling about them" (1 Maccabees 4:44-46). They also agreed that Simon would be their perpetual leader until the trustworthy Prophet would come (1 Maccabees 14:41).

The Messiah as Priest

The Messiah would also be the anointed High Priest who would be a perfect intercessor between God and the people. In the Book of Genesis, we learn about a mysterious personality named Melchizedek. He was the king of Salem (Jerusalem) and the priest of the Most High God. Abraham gave him tithes, which made Melchizedek's ministry greater than Aaron's (Genesis 14:18-20). He prefigured the priestly ministry of the Messiah.

King David recognized that the Messiah would be a King-Priest. He wrote of Him, "…You are a priest forever according to the order of Melchizedek" (Psalms 110:4). Zechariah says the Messiah shall be a priest on His throne (Zechariah 6:13).

While they didn't fully comprehend it, ancient rabbis understood that the Messiah, in his priestly ministry, would make atonement for the sins of the people. He would do this by suffering in their place according to the many Scriptures that spoke of this aspect of the Messiah's ministry. He would be the "Sin Bearer" of Isaiah [53], the "Cut Off One"of Daniel [9:24-26] the "Pierced One" of Zechariah [12:10], etc.

There is abundant evidence in early rabbinic writings, as well as the Dead Sea Scrolls, that the rabbis identified the Messiah as the "Suffering Servant" spoken of by the prophet Isaiah (Isaiah 42:1-4; 49:1-6; 50:4-9; 52:13-53:12).

There are also traditions of the Messiah appearing as a leper and a beggar for the purpose of suffering for the sins of Israel. The basic understanding was that the Messiah would reveal himself if the people were worthy, but he would depart if they were not.

One explanation was, "If they are worthy, He will come 'with the clouds of heaven' [Daniel 7:13]; if they are unworthy He will come 'poor and riding on a donkey' [Zechariah 9:9].[122]

Another says, "...there is a Messiah in every generation in this world, in reality, clothed in a body. And if the generation is worthy, he is ready to reveal himself; and if, God forbid, they are not worthy, he departs."[123]

It was only later in the twelfth century that the great commentator, Rashi, identified the Suffering Servant with Israel. This has been the official rabbinic interpretation from that time until now. But originally, the rabbis understood the Suffering Servant to be the Messiah.

---

122. Rachmiel Frydland, *What Rabbis Know About the Messiah* (Cincinnati, OH: Messianic Publishing Company, 1993), 5.
123. Raphael Patai, *The Messiah Texts* (Detroit, MI: Wayne State University Press, 1979), 31.

A book that provides an explanation of rabbinic legends concerning the Messiah is *The Messiah Texts* by Raphael Patai, published by Wayne State University Press, Detroit, Michigan.

The Messiah as King

The LORD promised David that he would have a descendant who would rule forever on the throne of Israel.

Samuel says, "When your days are fulfilled and you rest with your fathers, I will set up your seed after you, who will come from your body, and I will establish his kingdom. He shall build a house for My name, and I will establish the throne of his kingdom forever....And your house and your kingdom shall be established forever before you. Your throne shall be established forever" (2 Samuel 7:12-13,16).

When David's kingdom was destroyed by the Babylonians and the people were taken captive (606–586 BC), they looked for the "Greater Son of David" who would restore Israel to her former days of glory. Naturally, they emphasized this office of the Messiah rather than his prophetic and priestly offices.

They believed the Messiah would bring the exiles back to the land at the end of the age. He would restore the throne of the Jewish kingdom to the House of David, and establish the Messianic Kingdom on the earth. He would rule Israel and the nations with justice and righteousness.

Israel would be the head nation, and through them, God's blessing would come to the Gentiles. Jerusalem would be the world capital to which the nations would come to worship King-Messiah. Under the Messiah's rule, the nations would finally live together in peace and harmony.

Jewish tradition taught that human history would last for six thousand years and that the Messiah must come within that time frame. The first two thousand years were known as the years of desolation. The next two thousand years were known as the years of the *Torah*. The last two thousand years were called the Messianic Era. They were referred to as the "last days."

The coming of the Messiah would be preceded by great tribulation referred to as the "birth pangs" of the Messiah. While the rabbis hoped for his soon appearing, they personally did not want to be alive when he came because of the terrible suffering that would precede his coming.

A rabbi was asked by his student, "Give me a sign so I may know when the Messiah is near." The rabbi responded by telling a story. He told about a father and son who were walking in the desert. The son asked the father how they would know when they were approaching a town and their journey ending. The father said, "You will know a town is near when you see a cemetery."

The rabbi went on to explain to his student that they would know the coming of the Messiah is at hand when the Jewish people suffer great tribulation and death at the end of the age. Then Messiah would come and bring redemption to his people.[124]

One Scripture that speaks of the Jews returning to their ancient land at the end of the age is Deuteronomy 30:3 which says, "that the LORD your God will bring you back from captivity, and have compassion on you, and gather you again from all the nations where the LORD your God has scattered you."

Rabbi Blech says that Jewish mysticism has determined that Deuteronomy 30:3 is sentence number 5,708 in the Hebrew Bible, and that the year 1948, when Israel became a nation, is the year 5,708 on the Hebrew calendar.[125]

There was a difference of opinion regarding the person of the Messiah. Some groups thought he was pre-existent, and therefore, divine. The *First Book of Enoch* speaks of the Messiah as the "Head of Days" and the "Son of Man" who existed before creation (1 Enoch 46:1-3)

---

124. Blech, 325.
125. Ibid., 327-328.

Some writings speak of the King-Messiah as existing before the creation of the world who would be revealed to the elect when they were worthy.[126] The Hebrew prophet Micah said the Messiah would be born in Bethlehem but that his "goings forth are from of old, from everlasting" (Micah 5:2).

Other groups did not consider the Messiah as divine but as an ideal human who would save the Jewish people at the end of the age through normal means. This is the view today of Orthodox and Conservative Judaism. They cannot accept the Messiah as divine because, in their view, that would be idolatry.

However, the Hebrew prophet Zechariah says that when King-Messiah comes all the nations will worship Him in Jerusalem (Zechariah 14:16).

Reform Judaism does not believe in a personal Messiah but in a "Messianic Age" brought about through social and moral reform.

Another point of confusion regarding the Messiah was the two apparent contradictory portraits of the Messiah in the *Tanakh*. One portrait spoke of him as the Suffering Servant who would be put to death, bearing the sins of the people, and making atonement for them. These prophecies described the prophetic-priestly Messiah who came to be known as Messiah Ben Joseph.

The other portrait spoke of the Messiah as the "Greater Son of David" who would be the great king and deliverer. He was a political/military Messiah who was known as Messiah Ben David. This view taught that there would be two Messiahs.

The Christian view accepts the Jewish tradition that understood the Messiah to be divine. The New Testament explains that there would not be two Messiahs but that both portraits of the Messiah would be fulfilled in one person. There would be a time gap between the two roles the Messiah would play. This would require Him to appear on the earth at two different times.

The first time He would come as the religious Messiah to bring atonement for sin. He would come again as the political-military Messiah to establish the Messianic Kingdom on the earth.

---

126. Patai, 19.

We believe that Jesus of Nazareth is this Messiah, and that He is coming soon to redeem His people.

While Rabbi Blech does not recognize Jesus as the Messiah, he does agree that the Messiah will come in the "not-too-distant future."[127] At that time, the says, "The Jewish people will witness a spiritual re-awakening unlike any other in all of our history.

"A redemption already started by way of God's love for us will be brought to completion for a people that proudly proclaims its allegiance to His kingship, His rule, and His law. In that day the words of the prophet Zechriah will come to pass: "…the Lord will be One and His Name will be One."[128]

This brings to mind the words of Jesus, "Now when these things begin to happen, look up and lift up your heads, because your redemption draws near" (Luke 21:28).

---

127. Blech, 325.
128. Ibid., 331.

Chapter 9—Personal Study Guide

1. What is the name of the Hebrew Bible?

2. What are the names of the three divisions of the Hebrew Bible?

3. What view do the Jewish people have about the Hebrew Bible?

4. Explain the Jewish view of God.

5. Explain the *Shema*.

6. Explain the Jewish view of man and sin.

7. Explain the Jewish view of salvation.

8. Explain the Jewish view of Messiah.

Chapter 10

Basic Jewish Practices and Christianity

What people believe should impact how they live. This is especially true regarding what a person or group of persons believe about God. Our beliefs about God lead to practices and customs in our worship of God.

Both Christianity and Judaism have different worship practices and customs based on culture, history, and perceptions of God. Generally speaking, Gentile believers and Jews don't understand much about each other's worship practices and customs because of centuries of separation and mistrust.

The purpose of this chapter is to provide some basic information for righteous Gentiles (Christians) regarding the more important Jewish worship practices.

The Synagogue

In the Book of Exodus, the LORD directed the Hebrews to make a sanctuary where He would come and dwell in their midst (Exodus 25:8). This Tabernacle of Moses was later replaced with Solomon's Temple. When Solomon's Temple was destroyed and the Jews were taken captive to Babylon, they had no special place to worship God.

While all of us can worship God from our heart, it is important that we have some physical place, even if it's just a closet in our house, that we can identify as our place of worship. The Jews developed the synagogue during their time of exile to meet this need.

The word "synagogue" is a Greek word meaning assembly or congregation. It refers to a company of people who congregate to worship God. It is also thought of as the place of assembly.

This is similar to the use of the word "church" in Christianity. The word "church" is usually used to refer to the building where Christians meet, but the real meaning of the word is the people themselves who meet in the building. Reform Jews prefer to use the word "temple" rather than synagogue to speak of their special place of worship.

The synagogue functions as a place of gathering, a place of worship and prayer, and a place of learning. It is the custom that public worship requires a quorum of ten, a *Minyan*. In Orthodox Judaism, only men are included in the *Minyan*. Conservative Judaism may include women in the *Minyan* while Reform Judaism does not require a *Minyan* for public worship.

The synagogue is structured according to the pattern of the ancient Temple which had three sections. These were the Outer Court were the people assembled, the Holy Place where the priests ministered, and the Holy of Holies which housed the Ark of the Covenant.

In the synagogue, the auditorium corresponds to the Outer Court, the pulpit, or *Bimah*, corresponds to the Holy Place, and the Ark which houses the *Torah* Scroll corresponds to the Holy of Holies. Synagogues face toward Jerusalem, which means in Western countries, they face east. In Orthodox synagogues, men and women sit in separate areas. They sit together in Reform and Conservative synagogues.

The central object in the synagogue is the Ark which is a beautiful cabinet housing the *Torah* Scroll. The *Torah* Scroll is covered with a velvet or silk material which is often decorated with a *Torah* crown, lions of the tribe of Judah, breastplate (from the days of the High Priest in the Temple), and other ornaments depending on the means of the congregation.

A highlight of the synagogue service is when the *Torah* Scroll is uncovered and brought to the *Bimah* to be read. The person reading the *Torah* does not actually touch the Scroll. This is out of reverence to God's Word as well as the fact that the words of the Scroll actually "sit" on the parchment rather than being absorbed into the Scroll itself.

To keep from touching the letters, which might cause them to chip, the reader uses a *Torah* pointer called a *Yad*, which means "hand." It is shaped liked a hand with a pointed finger at the end.

A portion of the *Torah* is assigned to be read each week of the year. In this way, the entire Scroll is read every year beginning and ending in the Fall at the conclusion of the Feast of Tabernacles (*Sukkot*).

After the Torah portion is read, the Scroll is returned to the Ark where it is kept until the next reading. In addition to reading from the Torah, a selected portion is also read from the Prophets (*Haftarah*).

Kippah

The *kippah*, yarmulke in Yiddish, is a skull cap worn by Jewish men as a headcovering for the purpose of showing reverence to God. In fact the word *yarmulke* comes from a Hebrew phrase meaning, "in fear (awe) of God." This custom is practiced in the Eastern world where people still cover their heads as a sign of respect.

The custom is the opposite in the West where we uncover our heads as a sign of respect. For this reason, the tradition of a headcovering seems strange to those of us who live in the Western world. The practice of covering or not covering one's head is not an issue of the practice being right or wrong but simply different customs.

The biblical origin for wearing a headcovering is found in Exodus 28:4 where we learn the High Priest wore a turban as part of his priestly garments. The ordinary priests wore a ceremonial cap (Exodus 28:40). It was customary to cover the head as a sign of mourning (2 Samuel 15:30).

Wearing a headcovering was not a Jewish law, it was a custom. Sometimes the custom was strongly encouraged and widely practiced, while at other times it was not. Married women, however, were always expected to wear a headcovering as a sign of modesty and respect for their husbands.

One very influential rabbi in the fifth century was Huna ben Joshua. He said, "I never walk four cubits (less that two yards) with uncovered head because God dwells over my head" (*Babylonian Talmud*, Kiddushin 31a). The thinking was that since God was everywhere, those who feared Him should wear a headcovering to show respect. However, not all agreed that the headcovering was necessary.

While the custom of wearing a headcovering was generally accepted and practiced, it was not universally practiced except for married women. It was considered a scandal for a married woman's head to be uncovered. But it was not until the Middle Ages that the custom of a man covering his head became universally accepted. This was particularly expected during times of worship, prayer, and *Torah* study.

Today, Orthodox Jewish men always wear a headcovering. For aesthetic purposes, they often wear a hat over their *kippah*. The kind of hat they wear can indicate to which Orthodox group they belong.

Orthodox Jewish women also cover their head. Since a woman's hair is considered part of her personal beauty and attraction, it is reserved only for the eyes of her husband. Therefore, married Orthodox women wear a hat, headscarf, or wig in public.

Conservative Jews usually wear a *kippah* during religious services but do not consider it an obligation to wear one all the time as do the Orthodox. Reform Jews may wear a headcovering on certain occasions if they choose, but they do not consider it a requirement.

In the New Testament, the apostle Paul writes about headcoverings to the Gentile believers in Corinth. He says, "Every man praying or prophesying, having his head covered, dishonors his head. But every woman who prays or prophesies with her head uncovered dishonors her head, for that is one and the same as if her head were shaved. For if a woman is not covered, let her also be shorn. But if it is shameful for a woman to be shorn or shaved, let her be covered. For a man indeed ought not to cover his head, since he is the image and glory of God; but woman is the glory of man" (1 Corinthians 11:4-7).

In these instructions, Paul is addressing the customs of the time regarding acceptable standards for wearing a veil, not a hat as it is translated in most English versions of the text.

According to David Stern in the *Jewish New Testament Commentary*, the phrase "with his head covered" should literally be translated as "wearing something down over his head." (See the *Jewish New Testament Commentary* by David Stern, page 474.)

Paul is actually writing just the opposite of what the English translation says. He is not saying a man should not wear a headcovering such as a hat or *kippah*. He is saying a man should not wear a veil down over his head because this is the custom for married women (not "every woman" as it is translated) to show their modesty and respect for their husbands.

Paul further states that a married woman should not shave her head because this was a sign of disrespect and rebellion and was the practice of temple prostitutes.

For the believer, the issue is not whether one wears a headcovering or not. Believers are free to make their own choices in this regard and should do so in keeping with cultural norms and worship practices. The real issue is whether or not the believer lives a life of submission and awesome reverence to God. While what we wear on the outside is important for the sake of modesty and custom, how we are "dressed on the inside" is more important.

Tzitzit/Tallit

Whereas wearing a headcovering such as the *kippah* is a custom based on Jewish tradition, wearing a *tzitzit* is a biblical command. When God called the Hebrew people into covenant with Him, He intended for the entire nation to be a kingdom of priests.

We read in Exodus, "Now therefore, if you will indeed obey My voice and keep My covenant, then you will be a special treasure to Me above all people; for the earth is Mine. And you shall be to Me a kingdom of priests and a holy nation…"(Exodus 19:5-6).

After this proclamation, the LORD gave the people His holy commandments, including instructions for making a visual aid that would remind them of His commandments. When the people looked at this visual aid, they would be reminded of their high priestly calling. They were the royal priests of God and were to always remember and keep His commandments.

We find the instructions to make this visual aid in the Book of Numbers, "Again the LORD spoke to Moses, saying, 'Speak to the children of Israel: Tell them to make tassels (*tzitziot*) (*tzitzit*, singular) on the corners of their garments throughout their generations, and to put a blue thread in the tassels of the corners.

"And you shall have the tassel, that you may look upon it and remember all the commandments of the LORD and do them….' " (Numbers 15:37-39).

In ancient times, the Jewish men wore a four-cornered garment. God instructed the men to put tassels on the four corners with a blue thread in the tassels. As they look at the tassels they would be reminded to keep God's commandments.

White is the symbol of purity and blue the color of Heaven. The blue thread represented the presence of the Almighty in the midst of His people.

This was a wonderful visual aid that reminded the Jewish people that they were in covenant with God, and He would bless them as they obeyed His commandments. It was more than ritual.

Jewish sages taught that when a Jew kept the commandment regarding the tzitzit he would be able to behold the face of God.[129] In fact, Rabbi Aryeh Kaplan mentions that the word *tzitzit* means "to appear in visible form."[130]

---

129. Aryeh Kaplan, *Ttitzith* (New York: National Conference of Synagogue Youth, 1984), ix.
130. Ibid., x.

The basic idea is that when the Jewish man puts on his *tzitzit*, he would not just look upon "it." He would look upon "Him." He would behold the face of God, who would manifest Himself to His people as they obeyed His commandments and functioned as His priests on the earth.

Furthermore, the blue thread is referred to as the *shamash*, which is the Hebrew word for "servant." It symbolized the fact that the God of Heaven would become the suffering servant for the sins of mankind. We would look upon Him in human flesh as the perfect mediator and priest of God.

The blue thread was very expensive to make. The dye that was used to color the thread came from the blood of a hillazon snail. It took 12,000 of these snails to make just 1.4 grams of the dye. That's about enough to fill a thimble. In 200 BC, one pound of cloth, dyed blue, cost the equivalent of $36,000. By the year AD 300, that same pound of blue cloth cost about $96,000.

Because it was so expensive, garments made with this blue dye were worn only by royalty and priests. We can see clearly the significance of every Jewish male wearing the blue threaded *tzitziot*. They were the royal priests of God. During the time of Jesus, some of the Pharisees showed their wealth by the size of their tassels. Jesus rebuked them and said they enlarge the borders of their garments, not because they love God, but to be seen of men (Matthew 23:5).

In the second century after the time of Jesus, the Roman emperor Hadrian forbade the Jews to practice their faith. They were no longer allowed to wear the royal blue thread in their *tzitzit*. As times passed, the snails seem to have disappeared and the people no longer had the exact color of blue required for the *tzitziot*. Therefore, they could only use white thread for centuries, until recently.

Today, in Israel, a blue thread has been made which is acceptable by a growing number of rabbis. I personally have a *tallit* with the blue thread made by an orthodox Jewish tailor.

As times changed, men no longer wore four-cornered garments. Jewish men replaced the original garment with a four-cornered prayer shawl called a *tallit*. The *tallit* is important primarily because it is the means by which the Jewish men wear their *tzitziot*.

The *tallit* is the most prized garment of religious Jews. It is worn during the week in morning services, on the Sabbath, and on holidays. As the worshipper covers his head and body with the *tallit*, he offers a prayer to God and believes he is covered with the presence of the Almighty.

Some Jewish men wear a small *tallit* as an undergarment with the *tzitziot* exposed so the wearer can see them. When a Jewish man dies, he is wrapped in his *tallit* before being buried. One thread of the *tzitziot* is torn off to show that the man is now released from the command to wear *tzitziot*.

As mentioned, the *tallit* must have four corners. A hole is made in each corner through which the *tzitziot* is inserted. The threads are inserted through both sides of the hole so that there are a total of eight threads, one blue and seven white. A double knot is tied to hold the threads in place.

The blue thread is then wrapped around the white threads four times (7, 8, 11, 13 wraps) with each wrapping separated by a double knot. The result is four different wrappings of the blue thread separated by five double knots.

In the Hebrew language, each letter has a numeric value. Without giving all the details, the number of wrappings and knots equal the numeric value of the Hebrew name for God (*YHWH*) as well as the numeric value of the Hebrew word "one" which we earlier said is *echad*.

The numeric value of the wrappings and knots was a constant visual reminder to the Jewish people that YHWH is the one true God.

Furthermore, the numeric value of the word *tzitzit* is 600. When adding the eight threads and five knots (13) to 600, we get the number 613. This is the number of commandments God gave in the *Torah* (365 affirmations and 248 prohibitions). In this way, the *tzitziot* were a constant reminder to keep God's commandments.

But no matter how hard God's covenant people tried, they often failed to keep His commandments. Even if they didn't actually break a commandment, they often wanted to in their hearts. God looked upon the heart and considered just the desire to break His commandments a sin. Keeping God's commandments could not make the people righteous simply because they couldn't keep them in deed or desire.

Because of man's failures, God wrapped Himself in human flesh in the person of Jesus of Nazareth. Jesus came as the perfect revelation and visible manifestation of the unseen God.

John writes, "And the Word became flesh and dwelt among us, and we beheld His glory, the glory as of the only begotten of the Father, full of grace and truth" (John 1:14). The New Testament further claims that Jesus was and is the image of the invisible God. (See Colossians 1:15, Hebrews 1:3.)

As a *Torah*-observant Jew, Jesus wore a four-cornered garment with *tzitziot* on the bottom. On one occasion while He was in Capernaum, a desperate woman who had a hemorrhage for twelve years sought Him out to be healed.

Matthew writes, "And suddenly, a woman who had a flow of blood for twelve years came from behind and touched the hem of His garment. For she said to herself, 'If only I may touch His garment, I shall be made well.' But Jesus turned around, and when He saw her He said, 'Be of good cheer, daughter, your faith has made you well.' And the woman was made well from that hour" (Matthew 9:20-22).

The focus of this story is the woman's desire to touch the hem of the garment that Jesus was wearing. She was not the only one wanting to touch the hem of His garment.

Matthew also writes, "When they had crossed over, they came to the land of Gennesaret. And when the men of that place recognized Him [Jesus], they sent out into all the surrounding region, brought to Him all that were sick, and begged Him that they might only touch the hem of His garment. And as many as touched it were made perfectly well" (Matthew 14:34-36). Luke adds, "And the whole multitude sought to touch Him, for power went out from Him and healed them all" (Luke 6:19).

What was the hem of the garment Jesus was wearing which the woman and the crowd desperately wanted to touch? And why were they healed when they touched it? The hem of His garment was the *tzitziot*.

Malachi spoke of the Messiah as the "Sun of Righteousness… with healing in His wings" (Malachi 4:2). The Hebrew words for wings and tassels are interchangeable. The wing is the edge or border (tassel) of the garment. Jesus had healing in His wings (tassels). Whenever the people touched it, in faith, believing Him to be the "Sun of Righteousness, Messiah," healing flowed from Him.

Jesus perfectly kept all 613 commandments. He never even wanted to break them. The white thread represented His purity. The blue thread symbolized His divine nature. He was the physical embodiment of the Almighty in the midst of His people.

We previously noted that the blue thread is called the *shamash*, which means servant. The four times it was wrapped around the white thread totaled thirty-nine individual wrappings (7, 8, 11, 13 wraps). The Roman soldiers laid thirty-nine stripes on the back of Jesus before His death. He was the human *Shamash*, the Suffering Servant for the sins of mankind.

As the cost of the blue dye was very high, Jesus paid a great price to redeem us. That price was His own blood shed as atonement for sin. As the prophet Isaiah wrote, "Surely He has born our griefs and carried our sorrows; yet we esteemed Him stricken, smitten by God, and afflicted.

"But He was wounded for our transgressions, He was bruised for our iniquities; the chastisement for our peace was upon Him, and by His stripes we are healed. All we like sheep have gone astray; we have turned, every one, to his own way; and the LORD has laid on Him the iniquity of us all" (Isaiah 53:4-6).

The New Testament presents Jesus as the true reality of the *tzitziot* who brings healing to us. He is the "Sun of Righteousness with healing in His wings."

To the Christian believer, Jesus is God's heavenly *tallit* and *tzitziot* who desires to clothe us with His own perfect righteousness. He is God's garment of salvation and robe of righteousness. When we wrap ourselves in Jesus, draw near to Him, we can behold the presence of God in our lives.

He brings healing to us as He did for the woman in Capernaum, not by magic when we touch His garment, but by faith in Him as Messiah and Lord. His blood brings atonement and healing. He credits His own perfect righteousness to us and makes us priests of the Most High God.

As Peter writes, "But you are a chosen generation, a royal priesthood, a holy nation, His own special people, that you may proclaim the praises of Him who called you out of darkness into His marvelous light" (1 Peter 2:9). John adds that Jesus has redeemed us to God by His blood and made us kings and priests to our God (Revelation 5:9-10).

When Jesus returns to establish the Kingdom of God on the earth, He will wear a robe, which is surely a *tallit*. That robe will have His name in the position of the *tzitziot*, "King of kings and Lord of lords" (Revelation 19:16).

At His return, Jesus, our Jewish Lord, will rule from Jerusalem as King Messiah over Israel and the nations. Jewish men will once again wear the *tallit* with the blue thread to acknowledge that God is in his midst in the person of Jesus. All the nations will seek God's blessing through Messiah Jesus and the Jewish people. This is the future of Christian-Jewish relations.

Zechariah writes of this time and says, "Yes, many peoples and strong nations shall come to seek the LORD of hosts in Jerusalem, and to pray before the LORD. Thus says the LORD of hosts: 'In those days ten men from every language of the nations shall grasp the sleeve (wing, corner of a garment, *tzitzit*) of a Jewish man, saying, "Let us go with you, for we have heard that God is with you" ' "(Zechariah 8:22-23).

Tefillin

In addition to wearing *tzitziot*, the LORD also instructed the Hebrews to wear *tefillin*. *Tefillin* are small leather boxes containing Scriptures which the Hebrew people were to attach to their hands and foreheads.

The LORD said, "Therefore you shall lay up these words of Mine in your heart and in your soul [mind], and bind them as a sign on your hand, and they shall be as frontlets between your eyes" (Deuteronomy 11:18). (See also Deuteronomy 6:8; Exodus 13:9,16.)

As with the *tzitziot*, the *tefillin* were visual reminders to the Hebrews to put God's Word in their hearts and minds. They were to meditate on God's Word and recite it in prayers. God did not tell the Hebrews how to make the *tefillin*. All they knew was that they were to write down certain Scriptures and somehow attach them to their hands and foreheads.

The religious leaders decided to make two small leather boxes that would contain the Scriptures commanding them to make *tefillin*. They used leather straps to attach the boxes to the hand and arm and forehead. They would then wear the *tefillin* on weekdays during the morning prayers as a sign of their covenant with God. They are not worn on the Sabbath or holidays because the Sabbath is also a sign (Exodus 31:17).

The leather box worn on the forehead is made differently than the one worn on the arm. The box for the forehead contains four compartments, and each holds a separate piece of parchment.

Certain Scriptures are carefully handwritten on the four parchments with a quill and then meticulously inserted into the compartments. These are:1) Exodus 13:1-10, 2) Exodus 13:11-16, 3) Deuteronomy 6:4-9, and 4) Deuteronomy 11:13-21).

The box for the hand and arm contains one compartment that holds the same Scriptures written on a single parchment. There is a further difference. The box for the forehead has the Hebrew letter *shin* on the outside of the box. The *shin* stands for Shaddai, which means "Almighty."

The worshipper places the box for the hand on the left arm and hand so it can be close to his heart. He ties it to the upper arm above his elbow and then wraps the leather seven times around his forearm. Next, he wraps the end of the strap around his hand and around his middle and ring finger in such a way as to make the *shin*.

As the worshipper wraps the leather around his ring finger, he recites the following Scriptures from the Book of Hosea, "I will betroth you to Me forever; Yes, I will betroth you to Me in righteousness and justice, in lovingkindness and mercy; I will betroth you to Me in faithfulness, and you shall know the LORD" (Hosea 2:19-20).

The symbolism of the *tefillin* reminds the worshipper that he is to put God's Word in his mind and heart because he is betrothed to God through a marriage covenant. In this regard, the *tefillin* are like a wedding bond between the Jewish people and their covenant God.

We know from the New Testament that *Torah* observant Jews wore *tefillin*. Matthew records the following words of Jesus, "But all their [legalistic Pharisees] works they do to be seen of men. They make their phylacteries [Greek word for *tefillin*] broad and enlarge the borders of their garments [*tzitziot*]" (Matthew 23:5).

Jesus was not speaking against the wearing of *tefillin* and tzitziot but against their abuse. As a *Torah*-observant Jew, we know that Jesus wore *tzitziot*. He also would have worn *tefillin* as part of His religious clothing.

Although Americans have a Western image of Jesus and picture Him as a European, Jesus was a Jew of the first century who followed the customs of His people. Most Christians have a cosmic view of Christ in the heavens, but one wonders how well the Church would receive Jesus the Jew.

Jesus was the perfect revelation of the symbolism pictured by the *tefillin*. Jesus not only had God's Word in His mind and heart, He was the human manifestation of the Word of God (John 1:1,14; Revelation 19:13). He has bound believers to God by His blood and made them His bride (Revelation 19:7-9; 21:2,9). He is the great High Priest who ever lives to make intercession for them, and believers can pray to the Father in His name (Hebrews 7:25; John 14:13-14).

It is not the custom for righteous Gentiles (Christians) to wear *tefillin*. However, they certainly should live the kind of life *tefillin* symbolize. They certainly should meditate on God's Word and put it in their minds and hearts (Joshua 1:8; Psalm 1:1-3; 119:11). God's people certainly should obey the Lord and live a life that is pleasing to Him (Romans 12:1-2; 1 Corinthians 6:19-20). In this way, believers can be a human manifestation of the symbolism of *tefillin*.

Mezuzah

The word *mezuzah* means "doorpost." It refers to the commandment God gave the Hebrews to write His words on the doorposts of their houses. The LORD gave this instruction at the same time He told them to wear *tefillin*.

We read in Deuteronomy, "Hear, O Israel: The LORD our God, the LORD is one! You shall love the LORD your God with all your heart, with all your soul, and with all your strength. And these words which I command you today shall be in your heart. You shall teach them diligently to your children, and shall talk of them when you sit in your house, when you walk by the way, when you lie down, and when you rise up.

"You shall bind them as a sign on your hand, and they shall be as frontlets between your eyes. You shall write them on the doorposts of your house and on your gates" (Deuteronomy 6:4-9). (See also Deuteronomy 11:13-21.)

In ancient times, people decorated the entrance door of their house with some type of symbol or words which bore witness to their neighbors regarding their beliefs and values. It was a way for the people to identify with a god or other cause.[131] They would simply write the name of their god or a symbol on the doorpost of their house.

People often do this today. When someone comes to the door of a house, they see the symbol or words, and know what beliefs, values, or causes with which the members of the household identify. This modern way of "putting something on the doorpost" dates to ancient times.

Because of this use of doors, when the LORD delivered the Hebrews out of Egypt, He told the people to put the blood of the Passover lamb on the doorpost. This showed their identification with the God of Abraham, Isaac, and Jacob, which caused the LORD to spare them from death. (See Exodus 12.)

After God delivered the Hebrews from Egypt, He required them to write His words where the blood had been applied as a constant reminder to His covenant people that they were to love Him and keep His commandments.

As time went by, it became impractical to actually write the words directly on the doorposts. Instead a trained scribe called a *sofer* wrote the words on a small scroll which was inserted into a container which was then affixed to the doorpost.[132] The container, along with the scroll, came to be called the *mezuzah*, as it is today.

Over the years, the rabbis established rules for making and affixing the *mezuzah*. The scribe uses a quill taken from a kosher

---

131. Barney Kasdan, *God's Appointed Customs* (Baltimore, MD: Lederer Messianic Publishers, 1996), 90.
132. Dosick, 248.

fowl, and with specially prepared inks, writes the text of Deuteronomy 6:4-9 and Deuteronomy 11:13-21 on kosher parchment that comes from the skin of a lamb or goat.[133]

The scribe then writes the word *Shaddai*, for Almighty, on the outside of the parchment, rolls up the scroll, and inserts it in the container. The container is made of various shapes with artistic designs to add to its beauty. Furthermore, the *shin* is inscribed on the outside of the container as a reminder that the LORD is the guardian of the house.

The *mezuzah* is affixed to the right doorpost of the house at eye level. In ancient times, leading rabbis could not agree if the *mezuzah* should be affixed vertically or horizontally. They finally agreed to compromise and ruled that the *mezuzah* should be placed at an angle with the top slanting to the left towards the opening of the door.[134]

Today, the more observant Jew will also place a *mezuzah* on the doorpost of each room in the house. The one exception is the bathroom, which is not considered appropriate.

It is customary when entering a house or room to kiss the fingers and then touch the *shin* as a way of showing respect for God. In recent years, a *mezuzah* has been affixed to the entrances of public buildings in Israel as well as hotel rooms.

While there is no direct mention of the *mezuzah* in the New Testament, Joseph and Mary would have certainly had a *mezuzah* affixed to the door of their house. Little did they know that Jesus would be the redeemer of mankind by shedding His own blood as the human Passover lamb.

Furthermore, when Jesus was asked which was the greatest of all the commandments, He recited the passage from Deuteronomy 6. This was written on the door of every Jewish house. (See Matthew 22:34-40.)

---

133. Alfred Kolatch, *The Jewish Book of Why* (New York: Jonathan David Publishers, 1981), 114.
134. Dosick, 249.

On another occasion, Jesus referred to Himself as the door (John 10:9). He was speaking about the open entrance to the sheepfold. The true shepherd would stay in the entrance to guard and protect the sheep. For the follower of Jesus, He opens the way for us to enter into the house of God. The New Testament says that we are God's spiritual house (Ephesians 2:19-22), and Jesus is our guardian who is able to protect us against the enemies of our soul.

Jude writes, "Now to Him who is able to keep you from stumbling [falling], and to present you faultless before the presence of His glory with exceeding joy, to God our Savior, who alone is wise, be glory and majesty, dominion and power, both now and forever. Amen" (Jude 24-25).

While it is not the tradition for Christians to affix a *mezuzah* to the doorpost of their houses, it is certainly acceptable as a way of expressing identification with the God of Abraham, Isaac, and Jacob—as well as the Jewish people, to whom Christians owe such a great debt.

But whether one practices this custom or not, believers should open the door of their hearts and houses to the Almighty. Christians should be a "living *mezuzah*" in their words, thoughts, and deeds so that God will be glorified in their lives, His spiritual house. This is what Jesus had in mind when He said, "Behold, I stand at the door and knock. If anyone hears My voice and opens the door, I will come in to him and dine with him, and he with Me" (Revelation 3:20).

Mikveh

A *mikveh* is a body of water used for a ritual bath for purposes of purification. God required His people to be pure (ceremonially clean from that which defiled) in order to participate in worship through the religious rituals He gave them.

Even before God gave the *Torah*, He instructed the people to wash their clothes as an act of ritual cleansing before He would appear to them at Mount Sinai. Exodus reads, "Then the LORD said to Moses, 'Go to the people and consecrate them today and tomorrow, and let them wash their clothes. And let them be ready for the third day. For on the third day the LORD will come down upon Mount Sinai in the sight of all the people.' " (Exodus 19:10-11).

Also, the priests were to wash themselves before they could minister before the LORD at the Tabernacle (Exodus 29:4; Leviticus 8:6 and 16:4).

The *mikveh* was necessary because God declared that some circumstances would cause a person to be ritually impure and thus not be able to participate in worship. These are given in Leviticus 11–15 and Numbers 19 and 30, and all have to do with the loss of life.

Since God is life, any circumstance connected with the loss of life required ritual cleansing. These are: 1) touching anything dead (Leviticus 11; Numbers 19), 2) a woman following childbirth because she is not readily able to conceive (Leviticus 12), 3) leprosy (Leviticus 13–14), 4) any discharge of body fluids (Leviticus 15), and 5) a woman during her menstrual period (Leviticus 15).

God provided the *mikveh* as a means for those who were impure to wash themselves as an outward act of ceremonial cleansing so they could participate in the religious rituals. This was so important that when King Solomon built the Temple, he constructed ritual baths for the priests (1 Kings 7:26).

There were also many *mikvahot* at the southern entrance to the Temple mount so the people could wash themselves before entering the Temple area. *Mikvahot* have also been discovered at Qumran and even at Masada.

During the time of the prophets, God spoke more clearly of the spiritual significance of the *mikveh*. It would not only be for ritual defilement but also for spiritual defilement.

God declared through the prophet Ezekiel, "Then I will sprinkle clean water on you, and you shall be clean; I will cleanse you from all your filthiness and from all your idols. I will give you a new heart and put a new spirit within you; I will take the heart of stone out of your flesh and give you a heart of flesh. I will put My Spirit within you and cause you to walk in My statutes, and you will keep My judgments and do them" (Ezekiel 36:25-27).

Pagans (Gentiles) who converted to Judaism were required to immerse themselves in a *mikveh* as a sign that they had been spiritually reborn as Ezekiel stated.[135] Their immersion was an outward sign of the new heart and spirit God gave them as they turned from their sins and embraced the God of Abraham, Isaac, and Jacob.

Because the *mikveh* was an outward sign of the washing away of impurities, it required running water such as a spring, lake, river, ocean, pond, etc. It could not be a dead, stagnant pool. The natural flow of the water was a visual picture of one's impurities, or sins, being carried away. The *mikveh* was the "waters of life."[136]

In modern times, if there is no *mikveh* of natural flowing water, one must be constructed according to strict rabbinic rules. The *mikveh* must be designed so that water can flow to symbolize the washing away of impurities or spiritual defilement.

It must be filled with enough water to enable the person to completely immerse himself or herself. It must be constructed for privacy since the person entering the *mikveh* is completely naked so that the water can touch every part of the body.

Before entering the *mikveh*, the person must take a bath or shower to show that the immersion is for the ceremonial cleansing, not physical cleansing. The person completely immerses himself or herself in a fetal position in the womb-like waters of the *mikveh* as an act of being reborn in spirit.[137]

In modern times, Orthodox Jewish men often enter the *mikveh* before the Sabbath and at other special times such as feast days, before their wedding, etc. However, the two primary uses of

---

135. Ibid., 269-270.
136. Leo Trepp, *The Complete Book of Jewish Observance* (New York: Berhman House, Inc. and Summit Books, 1980), 294-295.
137. Dosick, 269-271.

the *mikveh* in our day are by women seven days after their monthly cycle and by Gentile converts to Judaism.

There is a clear connection between the Jewish *mikveh* and Christian baptism. Matthew tells us about John the Baptist who called people to repent of their sins and enter the waters of *mikveh* in the Jordan River.

Matthew writes, "In those days John the Baptist came preaching in the wilderness of Judea, and saying, 'Repent, for the kingdom of heaven is at hand!'...Then Jerusalem, all Judea, and all the region around the Jordan went out to him and were baptized by him in the Jordan, confessing their sins" (Matthew 3:1,5).

Jesus connected the *mikveh* to a spiritual birth when He conversed with Nicodemus. He said, "...Most assuredly, I say to you, unless one is born of water and the Spirit, he cannot enter the kingdom of God. That which is born of the flesh is flesh, and that which is born of the Spirit is spirit. Do not marvel that I said to you, 'You must be born again.'" (John 3:5-7).

Jesus was attending the Feast of Tabernacles in Jerusalem at the time of the pouring of the water ritual. He said, " 'He who believes in Me, as the Scripture has said, out of his heart will flow rivers of living water.' But this He spoke concerning the Spirit, whom those believing in Him would receive; for the Holy Spirit was not yet given because Jesus was not yet glorified" (John 7:38-39).

Peter preached to the Jews on the day of Pentecost, "...Repent, and let every one of you be baptized in the name of Jesus Christ for the remission of sins; and you shall receive the gift of the Holy Spirit" (Acts 2:38).

The apostle Paul also made the connection between the *mikveh* and the new birth. He wrote that it is, "...Not by works of righteousness which we have done, but according to His mercy He saved us, through the washing of regeneration [spiritual birth] and renewing of the Holy Spirit" (Titus 3:5).

While the waters of *mikveh* do not save us, they bear witness to our spiritual rebirth through faith in Messiah Jesus who said, "Go therefore and make disciples of all the nations, baptizing them in the name of the Father and of the Son and of the Holy Spirit" (Matthew 28:19).

Once again, it is clear that a Christian practice has its roots in biblical Judaism. In fact there is nothing in New Testament Christianity that is not Jewish.

There is another Jewish tradition that many Christians have discovered. It is the dietary laws in the Hebrew Scriptures.

Kashrut (*Kosher*)

The word *kashrut*, more commonly known as *kosher*, means "fitness." It refers to the dietary laws God gave the Jewish people to distinguish them from their pagan, Gentile neighbors. Instructions concerning these are given in detail in Leviticus 11 and Deuteronomy 14.

While there are proven health benefits in keeping these dietary laws, the real reason God gave them was spiritual. After giving the laws, God said, "For I am the LORD who brings you up out of the land of Egypt, to be your God. You shall therefore be holy, for I am holy" (Leviticus 11:45). (See also Exodus 22:31; Deuteronomy 14:21.)

The word holy means "separate." God had set apart the Jewish people from the pagan nations to be a special people who would worship Him and Him alone.

While God obviously provided food for one's health and pleasure, in ancient times eating had much greater meaning then than it does today. Eating was also considered a form of worship, communion, and fellowship with one's god.[138]

The table where food was eaten was considered an altar with spiritual significance. The pagans ate anything, and some scholars believed they used animals God declared unclean in their worship.

---

138. Trepp, 62.

In view of the spiritual connection to food, God revealed to Noah (Genesis 7-8), and later to Moses, those creatures which were clean and fit to eat and those which were unclean. God gave dietary laws as a visible means for His covenant people to express their desire to worship Him and live a morally clean life that would distinguish them from their morally unclean pagan neighbors. Rabbi Dosick explains, "*kashrut* is far less about eating than it is about behaving."[139] There may be more to eating than we realize.

The first dietary law God gave in the Bible was to Adam and Eve before they sinned. He said, "…See, I have given you every herb that yields seed which is on the face of all the earth, and every tree whose fruit yields seed; to you it shall be for food" (Genesis 1:29). From this statement in Genesis, God declared that all vegetables, fruits, grains, and nuts are *kosher*, fit for human consumption.

After the flood, God allowed man to eat certain flesh but prohibited the eating of blood. The LORD said to Noah, "But you shall not eat flesh with its life, that is, its blood" (Genesis 9:4). (See also Leviticus 7:26-27; 17:10-14.)

Because life is sacred, and the life of the flesh is in the blood (Leviticus 17:11), God considers blood to be sacred. It is the symbol of life itself. Therefore, eating a creature's blood is eating the very life-force of the creature, not just its flesh for food. Furthermore, blood contains the animal's characteristics and diseases that one takes into the body when blood is eaten.

God prohibited the eating of blood simply because blood represents the life of the creature and carries its nature and diseases. Since the Creator is the only source of life and strength for those made in His image, He forbade the eating of blood.

When God gave the dietary laws to the Jews, He also forbade them to eat fat (Leviticus 3:17; 7:23). The spiritual reason for this is that the fat was offered to God as part of their sacrifices.

---

139. Dosick, 268.

For health purposes we now know that eating animal fat leads to heart disease, which certainly does not glorify God in our bodies which belong to God (1 Corinthians 6:19-20). We also have learned in recent years that the poisons and toxins that animals eat are stored in their fat cells, which humans then ingest.[140]

Additionally, observant Jews do not eat the hindquarter of an animal, since it contains the sciatic nerve. The hindquarter contains the most popular cuts of meat such as filet mignon, sirloin steak, porterhouse steak, and T-bone steak.

The reason why observant Jews do not eat the hindquarter is found in the story of Jacob wrestling with the angel of the LORD as recorded in Genesis 32:22-32. God touched Jacob's hip so that he walked with a limp. From that time forward, Orthodox Jews avoid eating this meat.

God's primary dietary laws are recorded in Leviticus 11 and Deuteronomy 14. The instructions regarding eating animals are given in Leviticus 11:1-8 and Deuteronomy 14:3-8.

The Scripture says that the LORD gave these words to Moses and Aaron, "Speak to the children of Israel, saying, 'These are the animals which you may eat among all the animals that are on the earth: Among the animals, whatever divides the hoof, having cloven [split] hooves and chewing the cud—that you may eat.' " (Leviticus 11:2-3).

The LORD declared that certain animals were clean and certain were unclean (Genesis 7:2). The ones He declared clean were fit (*kosher*) to sacrifice and to eat. The clean animals God permitted the people to eat were those that both chewed their cud and had cloven (split) hoofs. Examples are cow, sheep, goat, deer, and any other animal that chews its cud and has divided hoofs.

From a health standpoint, it is interesting to note that all clean animals are herbivores—vegetarians. They do not eat the flesh of

---

140. Gordon S. Tessler, *Clean and Unclean Foods* (Raleigh, NC: Trumpets of Zion Ministries, 1991), 20.

other animals. They eat the "Genesis diet" which God gave to Adam and Eve.

Clean animals are less likely to have the diseases carried by other animals. They have several stomachs and a long digestive tract which helps them detoxify the food they eat, thereby making them fit for human consumption.[141] By eating clean animals, the Jews were not only expressing their desire to be morally clean, but they also benefited by being physically clean.

God declared unclean those animals that do not chew their cud and have split hoofs. Examples are pig, camel, horse, rabbit, squirrel, and any other animal that does not meet both requirements. Unclean animals eat the flesh of other animals, which means they are more likely to ingest their diseases.

Additionally, since they do not properly chew their food and have short digestive tracts, unclean animals keep the diseases ingested in their own organs, which makes them unfit (not *kosher*) for human consumption.

The LORD also forbade the eating of any animal that had died without being properly slaughtered because of the blood it retained in its body (Exodus 22:31).

The dietary instructions regarding fish are given in Leviticus 11:9-12 and Deuteronomy 14:9-10. Leviticus reads, "These you may eat of all that are in the water: whatever in the water has fins and scales, whether in the seas or in the rivers—that you may eat. But all in the seas or in the rivers that do not have fins and scales, all that move in the water or any living thing which is in the water, they are an abomination to you" (Leviticus 11:9-10).

According to these instructions, a clean fish must have both scales and fins. Examples are halibut, salmon, haddock, tuna, bass, flounder, perch, snapper, trout, and any other fish that has both scales and fins.

Unclean fish are scavengers that ingest high levels of toxins which they carry in their systems. For this reason, they are not fit

---

141. Ibid., 9-12.

(*kosher*) for human consumption. Unfortunately, they are the most popular fish and include all shellfish such as lobster, shrimp, crab, clams, scallops, etc. This also includes catfish, shark, porpoise, and whale. There is a difference of opinion about swordfish, because it has scales when it is young but loses them as it gets older.

The dietary laws for eating fowl and insects are recorded in the remaining verses of Leviticus 11 and Deuteronomy 14:11-20. While God gives no specific criteria, those which He forbids are scavengers which eat what no other fowl or insect will eat. They not only make one ritually unclean but also physically unclean. Examples of clean fowl are chicken, turkey, duck, and goose.

While God's people must have known there were health benefits from eating that which God declared clean, they understood that He gave these laws to remind them that He had set them apart for Himself. They were to live a holy life because He is holy.

Over time, the rabbis established certain rules to follow when slaughtering animals. The purpose was to kill the animal so that most of the blood would be drained out. The rabbis also wanted to find the most humane method to kill the animal.

Today, the job of ritual slaughtering is done by a skilled, religious authority. He uses a sharp knife, and with one swift stroke, cuts the animal's throat. This severs the animal's jugular vein, thus causing instant death without the animal feeling pain.

To eliminate the rest of the blood, the meat is soaked in water for about half an hour. It is then placed on a grate and covered with salt for about one hour at which time the remaining blood drains out of the meat. The meat is thoroughly washed to remove the salt and any remaining traces of blood. An alternate method to soaking and salting is to simply cook the meat on a grill which allows the blood to naturally drip from the meat.

One further Jewish tradition is the separation of meat and milk products. This custom is based on a statement in the *Torah* which says, "...You shall not boil a young goat in its mother's milk" (Exodus 23:19). (See also Exodus 34:26; Deuteronomy 14:21.)

While many scholars believe this tradition was a Canaanite fertility rite that is irrelevant to modern times, the rabbis applied this by forbidding the eating of meat and milk products at the same meal. To make sure this rule was followed, observant Jews use separate refrigerators and separate containers, dishes, and eating utensils for meat and milk products.

In the Bible, God blessed the creatures He declared clean and fit for consumption. While scholars differ on how they interpret the dietary laws, some believe that when the Bible speaks about food, it means creatures God called clean.

Furthermore, since God already blessed these creatures as food, there was no need to "bless the food." Instead the people blessed God for the food. The LORD said to His people, "When you have eaten and are full, then you shall bless the LORD your God for the good land which He has given you" (Deuteronomy 8:10).

For centuries, Christian scholars have told us that Jesus and the writers of the New Testament did away with God's dietary laws. On the surface, the New Testament seems to support this view. However, when we examine the appropriate New Testament Scriptures from the Hebraic perspective, this is not correct.

Looking through Hebrew eyes at New Testament statements concerning food challenges Western scholarly traditions. There are different interpretations, depending on the traditional and cultural views held by the student of the Bible.

First, we find Jesus in a discussion with some of the Pharisees who criticized His disciples for not washing their hands according to the traditions of the elders. Mark 7 reads, "Then the Pharisees and some of the scribes came together to Him, having come from Jerusalem. Now when they saw some of His disciples eat bread with defiled, that is, with unwashed hands, they found fault. For the Pharisees and all the Jews do not eat unless they wash their hands in a special way, holding the tradition of the elders.

"When they come from the marketplace, they do not eat unless they wash. And there are many other things which they have received and hold, like the washing of cups, pitchers, copper vessels, and couches. Then the Pharisees and scribes asked Him, 'Why do Your disciples not walk according to the tradition of the elders, but eat bread with unwashed hands?' " (Mark 7:1-5) (See also Matthew 15:1-20.)

We see clearly that this discussion is not about food but about keeping the traditions of the elders concerning the washing of hands. When the Jews went through the marketplace, they could not avoid touching things that were considered ritually impure. As a result, some Pharisees established strict rules for washing the hands up to the wrist before eating a meal. They expected everyone to meticulously follow these rules, and they condemned those who did not. They thought unwashed hands would make clean food unclean. This prompted Jesus to rebuke them for putting their traditions above the Word of God.

While Jesus did not condemn their traditions, His concern was the priority the Pharisees put on their traditions. He then explained to His disciples that it was not food they put in their bodies that defiled them but that defilement came from the heart.

Mark continues the words of Jesus, " '...Are you thus without understanding also? Do you not perceive that whatever enters a man from outside cannot defile him because it does not enter his heart but his stomach, and is eliminated, thus purifying all foods?'

"And He said, 'What comes out of a man, that defiles a man. For from within, out of the heart of men, proceed evil thoughts, adulteries, fornications, murders, thefts, coveteousness, wickedness, deceit, lewdness, an evil eye, blasphemy, pride, foolishness. All these evil things come from within and defile a man.' " (Mark 7:18-23).

From the Hebraic perspective, the statement "thus purifying all foods" has been misinterpreted for centuries. Christian scholars have understood the saying to mean that Jesus was doing away with the dietary laws in the Hebrew Scriptures. This is impossible. Since Jesus and His followers were *Torah*-observant Jews, they would not think of violating God's commands. They were people of their time and culture and lived according to God's laws.

The point of this discussion is not that Jesus and His disciples could eat anything they desired. The point is whether or not clean food is made unclean just because the disciples did not wash their hands according to the traditions of the elders. Jesus was focusing on the real issue of the heart. This is where the Pharisees should put their priority, not on their handwashing ritual.

Another place where it seems the New Testament does away with the dietary laws is in the Book of Acts. In this setting, God prepared Peter to receive Gentiles, whom the Jews considered unclean. This was a major crisis for Peter, who was being challenged by the Lord to preach the Gospel to people he had despised. This would require God to communicate in a dramatic way to Peter.

Cornelius the Gentile was a God-fearer. This means that he had embraced the Jewish God but had not formally converted to Judaism by being circumcised and baptised. Cornelius had a vision in which an angel of God instructed him to send for Peter who would come to his house and preach the gospel.

Cornelius sent three of his men to the house where Peter was staying. About the time they arrived at his house, it was lunchtime and Peter had gone up to the roof to pray. He fell into a trance and saw a large sheet full of unclean creatures. He then heard a voice telling him to eat them. Naturally, Peter was shocked and couldn't believe that the Lord would instruct him to eat these *non-kosher* creatures.

We read the following account in Acts, "The next day, as they went on their journey and drew near to the city, Peter went up on the housetop to pray, about the sixth hour [noon]. Then he became very hungry and wanted to eat; but while they made ready [prepared lunch], he fell into a trance and saw heaven opened and an object like a great sheet bound at the four corners, descending to him and let down to the earth. In it were all kinds of four-footed animals of the earth, wild beasts, creeping things, and birds of the air.

"And a voice came to him, 'Rise, Peter; kill and eat.' But Peter said, 'Not so, Lord! For I have never eaten anything common or unclean.' And a voice spoke to him again the second time, 'What God has cleansed you must not call common.' This was done three times. And the object was taken up into heaven again.' " (Acts 10:9-16).

It is interesting that Peter says he had never eaten *non-kosher* creatures. In reference to the Scripture just discussed in Mark, if Jesus was doing away with the dietary laws, Peter would have certainly had a few *non-kosher* meals. This is further confirmation from the Bible itself that Jesus did not say it was acceptable for His disciples to eat unclean creatures.

We also note that the sheet of unclean food was let down three times. As we study this closely, it becomes obvious why this number. It is because at the same time the sheet of unclean creatures was being lowered three times, three unclean Gentiles were knocking at the door to Peter's house.

The Holy Spirit told Peter that these men were there to see him and that he should receive them. This was a major challenge for Peter, who would not normally allow unclean Gentiles into his home.

The Lord gave Peter the vision of the unclean creatures to prepare him to receive the unclean Gentiles. Peter not only invited the men into his home, but he housed them overnight. Then on the next day, he went with them to Caesarea where he entered the house of Cornelius, another unclean Gentile.

Before Peter began to preach, he said to Cornelius and all those assembled, "…You know how unlawful [ritually forbidden] it is for a Jewish man to keep company with or go to one of another nation [unclean Gentile]. But God has shown me that I should not call any man common or unclean" (Acts 10:28). From Peter's own mouth we see that the vision of the unclean creatures was not about food, it was about people.

Peter then preached the gospel to these unclean Gentiles who were gloriously filled with the Holy Spirit and baptized. The Jews with Peter were as shocked to see this as Peter had been to see the vision of the unclean creatures.

Unclean Gentiles were cleansed by accepting Jesus as their Lord and Savior. Peter learned that people whom God has cleansed must not be called common. Jews and Gentiles were united as one in Messiah. But working out this unity in everyday living was a challenge to the new community of faith.

The Jerusalem Council

A problem arose in the early church community regarding fellowship between the Jewish believers and the Gentiles who were embracing Jesus and worshipping with their Jewish brethren. There were many Gentiles like Cornelius who admired the Jewish faith and embraced the God of the Jews.

The Jews and Gentile believers worshipped together at the synagogue on Shabbat. A controversy developed over how much Jewish rituals should the Gentiles be expected to follow. The more zealous Jewish believers wanted the Gentile converts to keep all the *Torah* and actually become Jews. Paul and Barnabas argued against this view. A counsel was called in Jerusalem and James gave the following decision:

"Therefore I judge that we should not trouble those from among the Gentiles who are turning to God, but that we write to them to abstain from things polluted by idols, from sexual immorality, from things strangled, and from blood. For Moses has had throughout many generations those who preach him in every city, being read in the synagogues every Sabbath" (Acts 15:19-21).

The leaders of the Jerusalem Council wrote a letter explaining their decision. They said, "For it seemed good to the Holy Spirit, and to us, to lay upon you no greater burden than these necessary things: that you abstain from things offered to idols, from blood, from things strangled, and from sexual immorality. If you keep yourselves from these, you will do well" (Acts 15:28-29).

The Jerusalem Council decreed four basic requirements of the believing Gentiles. The first was that they abstain from things polluted by idols. This was meat that had been sacrificed to idols and was later sold in the marketplace. The second requirement was that they avoid sexual immorality. Third, that they not eat "what is strangled," that is, meat from animals not slaughtered in a *kosher* way that allows the blood to flow out. The fourth requirement was that the Gentile brethren not eat blood.

These four requirements were not related to salvation but were practical guides to foster fellowship between the believing Jews and Gentiles. The leaders in Jerusalem did not want to unusually burden the Gentile believers with Jewish rituals and obligations that might hinder the Gentiles from turning from idols to the living God.

However, there were certain minimum requirements of the Gentile believers that related to practices that were particularly offensive to the Jewish believers. These were the four conditions decreed by the Jerusalem Council which they called the "necessary things." It is interesting to note that three of the four "necessary things" had to do with food.

James explained that the reason these four minimum requirements were necessary was due to the fact that the *Torah* given to Moses was read in the synagogue every Sabbath. Since the Gentile believers attended these services where they worshipped God and fellowshipped with their Jewish brethren, they should be sensitive to them in these four areas of Jewish belief and practice. As the

Gentile believers learned the Torah and grew in their faith, they would voluntarily incorporate more of the *Torah* into their lives, particularly the aspects of *Torah* that so clearly related to Jesus.

The original church was one community of the King consisting of believing Jews and believing Gentiles. The believing Jews continued to be Jews and were *Torah*-observant. Luke writes, "And when they [the Jerusalem Council] heard it, they glorified the Lord. And they said to him [Paul], 'You see, brother, how many myriads [tens of thousands] of Jews there are who have believed, and they are all zealous for the law'" (Acts 21:20). The Jews were not required to keep the *Torah* for salvation. *Torah* was instruction and teaching on how to walk with God

The believing Gentiles continued to be Gentiles but understood that they were grafted into the Jewish people and had become part of the commonwealth of Israel (Romans 11; Ephesians 2:11-22). While they were not required to become Jews nor keep the *Torah* for salvation, they did observe the minimum "necessary things" and voluntarily embraced more of the *Torah* as they grew to understand how the Torah was the root of their new faith.

Chapter 10—Personal Study Guide

1. Explain the structure of the synagogue and the highlight of worship at the synagogue.

2. Explain the purpose and use of the *Kippah* and any connection it has to Christianity.

3. Explain the purpose and use of the *Tzitzit* and any connection it has to Christianity.

4. Explain the purpose and use of *Teffilin* and any connection it has to Christianity.

5. Explain the purpose and use of the *Mezuzah* and any connection it has to Christianity.

6. Explain the purpose and use of the *Mikveh* and any connection it has to Christianity.

7. Explain the dietary laws given in Leviticus 11 and Deuteronomy 14.

8. Explain Mark 7 in light of the dietary laws.

9. Explain Acts 10 in light of the dietary laws.

10. Explain the purpose of the "necessary things" decreed by the Jerusalem Council.

Chapter 11

Jewish Life Cycle

Whereas the Gentile way of life which was incorporated into Christianity is not based on a biblical order, Jewish life goes through certain clearly defined stages. When observed, these stages of life keep Jews connected to their biblical covenants and rich traditions. The various stages of Jewish life make up what is referred to as the "Jewish Life Cycle." For example, one famous rabbi used to say:

"At five, the Jewish child is ready for the study of *Torah*. At ten for the study of *Mishnah*. At thirteen the child is considered responsible to perform *Mitzvot* (deeds). At fifteen the child is ready to study the *Talmud*. At eighteen the youth is ready for marriage, and at twenty for the pursuit of a livelihood.

At thirty, the Jew is considered to be at the peak of his or her strength and reaches the time of understanding at age forty. The Jewish person enters his or her senior years at age sixty and enters the period of wisdom and counsel at age eighty. Jews anticipate the grave at age ninety and pass from the scene at age one hundred."[142]

While we all understand that life is complicated and cannot be so easily categorized, the point is that there are certain significant events in the lives of Jews that set them apart as Jews. The purpose of this chapter is to get an understanding of the more important milestones in the stages of Jewish life.

Covenant of Circumcision (*Brit Milah*)

The first milestone, that is for baby boys, is circumcision (removing the foreskin of the penis). While this was a common practice of ancient nations, the LORD sanctified this practice and

---
142. Trepp, 214.

gave it new meaning and purpose. It was to be the sign of God's covenant with Abraham and his descendants.

When God called Abraham to leave Babylon, He made a covenant with Abraham. This was a sacred blood covenant that was literal, everlasting, and unconditional. In this covenant, God promised to give Abraham a land, make him a great nation, and bless the world through the Messiah who would come from the seed of Abraham. (See Genesis 12:1-3.)

Since this was a blood covenant, God required Abraham to circumcise himself, and all Jewish males after him were to be circumcised on the eighth day as a visual sign of the covenant. Because circumcision required the cutting of flesh and the shedding of blood, it was God's way of causing every natural descendant of Abraham to be born under the sign of the sacred blood covenant.

In Genesis 17, the LORD says to Abraham, " 'And I will establish My covenant between Me and you and your descendants after you in their generations, for an everlasting covenant, to be God to you and your descendants after you. Also I give to you and your descendants after you the land in which you are a stranger, all the land of Canaan, as an everlasting possession; and I will be their God.'

"And God said to Abraham. 'As for you, you shall keep My covenant, you and your descendants after you throughout their generations. This is My covenant which you shall keep, between Me and you and your descendants after you: Every male child among you shall be circumcised; and you shall be circumcised in the flesh of your foreskins, and it shall be a sign of the covenant between Me and you.

" 'He who is eight days old among you shall be circumcised, every male child in your generations, he who is born in your house or bought with money from any foreigner who is not your descendant. He who is born in your house and who is bought with your money must be circumcised, and My covenant shall be in your flesh for an everlasting covenant' " (Genesis 17:7-13).

God's command was to circumcise the Jewish male on the eighth day of his life. There were two reasons for God choosing the eighth day.

The first reason is spiritual and relates to the fact that the number eight is symbolic of "new beginnings." The baby was to begin its new life in covenant with the Almighty through the shedding of blood

The second reason is natural and relates to the physical health of the baby. Modern science has learned what God always knew regarding the clotting of blood in the human body. Vitamin K is the element which causes the blood to clot. It does not fully develop until the eighth day. This means that babies who are cut or bleed before the eighth day could bleed to death. Thus the eighth day is the first day that an infant boy can be safely circumcised.

We stated in a previous chapter that physical circumcision was an outward sign of the more important spiritual circumcision of the heart. A Jew could be physically circumcised as a sign of the covenant, but it was also necessary for his heart to be circumcised.

Moses said to his own Jewish brethren, "Therefore circumcise the foreskin of your heart, and be stiff-necked no longer" (Deuteronomy 10:16). He also explained that this spiritual circumcision came from God, "And the LORD your God will circumcise your heart and the heart of your descendants, to love the LORD your God with all your heart and with all your soul, that you may live" (Deuteronomy 30:6). Jeremiah added, "Circumcise yourselves to the LORD, and take away the foreskins of your heart..." (Jeremiah 4:4).

Circumcision is probably the most important of the various stages in the life of a Jewish male. It takes precedence over every religious event, including the keeping of the Sabbath and *Yom Kippur*. The only exception to circumcising the infant on the eighth day is if the procedure would jeopardize the health of the infant. In this case, the infant would be circumcised as soon as possible after the eighth day.

Since circumcision is not a complicated medical procedure, it is normally done in the home and during the morning hours. Traditionally, the father circumcises his own son. However, as is understandable, few fathers are able to perform the procedure so it is usually done by a trained specialist called a *mohel*.

On the morning of the eighth day, the infant's mother gives the baby to the godmother who hands him to the godfather. The godfather carries the infant into the room where the men are waiting and the circumcision is to take place. He hands the baby to one who places the infant on a chair which is called the "Chair of Elijah."

After calling on Elijah to witness the circumcision, another man hands the baby to the father who then gives the infant to the godfather. The godfather holds the baby in his lap on a pillow during the circumcision procedure, which only takes a few minutes. The appropriate prayers and blessings are recited, the baby is given his Hebrew name, and a festive meal ends the celebration.

While Judaism has never recognized the practice of circumcising girls, as is the custom of many Arab and African countries, modern Jewish households often have a ceremony celebrating the birth of a girl.

Since circumcision is a Jewish religious practice, it is not suprising to find this ritual mentioned in the New Testament. The Gospel of Luke tells us of the time when John the Baptist was circumcised and received his Hebrew name—Yochanan. He would be called, "*Yochanan the Immerser*."

Luke writes, "So it was, on the eighth day, that they came to circumcise the child; and they would have called him by the name of his father, Zacharias. His mother answered and said, 'No; he shall be called John.' But they said to her, 'There is no one among your relatives who is called by this name.' So they made signs to his father—what he would have him called. And he asked for a writing tablet and wrote, saying, 'His name is John.' So they all marveled " (Luke 1:59-63).

Luke also writes about the circumcision of Jesus, "And when eight days were completed for the circumcision of the Child, His name was called Jesus, the name given by the angel before He was conceived in the womb" (Luke 2:21).

The apostle Paul was circumcised according to Jewish practice as we learn from his own words (Philippians 3:5). Yet, many falsely accuse Paul of being anti-*Torah* and starting the Christian religion as a split from Judaism. Nothing could be further from the truth. Paul's writings have been misunderstood for centuries by Gentile scholars who wanted to strip Christianity of its Jewish roots as well as the rabbinic community who wrongly interpreted Paul's writings as being anti-Jewish.

Paul was not against circumcision. He was against those who said that physical circumcision was necessary for salvation, which he calls justification. There were certain Jews who said the Gentiles had to be circumcised to be saved.

Paul wrote to the Gentile believers in Galatia that this was not true. He said, "Indeed I, Paul, say to you that if you become circumcised, Christ [Messiah] will profit you nothing. And I testify again to every man who becomes circumcised that he is a debtor to keep the whole law.

"You have become estranged from Christ [Messiah], you who attempt to be justified by law; you have fallen from grace. For we through the Spirit eagerly wait for the hope of righteousness by faith. For in Christ [Messiah] Jesus neither circumcision nor uncircumcision avails anything, but faith working through love" (Galatians 5:2-6).

Another statement from Paul that has been misunderstood for the same reasons is as follows, "For he is not a Jew who is one outwardly, nor is circumcision that which is outward in the flesh; but he is a Jew who is one inwardly; and circumcision is that of the heart, in the Spirit, not in the letter; whose praise is not from men but from God" (Romans 2:28-29).

Again, Paul was not writing against circumcision. He was writing against the teaching that a person had to be circumcised in order to be saved. His point in all of his writings about circumcision is simply that Jews should be circumcised according to the *Torah*, Gentiles do not have to be circumcised, and that the real circumcision that mattered to God was in the heart.

Paul's statements are in perfect agreement with the Hebrew Scriptures, and any honest Christian scholar or rabbi would have to agree when he understands the context of Paul's statements. The thought would never have entered Paul's mind that a Jew should not be circumcised. The proof of this has to do with Paul and his young disciple named Timothy.

Timothy had a Jewish mother and a Gentile father. Timothy was not circumcised when he was eight days old. Since Paul was taking Timothy with him to minister to Jews, he had Timothy circumcised (Acts 16:1-3).

Paul had another disciple named Titus. Paul refused to circumcise Titus, who was a Gentile (Galatians 2:3). He was not against circumcision; he simply understood it was not necessary for Gentile believers.

Followers of Jesus must heed the same words Moses gave to the Jews centuries ago, "Circumcise the foreskins of your hearts." Jesus spoke of this as a spiritual rebirth and said to Nicodemus, "You must be born again" (John 3:1-10).

The infant male is given his Hebrew name at the time he is circumcised—the physical sign of the covenant. When God made covenant with Abraham, He gave Abraham and Sarah new names (Genesis 17:5,15).

Jews with a European background name their children after deceased relatives. Jews from the Middle East name their children after living relatives. We see this custom in the New Testament with John the Baptist and Jesus.

Redemption of the Firstborn (*Pidyon Haben*)

In ancient times, parents sacrificed their firstborn son to their gods. When the one true God spoke to Abraham, He required Abraham to sacrifice Isaac, his firstborn, as a sign of his devotion to God (Genesis 22). We learn from the outcome that God did not actually intend Abraham to kill Isaac.

This was God's way of testing Abraham according to the cultural practice of the times in which Abraham lived. God did not sanction human sacrifice, but He did require the firstborn son to be offered to Him in divine service.

The background for the redemption of the firstborn is the story of the Exodus. The last plague God sent against the Egyptians was death to the firstborn son of the Egyptians. Yet, He spared the firstborn sons of the Hebrews because they put the blood of the Passover lamb on the doorpost of their houses according to God's instructions. As a result, the firstborn sons of the Hebrews belonged to God and were to serve Him as His priests.

God said, "...you shall set apart to the LORD all that open the womb, that is, every firstborn that comes from an animal which you have; the males shall be the LORD'S. But every firstborn of a donkey you shall redeem with a lamb; and if you will not redeem it, then you shall break its neck. And all the firstborn of man among your sons you shall redeem" (Exodus 13:12-13).

The firstborn sons were to serve God and the people as the priests of God. However, they proved unworthy. When Moses was on Mount Sinai receiving the *Torah* from God, the people down below, including the firstborn sons, worshipped the golden calf (Exodus 32).

Only the Levites refused to worship the golden calf. Therefore, God chose the Levites to be His ministers in place of the rebellious firstborn sons (Numbers 3:12). However, this presented a problem.

When God told Moses to count the number of firstborn sons and the number of Levites, Moses discovered there were 22,000 Levites and 22,273 firstborn sons (Numbers 3:39, 43). There were more firstborn sons than there were Levites.

So God commanded that the extra 273 firstborn sons be redeemed (bought back from God). He set the price at five shekels for each of the firstborn sons, and the money was given to Aaron, who was the High Priest. (See Numbers 3:46-51.) From that time on, firstborn sons were redeemed when they were one month old (Numbers 18:15-16).

Today, the custom of redeeming the firstborn is only practiced by traditional Orthodox Jews. When the infant, firstborn son reaches the thirtieth day of his life, the parents bring him to a Kohen, who is considered to be a modern descendant of the priestly clan of Levites.

The Kohen, or Levite, asks the parents if they want to give their son in service to the LORD or redeem him. They redeem the son by giving the Kohen five silver dollars or shekels. The Kohen offers certain prayers and blessings and the ceremony is complete. If the firstborn is a girl, some non-Orthodox Jews simply present the infant as an expression of thanksgiving for her birth.

Since the New Testament is a Jewish book, it is not surprising to find the *pidyon haben* practiced by the family of Jesus. The story is recorded in the Book of Luke, where we learn that Mary went to the Temple for her rite of purification and to redeem Jesus as her firstborn Son.

Luke writes, "Now when the days of her purification according to the law of Moses were completed, they brought Him [Jesus] to Jerusalem to present Him to the Lord (as it is written in the law of the Lord, 'Every male who opens the womb shall be called holy to the Lord'), and to offer a sacrifice according to what is said in the law of the Lord, 'A pair of turtledoves or two young pigeons.'" (Luke 2:22-24).

The LORD gave the Hebrews certain laws of purity which are recorded in Leviticus 12. One of the laws stated that when a woman gave birth to a son, she would be ritually unclean for forty days. At the end of the forty day period, she was to bring a sacrifice to the priest at the Temple as the means for her to be ceremonially cleansed. The fact that Mary presented pigeons tells us that she and Joseph were very poor.

Mary also offered Jesus according to the commandment God gave to redeem the firstborn. Luke explains, "And behold, there was a man in Jerusalem whose name was Simeon, and this man was just and devout, waiting for the Consolation of Israel, and the Holy Spirit was upon him. And it had been revealed to him by the Holy Spirit that he would not see death before he had seen the Lord's Christ [Messiah]. So he came by the Spirit into the temple.

"And when the parents brought in the Child Jesus, to do for Him according to the custom of the law, he took Him up in his arms and blessed God and said: 'Lord, now You are letting Your servant depart in peace, according to Your word; for my eyes have seen Your salvation which You have prepared before the face of all peoples, a light to bring revelation to the Gentiles, and the glory of Your people Israel' "(Luke 2:25-32).

Simeon must have been a priest who was able to give the blessing to the LORD concerning the firstborn. According to the custom of the law, Joseph and Mary would have paid Simeon the five *shekels* to redeem Jesus.

However, when Simeon saw Jesus he knew Jesus was no ordinary firstborn. He recognized, with the assistance of the Holy Spirit, that Jesus was the true redeemer of mankind whom the custom only foreshadowed.

It was this custom that Simon Peter had in mind when he wrote, "knowing that you were not redeemed with corruptible things, like silver or gold, from your aimless conduct received by tradition from your fathers, but with the precious blood of Christ [Messiah], as of a lamb without blemish and without spot" (1 Peter 1:18-19).

Paul writes, "I beseech you therefore, brethren, by the mercies of God, that you present your bodies a living sacrifice, holy, acceptable to God, which is your reasonable service. And do not be conformed to this world, but be transformed by the renewing of your mind, that you may prove what is that good and acceptable and perfect will of God" (Romans 12:1-2).

Bar/Bat Mitzvah

Another major milestone in the life of a Jewish young person is the *Bar/Bat Mitzvah*. *Bar Mitzvah* literally means "son of the commandments." *Bat Mitzvah* means "daughter of the commandments." This is a very meaningful time in the life of a young person as it marks his or her age of religious accountability. The age of accountability for the young man is thirteen. It is twelve for the young woman.

This is the age when young people have physically developed to take on the responsibilities of an adult. The rabbis also considered it to be the age when young people are mature enough to take personal responsibility for their religious lives. Before their *Bar/Bat Mitzvah*, the father was responsible for the religious training of the children. Now they must make their own decisions and fully enter into the religious life of the Jewish community as an adult.

While there is no command in the *Torah* regarding the *Bar/Bat Mizvah*, it is a custom that was practiced in the first century of our era.[143] In order to prepare for their *Bar Mitzvah*, it was customary for young boys to accompany their parents to Jerusalem to keep the feasts at the age of twelve.[144] The practice that is followed today developed in the Middle Ages.

In the past, traditional Jews conducted only a *Bar Mitzvah* ceremony. Reform Judaism introduced the *Bat Mitzvah*, which is now also practiced by some Orthodox and Conservative groups.

The *Bar Mitzvah* ceremony normally takes place at the synagogue on a Saturday morning service, close after the young man's

---
143. Ibid., 242.
144. Kasdan, 38.

thirteenth birthday. He is called to the podium to lead part of the service—including reciting blessings, reading from the *Torah* and the Prophets, and giving a short speech, which we Christian believers would call a "personal testimony."

This is a time of rejoicing as the young man takes his place among the religious community. Appropriately, the service is usually followed by a celebration.

It is most interesting that the New Testament tells the story of Jesus going to Jerusalem with His parents to keep the feast at the age of twelve in preparation for His own *Bar Mitzvah*, as was the custom in His day.

Luke writes, "His parents went to Jerusalem every year at the Feast of the Passover. And when He was twelve years old, they went up to Jerusalem according to the custom of the feast. When they had finished the days, as they returned, the Boy Jesus lingered behind in Jerusalem.

"And Joseph and His mother did not know it; but supposing Him to have been in the company, they went a day's journey, and sought Him among their relatives and acquaintances. So when they did not find Him, they returned to Jerusalem, seeking Him.

"Now so it was that after three days they found Him in the temple, sitting in the midst of the teachers, both listening to them and asking them questions. And all who heard Him were astonished at His understanding and answers" (Luke 2:41-47).

It took Joseph and Mary one full day before they realized that Jesus was not with them. They assumed He was with relatives in the crowd of pilgrims. When they returned to Jerusalem, they found Jesus participating in His own *Bar Mitzvah*. He was learning from the rabbis as well as astounding them with His answers to their questions.

Jesus was the perfect "Son of the Commandments." He said, "And He who sent Me is with Me. The Father has not left Me alone, for I always do those things that please Him" (John 8:29).

While Gentile believers do not celebrate a *Bar Mitzvah*, we recognize there is an age of accountability for young people where they must make their own decisions regarding their relationship with God.

Jesus said, "If you love Me, keep My commandments. ...He who has My commandments and keeps them, it is He who loves Me. And He who loves Me will be loved by My Father, and I will love him and manifest Myself to him" (John 14:15, 21). May every Christian be a true *Bar/Bat Mitzvah*.

The Jewish Wedding

A major milestone in the life of anyone is his or her wedding. The information presented in this discussion is taken from the author's publication, *Here Comes the Bride: Jewish Wedding Customs and the Messiah*.

The Jewish people have a rich tradition that dates back to ancient times. While there are many similarities to our Western ways, there are other marriage customs that are foreign to our way of thinking. For example, the Bible considers marriage a sacred blood covenant (Malachi 2:14) requiring a formal marriage contract between the two parties.

Furthermore, the father often chose the bride for the son at an early age. He sometimes used the services of a matchmaker who was the expert in finding just the right bride for the father's son.

In the biblical period, the Jewish wedding consisted of three phases. These were the: 1) betrothal phase, 2) wedding phase, and 3) celebration phase.[145]

In the initial betrothal phase, the young man prepares a contract or covenant which he presents to the young woman he wants to marry. This marriage contract is called a *Ketubah*. It is a formal

---

145. Richard Booker, *Here Comes the Bride* (Houston, TX: Sounds of the Trumpet, 1995), 1.

written document which stipulates the terms of the marriage proposal he is making.

Once the *Ketubah* is prepared, the man then goes to the house where the young woman lives and makes the proposal to her and her father.

The most important part of the proposal is the bride price. This is the price the young man is willing to pay the father for his permission to marry his daughter. If the marriage contract and the bride price are acceptable to the father, the young man would pour a cup of wine for his beloved. This cup of wine represents the blood covenant commitment and union they would have as husband and wife. If she accepts the proposal, she drinks the cup as her way of saying "yes" to the young man.

After the young man returns home, and before their actual wedding, the bride takes a *Mikveh* as part of a ceremonial cleansing to prepare herself for the days ahead.

At this point, the young couple are betrothed. In Bible times, and even in some cultures today, the betrothal phase made them legally married, although they were not yet ready to live together as husband and wife. The marriage was consummated later after the wedding during the celebration phase.

Before leaving the house of his newly betrothed, the young man assures her that he is now going home to prepare a place for her. And as soon as it is prepared, he will come again for her. The bridegroom then returns home and begins building a room onto his father's house that will serve as their wedding chamber. In Jewish weddings today, the *chuppah* represents this wedding chamber.

It usually took a full year for the young man to complete the bridal chamber, and it was up to his father to determine when it was finished. Whenever someone asked the eager bridegroom the date of his wedding, he would reply, "I don't know, only my father knows."

While the bridegroom is busy preparing a place for them to live, the bride is busy making herself ready. Although she doesn't know exactly when he will come for her, she wants to be ready. She reorders her entire life to prepare for his coming.

Whenever she leaves her house she wears a veil to let other young men know she is no longer available. She belongs to another because she has been bought with a price. She is set apart and consecrated to her bridegroom. Her veil is a constant reminder that she is betrothed to one who is preparing a place where they will enter into the joys of their covenant relationship through marriage.

When the bridegroom's father thought the wedding chamber was complete, he would tell his son to go get his bride. It was the custom for the bridegroom to "steal away" his bride like a thief in the night.[146]

Now the young girl never knew exactly when he was coming so she made special preparations to make sure she was ready. She kept her lamp and oil beside her bed, along with her veil and other belongings. Her bridesmaids would also be waiting, making sure they had plenty of oil in their lamps.

As the bridegroom nears the house of his awaiting bride, his best man gives a shout and blows the shofar (ram's horn) to let the bride know her bridegroom is coming.[147] When they arrive, the bridegroom takes his bride to his house and the wedding chamber he has prepared for her.

When the wedding party arrives at the house of the bridegroom's father, the couple go into the wedding chamber where they consummate the marriage and establish their covenant union. The celebration lasts for seven days with many invited guests. It is a festive time with singing and dancing, followed by a joyous feast called the "marriage supper" which is given to honor the newly married couple.

Much of this ancient tradition is still practiced today in Jewish weddings, with some modifications. The *Ketubah* is still considered

---

146. Ibid., 8.
147. Ibid., 9.

an important element of Jewish weddings. However, it is more symbolic and has been replaced by the modern marriage license.

In addition, the young couple marry whenever they can make the necessary arrangements. Furthermore, they normally have their own house or apartment where they begin their new life together.

The wedding ceremony itself is conducted under a *chuppah*— a canopy symbolizing the house where the new couple will dwell. It includes the sermon from the rabbi, exchanges between the bridegroom and bride, the reciting of blessings, and drinking several cups of wine to symbolize their union. At the conclusion of the ceremony, the groom breaks a glass as a reminder of the destruction of the Temple in Jerusalem. A great feast follows with much rejoicing.

The parallels of the Jewish wedding to Christianity should be obvious. God, our heavenly Father, chose a bride for His Son Jesus. Paul writes, "Blessed be the God and Father of our Lord Jesus Christ [Messiah], who has blessed us with every spiritual blessing in the heavenly places in Christ [Messiah], just as He chose us in Him before the foundation of the world, that we should be holy and without blame before Him in love" (Ephesians 1:3-4).

God Himself sent the Holy Spirit as the matchmaker from from Heaven who would make us one with Him. Jesus came to the house of the bride (earth), and offered a marriage contract to us. That marriage contract is the New Covenant, which stipulates the terms and conditions for our salvation.

The price Jesus offered to purchase us was His own blood. Paul writes that God had purchased us with His own blood (Acts 20:28).

When we accept the terms of the New Covenant, we show our desire to join ourselves to Jesus by drinking the cup of the New Covenant, which is the cup of communion or the Lord's Supper.

Matthew writes, "And as they were eating, Jesus took bread, blessed and broke *it*, and gave it to the disciples and said, 'Take, eat; this is My body.' Then He took the cup, and gave thanks, and gave *it* to them, saying, 'Drink from it, all of you. For this is My blood of the new covenant, which is shed for many for the remission of sins' " (Matthew 26:26-28).

After Jesus was resurrected, He gave the following words of assurance to His followers, "In My Father's house are many mansions; if it were not so, I would have told you. I go to prepare a place for you. And if I go and prepare a place for you, I will come again and receive you to Myself; that where I am, there you may be also" (John 14:2-3).

Jesus is preparing a place for His bride in the New Jerusalem. He will come for us when He is finished. Although we don't know when this will be (Matthew 24:36), we live our lives in anticipation of His coming. We no longer belong to ourselves. We belong to God.

As Paul writes, "For you were bought at a price; therefore glorify God in your body and in your spirit, which are God's (1 Corinthians 6:20). Our holy lives are like the veil that says to the world we are betrothed to Jesus and are waiting for Him to come and take us to "Father's House."

Just before He comes, Jesus will warn us that His coming is near by the blowing of the *shofar*. Paul writes, "For the Lord Himself will descend from heaven with a shout, with the voice of an archangel, and with the trumpet [*shofar*] of God. And the dead in Christ [Messiah] will rise first. Then we who are alive and remain shall be caught up together with them in the clouds to meet the Lord in the air. And thus we shall always be with the Lord" (1 Thessalonians 4:16-17).

The wedding chamber Jesus is preparing for His bride is the New Jerusalem—our heavenly *chuppah*. John wrote, "Then I, John saw the holy city, New Jerusalem, coming down out of heaven from God, prepared as a bride adorned for her husband" (Revelation 21:2).

There will be a great marriage feast with much rejoicing. It will be a glorious celebration. John writes, "Let us be glad and rejoice and give Him glory, for the marriage of the Lamb has come, and His wife has made herself ready. And to her it was granted to be arrayed in fine linen, clean and bright, for the fine linen is the righteous acts of the saints.

"Then he said to me, 'Write: Blessed are those who are called to the marriage supper of the Lamb!' And he said to me, 'These are the true sayings of God' "(Revelation 19:7-9).

Death and Mourning

The last milestone of death is one we all must face. What we believe about death not only affects how we die, but also how we live. Death is man's ultimate fear.

While different religions have their theories about death, the Bible is the only authoritative book on the subject because it claims to be inspired by God. The Creator is the only One who would know what happens to His creatures after they die.

While the Hebrew Bible certainly indicates that there is life after death, it does not give the subject primary emphasis nor does it give any detailed explanation of the hereafter. The writer of Ecclesiastes says, "…the dust [body] will return to the earth as it was, and the spirit will return to God who gave it" (Ecclesiastes 12:7).

Several places speak about a resurrection of the body. Job wrote, "For I know that my Redeemer lives, and He shall stand at last on the earth; and after my skin is destroyed, this I know, that in my flesh I shall see God" (Job 19:25-26).

Michael gave Daniel the following word of hope and comfort, "But you, go your way till the end; for you shall rest, and will arise to your inheritance at the end of the days" (Daniel 12:13).

The *Talmud* seems to teach that when a person dies, his or her soul lives on either with God or apart from God. Then at the end of the age, there will be a literal physical resurrection when the soul will rejoin the body.

It was not until the intertestamental period that the rabbis developed a fuller theology on death and the afterlife. During this time, the Greeks and Romans ruled over the Jews. The people could not understand why their oppressive rulers seemed to enjoy "the good life" while they experienced many hardships and sufferings, even though they tried to please God.

The rabbis taught that God did not always reward the righteous in this life but would surely do so in the world to come.[148] The Scripture supports this view and says, "Surely there is a reward for the righteous; surely He is God who judges in the earth" (Psalm 58:11).

Furthermore, as the people suffered under the rule of the Gentiles, they longed for the Messiah who would deliver them and re-establish the nation of Israel and the throne of David.

Yet, many were concerned that Messiah would come after they died. This meant they would miss the Messianic Kingdom spoken of by the prophets.

The rabbis assured the people that they would be resurrected at the end of the age to participate in the redemption of Jerusalem. Daniel confirms this teaching.

Both biblical Judaism and New Testament Christianity teach the eternity of the soul and the physical resurrection of the body at the end of the age when Messiah appears. The righteous will be resurrected to everlasting life and the unrighteous to everlasting shame and damnation.

Daniel records these words from Michael, "And many of those who sleep in the dust of the earth shall awake, some to everlasting life, some to shame and everlasting contempt" (Daniel 12:2).

In the New Testament era, the Pharisees gave much emphasis to these teachings, but the Sadducees denied them. Jesus accepted the teachings of the Pharisees on the subject and added further

---

148. Dan Cohn-Sherbok, *The Jewish Faith* (Valley Forge, PA: Trinity Press International, 1993), 112.

enlightenment claiming to have the power of life and death within Himself (John 11:25-26).

It was also during the intertestamental period that the rabbis developed the teaching that the soul of the deceased went to a place called *Sheol*.

The rabbis taught that Sheol was divided into two compartments. The top compartment was called Abraham's Bosom or Paradise and was the place where the righteous went until their soul rejoined their bodies at the end of the age. The unrighteous went to the bottom part of Sheol which was a place of torment.

This terrible place of judgment was named Geyhinnom, after the Valley of Hinnom, which was the garbage dump just outside the walls of Jerusalem. Since there was a fire always burning in the Valley of Hinnom, it became the symbol of Hell (Isaiah 66:24; Mark 9:44-48). Jesus accepted this teaching and used it in a parable which is recorded in Luke 16:19-31.

Because God created the body to contain man's spirit (Proverbs 20:27), Judaism honors the body of the deceased.

It is the tradition of Judaism to bury the deceased within twenty-four hours of death, unless the burial day would be on the Sabbath or close relatives require additional travel time to get to the funeral.

A Jewish burial society and/or professional mortuary handle the details. Because the *Torah* gives such high regard to blood, Jewish burial tradition does not normally permit embalming nor autopsies.

Also, since God created the body from the dust of the earth, traditional Judaism does not sanction cremation but burial in the ground. This is based on Genesis 3:19 which says, "...for dust you are and to dust you shall return."

The body of the deceased is cleaned and washed in a prescribed manner according to Jewish traditions and customs. Those attending the body clothe it in a white linen shroud that has no pockets. This is a dramatic statement that we take nothing with us when we leave this world. Males are traditionally buried with their *Tallit* draped over their shoulders. One of the *tzitzit* is cut to symbolize that the deceased is no longer obligated to keep the commandments.

While Gentiles are usually buried in the most expensive casket the family can afford, Jews are traditionally buried in a simple pine box. Rabbi Dosick explains that the reason is because the wood will quickly decay, thus more rapidly returning the body to the dust of the earth. He goes on to say that the simple pine box also demonstrates that we are all equal in death.[149]

Jewish funeral services normally have a closed casket to show respect for the body. The more Orthodox services do not allow flowers or singing as these are symbols of joy. During the memorial service, the relatives of the deceased tear a small part of their clothing to show their grief for losing their loved one. Funeral homes normally provide a black ribbon to tear in place of the clothing.

At the burial site, it is customary for family members to throw a small handful of dirt over the casket. Before leaving the gravesite, the mourners recite the *Kaddish* as an expression of their faith in God. While the *Kaddish* is often referred to as a prayer for the dead, it is a prayer glorifying God even in times of great sorrow. This great prayer of praise comes from Ezekiel 38:23. It is to be said for the next eleven months.

The *Kaddish* reads as follows:

"May His great name grow exalted and sanctified in the world that He created as He willed. May He give reign to His kingship in your lifetimes and in your days, and in the lifetimes of the entire family of Israel, swiftly and soon. Amen.

"Blessed, praised, glorified, exalted, extolled, mighty, upraised, and lauded be the Name of the Holy One, Blessed is He beyond any blessing and song, praise and consolation that are uttered in the world. Amen.

---
149. Dosick, 305.

"May there be abundant peace from Heaven, and life, upon us and all Israel. Amen. He who makes peace in His heights, may He make peace upon us, and upon all Israel. Amen."

Jewish mourning for the dead is divided into three distinct periods designed to help the mourners deal with their grief before gradually returning to normal life.

The first seven days are the most intense during which the mourners, according to tradition, sit on low stools to symbolize their grief. The more observant Jews will not wear leather, because in ancient times these were symbols of luxury, and they cover the mirrors to avoid any show of vanity. The basic idea is to shield the mourners from the normal everyday activities so they can express their grief. This seven day period is know as the *shivah*, meaning "seven."

After this intense time of grieving is another period lasting twenty-three days. It is called *shloshim*, meaning "thirty." During this period, the mourners return to their normal activities but usually refrain from attending celebrations and other joyous events where there is music and dancing.

The grieving period continues for a complete year from the date of death. The *Kaddish* is said for the first eleven months. It is not said the twelfth month, because the sages taught that the soul which did not merit heaven stayed in a place of purgatory until the soul was cleansed. The sages believed this soul-cleansing was completed during the twelve month period. Therefore, it was not necessary to say *Kaddish* in the twelfth month.

On the first anniversary of the death, a gravestone is set in place and dedicated. This brings to a close the formal period of mourning so that the mourners can fully resume their normal lives. It is tradition to place small stones, or pebbles, on the gravestone to honor the memory of the deceased. Furthermore, it is customary to commemorate the loss of the loved one each year on the anniversary of the day of death.

Jesus was buried according to the Jewish customs of His day. Joseph of Arimathea and Nicodemus were important members of the Jewish Supreme Court (the Sanhedrin). They took Jesus' body and wrapped it in linen bands with a mixture of myrrh and aloes weighing about one hundred pounds. (See John 19:38-40.) The amount of spices used to anoint the body was a measure of the value of the deceased.

It was the custom for the body to be washed and straightened, and then bandaged tightly from the armpits to the ankles in strips of linen about a foot wide. Aromatic spices, often of a gummy consistency, were placed between the wrapping. They served as a bonding agent to glue the wrappings into a solid covering. The face was left uncovered, but a cloth was wrapped around the head of the body.

Aloe was a fragrant wood which had been pounded into dust. The myrrh was an aromatic gum which was mixed with the powdered wood. We might think of the myrrh as the "first-century superglue." When mixed together, the dry aloe stuck to the body, so that Jesus' body was embedded in the powdered spice.

The body lay with its face turned upwards and its hands folded on the chest. The face, neck, and upper shoulders were left bare. The head rested on a raised portion of the ledge which served as a pillow. Because Jesus' body was hurriedly prepared for the tomb, there was no time for an elaborate burial. Later, after the weekly Sabbath, the women came to anoint Jesus' face, neck, and shoulders.

But when the women came to the tomb, they found that it was empty. Jesus had risen from the dead. Matthew gives the following account, "Now after the Sabbath [at the end of the Sabbath], as the first day of the week began to dawn, Mary Magdalene and the other Mary came to see the tomb. And behold, there was a great earthquake; for an angel of the Lord descended from heaven, and came and rolled back the stone from the door, and sat on it.

"His countenance was like lightning, and his clothing as white as snow. And the guards shook for fear of him, and became like dead men. But the angel answered and said to the women, 'Do not be afraid, for I know that you seek Jesus who was crucified. He is not here; for He is risen, as He said. Come, see the place where the Lord lay.' "(Matthew 28:1-6).

Christians need not fear death because Jesus has conquered death. The New Testament promises eternal life and the hope of the resurrection to true believers who have given their lives to Him.

Paul writes, "Behold, I tell you a mystery: We shall not all sleep, but we shall all be changed—in a moment, in the twinkling of an eye, at the last trumpet. For the trumpet will sound, and the dead will be raised incorruptible, and we shall be changed. For this corruptible must put on incorruption, and this mortal must put on immortality.

"So when this corruptible has put on incorruption, and this mortal has put on immortality, then shall be brought to pass the saying that is written: 'Death is swallowed up in victory. O Death, where is your sting? O Hades, where is your victory?' The sting of death is sin, and the strength of sin is the law. But thanks be to God, who gives us the victory through our Lord Jesus Christ [Messiah].

"Therefore, my beloved brethren, be steadfast, immovable, always abounding in the work of the Lord, knowing that your labor is not in vain in the Lord" (1 Corinthians 15:51-58).

Chapter 11—Personal Study Guide

1. Explain the meaning and purpose of circumcision and any connection to Christianity.

2. Explain the meaning and purpose of the redemption of the firstborn and any connection to Christianity.

3. Explain the meaning and purpose of *Bar/Bat Mitzvah* and any connection to Chritianity.

4. Discuss the Jewish wedding tradition and how it relates to Christianity.

5. Discuss the Jewish view of death and mourning and how it relates to Christianity.

Chapter 12
Jewish Religious Cycle—the Sabbath

In the Hebrew Scriptures God provided a written record of the Messiah to enable the Jewish people to recognize Him when He appeared. Jesus of Nazareth claimed to be this Messiah and proved it by fulfilling in Himself the very Scriptures that spoke of the Messiah. Yet even though many thousands of Jews believed that Jesus was the Messiah, the powerful Jewish leadership in Jerusalem rejected Jesus for themselves and the nation.

Ironically, the Gentiles embraced Jesus. John writes, "He came to His own and His own did not receive Him. But as many as received Him, to them He gave the right to become children of God, to those who believe in His name" (John 1:11-12).

These Gentile followers of Jesus experienced a spiritual new birth and, along with the Jewish believers, became part of a company of people called "the church." The church did not replace the Jewish people in God's plan of redemption. Instead, the non-Jewish believers became part of the commonwealth of Israel with Abraham as their spiritual father (Ephesians 2:11-18).

The Great Divide

As the church became more "Gentilized," Jews and Christians began to go their separate ways. It wasn't long before the church was flooded with unbelievers who embraced the Christian faith but never received Jesus personally as their Lord and Savior. Their hearts did not change. These people brought their hate with them into this new Christian faith.

About the same time, some of the early church fathers developed a faulty theology that created an anti-Semitic mentality in the church that further divided the Christian world from the Jews. These early anti-Jewish declarations laid the foundation for the tragic future of Jewish-Christian relations that would see the church lose sight of its Jewish roots and persecute the Jews down through the centuries.

In our present day, God is doing a new thing. He is breaking down the walls of hate and misunderstanding that have divided the Jews and Gentile believers for centuries.

God is sovereignly calling Jewish people back to their ancient land and to their roots, as the time to favor Zion has come. At the same time, God is stirring in the hearts of Christians a holy love for the Jewish people and awakening them to the Jewish roots of their Christian faith.

As mentioned in the introductory chapter, many Christians are realizing that the origin of our faith is Jerusalem, not Athens, Rome, Geneva, Wittenberg, Aldersgate, Azuza Street, Springfield, Nashville, Tulsa, etc. As a result, Christians around the world are reaching out to the Jewish people in new and exciting ways. It is clearly God's appointed time, His prophetic season, to reconcile Jews and Christians "for such a time as this."

Because of the prophetic season in which we are living, many Christians are wanting to learn about their Jewish heritage. The purpose of this chapter is to study the Sabbath—the Day of the Lord. The information is taken from the author's publication, *Shabbat Shalom: A Guide for Christians to Understand the Sabbath*.

The Sabbath

The word "Sabbath" is found 135 times in the Bible. It is mentioned 75 times in the Hebrew Scriptures and 60 times in the New Testament. The word refers to the seventh day of the week and basically means to rest or take an intermission. The Hebrew word for Sabbath is *Shabbat*.

While the Sabbath is central in Jewish life, some believe that God gave the Sabbath for all mankind and only later gave it specifically to the Jews as their special day. In addition to this understanding, when Christianity became the official religion of Rome, Sunday was declared and actually enforced as the Sabbath for Christendom.

The basic purpose of the Sabbath is to provide a day for people to rest from their labors and spend time in fellowship with God and one another. Furthermore, the Sabbath was a sign of the covenant God had with the Jewish people. Exodus reads, "Speak also to the children of Israel, saying: 'Surely My Sabbaths you shall keep, for it is a sign between Me and you throughout your generations, that you may know that I am the LORD who sanctifies you' " (Exodus 31:13).

When God said He gave the Sabbath as a sign, He meant it would be a pledge or seal guaranteeing His commitment to keep His promises to the children of Israel to give them a land, to make them a great nation, and to redeem the world through them. God had made these promises to Abraham and his descendants, and the Sabbath was the guarantee that He would do what He said He would do for them. When the people rested on the Sabbath they were resting in the faithfulness of God to keep His word.

In Bible times, life was hard. Work was strenuous. There were no convenient, labor-saving devices such as washing machines, dishwashers, tractors, lawnmowers, disposable diapers, etc. People were exhausted just trying to make a living.

The Sabbath was a tremendous gift from God to people whose tired, aching bodies needed a rest. It was the one day of the week when they could spend time with God and family. They could break their monotonous routine. They could "take an intermission." They could refresh their spirits and souls. The Sabbath was a day of delight for the people.

Isaiah writes, "If you turn away your foot from the Sabbath [keep your feet from breaking the Sabbath], from doing your pleasure on My holy day, and call the Sabbath a delight, the holy day of the LORD honorable, and shall honor Him, not doing your own ways, nor finding your own pleasure, nor speaking your own words, then you shall delight yourself [find joy] in the LORD..."(Isaiah 58:13-14).

In this Scripture, God calls the Sabbath, "My holy day, the holy day of the LORD." Although the people were to honor God each day of their lives, this was the one day of the week set apart especially for this purpose. The Sabbath was God's gift of time to honor Him.

The people were not to go their own ways, find their own pleasures, and speak their own words. Instead, they were to spend the day studying, meditating, praying, and fellowshipping with God and one another as a family.

God would bless the people with great joy as a result of being in His presence. Psalm 16:11 reads, "...in Your presence is fullness of joy...."

The Sabbath was such a blessing that the God of Abraham, Isaac, and Jacob expected foreigners who accepted Him as their God to keep the Sabbath.

Isaiah explains, "Thus says the LORD: 'Keep justice, and do righteousness, for My salvation is about to come, and My righteousness to be revealed. Blessed is the man who does this, and the son of man [mankind] who lays hold on it; who keeps from defiling the Sabbath, and keeps his hand from doing any evil.

"Also the sons of the foreigner who join themselves to the LORD, to serve Him, and to love the name of the LORD, to be His servants—Everyone who keeps from defiling the Sabbath, and holds fast My covenant—" (Isaiah 56:1-2,6).

God links the Sabbath with the covenant He made with Abraham, Isaac, and Jacob. Foreigners [Gentiles] who turned from their idols and accepted the God of the Jews as the one true God entered into the covenant and became part of the commonwealth of Israel. As part of the covenant people of God, it was natural that they keep the Sabbath. God said He would bless the son of man (mankind in general) who keeps the Sabbath.

Of course just "keeping the Sabbath" would not please God. He expected the people to keep the Sabbath with a right heart. God blesses the one who "keeps his hand from doing evil." This is the person who honors the Sabbath both outwardly and inwardly by expressing love toward God and each other.

Jesus and the Sabbath

Contrary to traditional Christian and rabbinic teaching, Jesus faithfully kept the Sabbath. (See Luke 4:16-21.) In fact, he presented Himself as the spiritual reality of the Sabbath who would give true rest to our souls.

Jesus said, "Come to Me, all you who labor and are heavy laden, and I will give you rest. Take My yoke upon you and learn from Me, for I am gentle and lowly in heart, and you will find rest for your souls. For My yoke is easy and My burden is light" (Matthew 11:28-30). The writer of the Book of Hebrews refers to the rest believers can have in Jesus. (See Hebrews 4:1-11.)

Other than His claim to be the Messiah, Jesus had more problems with some of the religious leaders regarding the Sabbath than He did with any other issue. His concern was not with the Sabbath but with the many rules and regulations that made Sabbath keeping an end in itself. What God intended to be a delight had become a burden.

While keeping the Sabbath was primary for the rabbis, not all the groups agreed on how it should be kept. Some had more rules than others and were much more strict.

For these groups, keeping the Sabbath became an end in itself, in spite of the hardships their restrictions caused. They lost their focus as to the true purpose for the Sabbath. If there was a conflict between their rules and regulations and the needs of the people, they would enforce their rules to the detriment of the people.

Other leading religious groups were more lenient in their interpretation of how to keep the Sabbath. While they were certainly focused on keeping the Sabbath, they understood it was to be a delight and not a burden. They had fewer restrictions and recognized that man's higher interests and needs took precedence over their rules. Jesus identified more with this group. If there was a conflict between legitimate human needs and legalistic rulings to control people's behavior, Jesus would always give His priority to helping people.

Jesus' compassion for people brought Him into conflict with the religious Pharisees who had the more strict interpretation of the Sabbath. Jesus had problems with some of the misguided teachings regarding the Sabbath, not the Sabbath itself.

Paul and the Sabbath

Next to Jesus Himself, the apostle Paul is probably the most misunderstood man in all of human history. This is particularly true in regard to Paul's attitude towards the *Torah*. As with Jesus, Paul was a *Torah* observant Jew.

While there are some Scriptures that seem to indicate otherwise, Paul kept the Sabbath. The reason some Scriptures have been misunderstood is because they have not been interpreted in their original cultural context. That context is first century Judaism.

Since God gave the Sabbath as a sign of His covenant with the Jewish people, it would never have entered Paul's mind that God intended to change the Sabbath from Saturday to Sunday. It was officially changed to Sunday by Constantine in AD 321, as mentioned earlier in a previous chapter.

Yet several Scriptures seem clear that the church met on Sunday rather than Saturday. However, when read with a Jewish background, we learn otherwise. Let's consider the two examples that have been the most misunderstood. The first is the church at Troas.

We read in Acts 20, "Now on the first day of the week, when the disciples came together to break bread, Paul, ready to depart the next day, spoke to them and continued his message until midnight. There were many lamps in the upper room where they were gathered together....Now when he had come up, had broken bread and eaten, and talked a long while, even till daybreak, he departed" (Acts 20:7-8,11).

This seems clear that the church in Troas was having a "Sunday morning get-together." But this is not correct. Here's why. The Jews kept the Saturday Sabbath for centuries. They opened the Sabbath with a special prayer, followed by the lighting of candles and a meal. This was on Friday evening around 6:00 p.m. They ended the Sabbath with a special service called the *Havdalah*, or "closing of the Sabbath."

Jews still do this today. This was also around 6:00 p.m., or until the sighting of three stars. They would continue this "closing of the Sabbath" into the later evening hours, much like Christians gather for fellowship after a Sunday evening church service and talk and eat for hours. This special service included prayer, followed by a meal and fellowship. This was on Saturday night, which in Hebrew is called, *Motza'ei-Shabbat*.[150]

In this setting, Paul and the believers had come together for their regular Sabbath meeting. This is when the disciples came together to break bread at the close of the Sabbath. Since they were already meeting, and Paul was leaving the next day (Sunday), he kept talking until midnight and stayed until daybreak on Sunday when he departed. These Jewish believers could not be meeting on Sunday because that was a workday for the Jews. Paul was not in church on Sunday because he was making his way to Assos, the next stop on his journey.

The next misunderstood Scripture refers to the church at Corinth. Paul taught in Corinth on the Sabbath in a home next to the synagogue for a year and six months (Acts 18:1-11). Later, he wrote to this congregation about taking a collection.

We read Paul's instructions in 1 Corinthians, "Now concerning the collection for the saints, as I have given orders to the

---

150. David Stern, *Jewish New Testament Commentary* (Jerusalem: Jewish New Testament Publications, 1992), 297-298.

churches of Galatia, so you must do also: On the first day of the week let each one of you lay something aside, storing up as he may prosper, that there be no collections when I come" (1 Corinthians 16:1-2).

Once again, the phrase, "the first day of the week," refers to *Motza'ei-Shabbat*. It was the close of the regular Saturday evening gathering.

The Jewish believers, along with the Gentile followers of Jesus, observed the Sabbath as a day of rest and met for worship and fellowship in the evening after it was over.

Judaism prohibits handling money on the Sabbath. After the Sabbath was over, on the first day of the week, they were to take up a collection and have it ready for Paul's visit.

From the beginning of time, God gave the Sabbath as His special day of rest. While it is considered to be the holy day for the Jews, it is clear in the Bible that the Lord intended it to be the day of rest for all believers, be they Jew or Gentile.

Jewish Religious Cycle—the Sabbath

Chapter 12—Personal Study Guide

1. Discuss the meaning and purpose of the Sabbath.

2. Discuss how Jesus related to the Sabbath.

3. Discuss how Paul related to the Sabbath.

4. Explain what was happening in the following Scriptures in relationship to the Sabbath.
   A. Acts 20

   B. First Corinthians 16

5. How should the Church view the Sabbath?

Chapter 13
Jewish Religious Cycle—the Feasts

In addition to the Sabbath, the God of Israel instructed the Jews to celebrate certain festivals that would serve as visual aids of His plan of redemption. The Jews were to keep these feasts on prescribed months and days of the year as God ordained on the Jewish calendar.

The purpose of this chapter is to provide a basic survey of the feasts from a Christian view. The information for this chapter is taken from the author's book *Jesus in the Feasts of Israel*.

The Jewish Calendar

The Jews have two concurrent calendar years. The civil calendar is based on the Jews' agricultural season. It begins with the Hebrew month of *Tishri*, which corresponds to the months of September and October on the Gentile calendar. Thus, the Jewish new year begins in the fall of the Gentile calendar.

Since God created the evening and the morning as the first day (Genesis 1:5), the Jewish day begins at sunset, roughly 6:00 p.m., rather than at midnight. This difference in the beginning of the day can cause confusion for the Christian who normally reads the New Testament through Western, Gentile eyes. This means that Jewish holidays begin in the evening before the morning of the day on the Gentile calendar.

The Jewish religious calendar is a moon or "lunar" calendar based on the movement of the moon around the earth. Each new moon begins a new month. This information doesn't seem very spiritual until we learn that the Hebrew word for moon can be translated as "renewal." Every new moon is a reminder of the rebirth God has for all who will commit their lives to Him and be renewed in their hearts.

The difference between the civil calendar and religious calendar is 11 1/4 days each year. Because of this difference, the Jews add an extra month to their calendar every third year so that the feast days can be kept in the seasons called for by the Bible.

God set the feasts to be celebrated on specific days on the religious calendar. However, because the religious and civil calendars are different, the Feast holidays do not always fall on the same civil calendar date each year.

	Jewish Calendar		
Feast	**Religious**	**Civil**	**Name of Months**
Passover	1	7	*Nisan*—Mar-Apr
	2	8	*Iyyar*—Apr-May
Pentecost	3	9	*Sivan*—May-June
	4	10	*Tammuz*—June-July
	5	11	*Ab*—July-Aug
	6	12	*Elul*—Aug-Sept
Tabernacles	7	1	*Tishri*—Sept-Oct
	8	2	*Heshvan*—Oct-Nov
	9	3	*Kieslev*—Nov-Dec
Hanukkah	10	4	*Tebeth*—Dec-Jan
(Secular Holiday)	11	5	*Shebat*—Jan-Feb
Purim	12	6	*Adar*—Feb-Mar
(Secular Holiday)			

The Feasts

As mentioned, the feasts were religious holidays that God established as visual aids for the Hebrews to learn His plan of redemption through the Messiah. Every redemptive work of Jesus happened on a feast day. If for no other reason, this shows just how important it is for Christians to understand these festivals.

While we normally think of these holy days as the "Feasts of the Jews," they are really the "Feasts of the LORD." Leviticus reads, "…The feasts of the LORD, which you shall proclaim to be holy convocations, these are My feasts.…These are the feasts of the LORD, holy convocations, which you shall proclaim at their appointed times" (Leviticus 23:2,4).

God established seven of these feasts and scheduled them on the Hebrew calendar in such a way that the Jews would have to travel to Jerusalem three times a year to keep them. These three feast seasons were known as Passover (*Pesach*), Pentecost (*Shavuot*), and Tabernacles (*Sukkot*).

Passover

Historically, Passover marks the national liberation of the Hebrews from Egyptian slavery. *Pesach,* the Hebrew name for this feast, literally means, "the lamb."

In the story in Exodus, God instructed each family to take an unblemished lamb to their home on the tenth day of *Nisan*. They were to observe the lamb for five days to make sure it was without spot or blemish. Then on the fourteenth day, they were to kill the lamb and take some of its blood and place it on the two doorposts and the lintel of their house.

The Hebrews killed the lambs at three o'clock in the afternoon on the fourteenth. According to the instructions, they were not to break any bones in the lamb and were to consume it entirely. Nothing was to be left over for the next day. (See Exodus 12:10, 46.)

At that first Passover, the angel of death killed the firstborn male throughout the land. However, if the entrance to the door was covered with the blood of the lamb, the angel would "pass over" the house and the people inside would be spared. The whole story is told in Exodus 12.

The LORD instructed the Hebrews to celebrate the Feast of Passover as an everlasting memorial to their great deliverance from Egypt by the blood of the lamb. Leviticus reads, "These are the feasts of the LORD, holy convocations which you shall proclaim at their appointed times. On the fourteenth day of the first month at twilight is the LORD'S Passover" (Leviticus 23:4-5).

Today the Feast of Passover is celebrated by Jewish people around the world with a beautiful Passover *Seder* (service) which commemorates the liberation of their ancestors from Egypt.

The Passover *Seder* is a meal with special foods, ritual practices, and reading from the Scripture in accordance with God's instructions given in Exodus 12 and Leviticus 23:4-5. It is a wonderful picture of redemption celebrated by family and friends who gather to rejoice in this mighty act of God on their behalf.

There is an obvious Christian connection through Jesus to all of these feasts. John the Baptist introduced Jesus as the "…Lamb of God who takes away the sin of the world" (John 1:29).

From a New Testament perspective, Jesus fulfilled (correctly interpreted) the Feast of Passover in His crucifixion. He orchestrated all of the events of the last week of His life to accomplish in His flesh what the feasts symbolized.

As the lambs were set aside to be tested on the tenth day of the month, so Jesus entered Jerusalem on the tenth day to be set aside as the human Lamb of God.

The religious leaders observed Jesus for five days, from the tenth to the fourteenth, but they couldn't find anything wrong with Him. Finally, they took Jesus to the Roman governor, Pilate, who examined Jesus and said, "…I find no fault in Him" (John 19:4).

Jesus was crucified on the fourteenth, the same day the lambs had been killed for centuries. Furthermore, He died at the same time the lambs were killed. The Jews prepared the lambs for sacrifice at nine o'clock in the morning on the fourteenth. They then killed them at three o'clock that afternoon.

At the exact hour when the Jews were preparing their lambs for sacrifice, Jesus was nailed to the cross. Then at three o'clock as the people were slaughtering their lambs, Jesus died (Mark 15:25-37).

All the other details concerning the death of the lambs happened to Jesus. As just mentioned, God said not to break any bones in the Passover lamb. Likewise, John records that the Roman soldiers broke the legs of the two thieves who were crucified next to Jesus. But when they came to Jesus, they saw He was already dead and did not break His legs (John 19:31-36).

We also noted that God instructed the Jews to consume the whole lamb so that nothing would be left over for the next day (Exodus 12:10). Likewise, the Jews hurriedly had Jesus' body taken down before six o'clock so that He was not left on the cross the next day (John 19:31).

The apostle Paul connected Jesus to Passover when he said, "For indeed, Christ [Messiah] our Passover, was sacrificed for us" (1 Corinthians 5:7). While Christianity has taught that the feasts were Jewish holidays that have no meaning for the Church, Paul instructed the Christians at Corinth to "...keep the feast, not with old leaven, nor with the leaven of malice and wickedness, but with the unleavened bread of sincerity and truth" (1 Corinthians 5:8).

Unleavened Bread

The background for the Feast of Unleavened Bread is also found in Exodus 12. We learn when God delivered the Hebrews from Egypt, He brought them out with such haste, they didn't have time to cook their bread which normally would have included leaven.

Over time, leaven became symbolic of the Hebrew's old life of bondage in Egypt under Pharaoh and the Egyptian's way of life which was contrary to God. Unleavened bread symbolized their putting off this old life as they came out of Egypt.

God instructed the Hebrews to keep the Feast of Unleavened Bread as a memorial to their separation from Egypt. The people were not to eat leavened bread at Passover on the fourteenth of *Nisan* nor for the next seven days, according to Exodus 13:3-7.

The Feast of Unleavened Bread was celebrated the day after Passover and lasted from the fifteenth to the twenty-first. We read in Leviticus 23, "And on the fifteenth day of the same month is the Feast of Unleavened Bread to the LORD; seven days you must eat unleavened bread. On the first day you shall have a holy convocation; you shall do no customary work on it. But you shall offer an offering made by fire to the LORD for seven days. The seventh day shall be a holy convocation; you shall do no customary work on it" (Leviticus 23:6-8).

In later years, when preparing the food for this feast, the rabbis added the rule that food could only be eaten if it was cooked before the leavening process began. They determined that it took 18 minutes from the time the wheat is mixed with water until the time the yeast in the wheat begins to ferment.

The baking of this unleavened bread called *matzah* requires close supervision in order to meet the rigid requirements of the rabbis. Anyone who has eaten this specially prepared unleavened "bread of affliction" can't help but notice that it is bruised, striped, and pierced. To the Christian, the connection to Jesus is obvious.

The prophet Isaiah gave us a preview of the Messiah who would be smitten, bruised, and pierced for our sins. We read, "Surely He has born our griefs and carried our sorrows; yet we esteemed Him stricken, smitten by God, and afflicted.

"But He was wounded for our transgressions, He was bruised for our iniquities; the chastisement for our peace was upon Him, and by His stripes we are healed....for the transgression of My people He was stricken.

"And they made His grave with the wicked—but with the rich at His death, because He had done no violence, nor was any deceit in His mouth. Yet it pleased the LORD to bruise Him" (Isaiah 53:4-5, 8-10).

Jesus fulfilled this feast as the bread of life from Heaven who had no leaven [sin] in Him. Paul writes, "For He [God] made Him [Jesus] who knew no sin to be sin for us, that we might become the righteousness of God in Him" (2 Corinthians 5:21). John adds, "And you know that He was manifested to take away our sins, and in Him there is no sin" (1 John 3:5).

Jesus said, "...I am the bread of life. He who comes to Me shall never hunger, and he who believes in Me shall never thirst" (John 6:35).

As just stated, Jesus was crucified on the fourteenth, the day of the Feast of Passover. His body was taken down just before six o'clock that evening.

Joseph of Arimathea and Nicodemus prepared Jesus' body for burial and placed Him in Joseph's tomb just in time for Jesus to be buried on the fifteenth, which was the first day of the Feast of Unleavened Bread (John 19:38-42). This is the "high Sabbath" mentioned in John 19:31.

Jesus, the unleavened bread of God from Heaven, took all of our leaven of sin and was buried on the same day the Jews had been celebrating the feast for centuries. What they had been portraying in the Feast of Unleavened Bread was a visual aid pointing them to Jesus, who had come and fulfilled in His flesh the reality pictured by this feast.

Jesus took our leaven of sin in His spirit, our leaven of sorrows in His soul, and our leaven of sickness, disease, and death in His body. He took the full burden of all the liabilities of our human condition with Him into the grave.

Then Joseph rolled a large stone in front of the tomb. Finally, the tomb was secured by stretching a cord across the stone and sealing it at each end with a Roman seal (Matthew 27:57-66).

Jesus lay inside with our sins, sorrows, sickness, and diseases buried with Him. This is how Jesus fulfilled the Feast of Unleavened Bread.

Christians can apply this work of Jesus on their behalf by "putting off the old man of sin" as Paul writes in Ephesians, "that you put off, concerning your former conduct, the old man which grows corrupt according to the deceitful lusts" (Ephesians 4:22). As believers appropriate the work of Jesus as their Unleavened Bread, the old man of sin no longer controls us. He was buried with Jesus in Jerusalem.

Firstfruits

The Feast of Firstfruits is celebrated during the Feast of Unleavened Bread on the eighteenth day. The LORD said to Moses, "Speak to the children of Israel, and say to them: 'When you come into the land which I give to you, and reap its harvest, then you shall bring a sheaf of the firstfruits of your harvest to the priest.

"He shall wave the sheaf before the LORD, to be accepted on your behalf; on the day after the Sabbath the priest shall wave it'" (Leviticus 23:10-11).

According to these instructions, the Hebrews were to bring the first sheaves (*omer*) of the barley harvest and wave them before the LORD.

An *omer* was about four pints. Before any barley produce of the new crop could be eaten, or even touched, a measure had to be brought to the temple as an offering to the LORD. This offering is known as the *omer*. The period of time between this feast and the Feast of Pentecost is a time of "counting the *omer*."

A small plot of ground was set apart in the Kidron Valley to grow this firstfruits offering. When it came time to cut the sheaves, a large crowd of worshippers followed representative leaders to the place where the firstfruits were to be harvested.

Jewish Religious Cycle—the Feasts

The people sang, played their instruments, and danced before the LORD to celebrate His goodness. This was certainly an exciting time. If God accepted the firstfruits of the harvest, it meant He would accept the entire harvest.

Jesus fulfilled this feast when He was resurrected as the firstfruits from the dead on the seventeenth/eighteenth at the very time when the firstfruits harvest was being offered to God. His resurrection marked the beginning of the harvest of souls who have been set apart for God through Jesus.

Paul connected Jesus to the Feast of Firstfruits. He said "But now Christ [Messiah] is risen from the dead, and has become the firstfruits of those who have fallen asleep. For since by man came death, by Man also came the resurrection of the dead.

"For as in Adam all die, even so in Christ [Messiah] all shall be made alive. But each one in his own order: Christ [Messiah] the firstfruits, afterward those who are Christ's [Messiah's] at His coming" (1 Corinthians 15:20-23).

The New Testament presents Jesus as that human sheaf that God set apart for the purpose of conquering death and providing eternal life for all who would acknowledge Him as Lord and Savior. As such, He was the first to rise from the dead who would never die again, as we learn in Matthew 28:1-6.

Since His firstfruits resurrection was accepted by God our Father, believers have assurance that they too will be resurrected and accepted by God (Ephesians 1:6). True believers are accepted by God through Jesus, who is our firstfruits representative.

Because Jesus conquered death as the firstfruits from the grave, all who follow Him have the same promise of resurrection at the end of the age.

Paul writes, "Behold, I tell you a mystery; We shall not all sleep, but we shall all be changed—in a moment, in the twinkling of an eye, at the last trumpet.

"For the trumpet will sound, and the dead will be raised incorruptible, and we shall be changed. For this corruptible must put on incorruption, and this mortal must put on immortality.

"So when this corruptible has put on incorruption, and this mortal has put on immortality, then shall be brought to pass the saying that is written: 'Death is swallowed up in victory. O Death, where is your sting? O Hades, where is your victory?' The sting of death is sin, and the strength of sin is the law.

"But thanks be to God, who gives us the victory through our Lord Jesus Christ [Messiah]" (1 Corinthians 15:51-57). (See also Romans 8:11; 1 Thessalonians 4:13-17; 5:9-11.)

How exciting that believers can also apply this work of Jesus to their lives. We do this by "putting on the new man." Paul writes, "and that you put on the new man which was created according to God, in true righteousness and holiness" (Ephesians 4:24). The result will be the fruit of God's Spirit manifested in our lives (Galatians 5:16-25).

Jesus said, "For as Jonah was three days and three nights in the belly of the great fish, so will the Son of Man be three days and three nights in the heart of the earth" (Matthew 12:40).

In order to correctly understand the events surrounding His death, burial and resurrection, we need to realize this all happened according to the Jewish day which begins in the evening at sunset. Jesus was crucified on Passover, most likely, on Wednesday, the 14th of *Nisan* in the year AD 31, which was April 25 on the Gentile calendar.

He was buried at the close of Wednesday (around 6:00 p.m.) which would begin Unleavened Bread on Thursday the 15th of *Nisan*. As just mentioned, this was the high Sabbath to which John refers (John 19:31).

Western Christian scholars have mistakenly believed this high Sabbth to be the regular weekly Sabbath. This is why we have been taught that Jesus was crucified on Friday.

Jewish Religious Cycle—the Feasts

Jesus' body was in the tomb through Thursday (night 1, day 1), Friday (night 2, day 2), and Saturday (night 3, day 3). He was resurrected at the close of the Sabbath (Saturday evening the 17th) which began the first day of the week (Sunday the 18th).

This accounting of time is the only way Jesus could have fulfilled the sign of Jonah by being in the tomb for the full three days and three nights. It is also the only way His death, burial, and resurrection could be accomplished on Feast days.

Pentecost

The next major feast season is Pentecost. It is also referred to as the Feast of Weeks, Feast of Harvest, and the Day of Firstfruits (Exodus 23:16; 34:22; Numbers 28:26). This feast is celebrated on the sixth day of the Hebrew month of *Sivan*, which corresponds to the months of May and June on the Gentile calendar.

We learn from Leviticus, "And you shall count for yourselves from the day after the Sabbath, from the day that you brought the sheaf of the wave offering: seven Sabbaths shall be completed.

"Count fifty days to the day after the seventh Sabbath; then you shall offer a new grain offering to the LORD. You shall bring from your dwelling two wave loaves of two-tenths of an *ephah*. They shall be of fine flour; they shall be baked with leaven. They are the firstfruits to the LORD" (Leviticus 23:15-17).

We see from these instructions that the main activity on the Feast of Pentecost was the presentation of a wave offering of two loaves of baked bread to the LORD. They were to do this fifty days after the Feast of Firstfruits. Since the word Pentecost in Greek means "fifty," this feast gets its name from the fifty-day interval between the two feasts.

The wave offering expressed the Hebrews' dependence on God for the harvest and their daily bread. This was a thanksgiving offering.

Later when the Jews were dispersed among the nations, the Feast of Pentecost lost its primary significance as a harvest festival and was celebrated as a memorial to the time when God gave the

Torah at Mount Sinai. This is because the Jews have traditionally believed that God gave the *Torah* to Moses on the Day of Pentecost (Exodus 19:1,11). The Day of Pentecost did not originate with Christianity, but it is the Jewish feast day that God chose to send the Holy Spirit, as proof that Jesus had been glorified as Lord.

This was the day when the Jews were in Jerusalem celebrating the feast and the giving of the *Torah*. They were looking forward to the time when God would write the *Torah* on their hearts as the prophets said (Jeremiah 31:31-34).

From Luke's account in Acts 2 we see the marvelous timing of God. Thousands of devout Jews had journeyed to Jerusalem to celebrate the Feast of Pentecost. It was then that the followers of Jesus waiting in the upper room were filled with the Holy Spirit as prophesied by Joel (Joel 2:28-29).

These Jewish believers began to worship God in foreign languages that were spoken and understood by the Jewish pilgrims. There was such a loud noise accompanying this experience, that it attracted the attention of the Jewish visitors who went to see what the commotion was all about. Peter then stood up and preached a bold sermon to this Jewish crowd. About 3,000 responded to Peter's sermon by accepting Jesus as their Messiah and Lord.

This outpouring of the Holy Spirit was taking place on the very day when the Jews were offering the two wave loaves to God and celebrating the *Torah*, symbolizing their dependence on God. One wave loaf represented the Jews and the other the Gentiles who would also receive the Holy Spirit in like manner as recorded in Acts 10.

Christian believers can apply the spiritual reality of the Feast of Pentecost by being filled with the Spirit of God as Paul wrote, "…be filled with the Spirit" (Ephesians 5:18). The Spirit of God gives us power to minister the life of Jesus to those in need.

Trumpets

The last feast season is the Feast of Tabernacles. It includes the three feasts of Trumpets, Atonement, and Tabernacles. The

Jewish Religious Cycle—the Feasts

LORD gave the following instructions concerning the Feast of Trumpets, "…In the seventh month, on the first day of the month, you shall have a sabbath-rest, a memorial of blowing of trumpets, a holy convocation. You shall do no customary work on it; and you shall offer an offering made by fire to the LORD" (Leviticus 23:23-25).

We see from this Scripture reference that the Feast of Trumpets is on the first day of the seventh month on the religious calendar. This is the Hebrew month of *Tishri*, which corresponds to the months of September and October. *Tishri* is also the first month on the Jewish civil calendar and is the Jewish New Year. The Hebrew name for this new year is *Rosh Hashanah*. It is also know as *Yom Teruah*, the day of blowing of trumpets.

The main purpose of the Feast of Trumpets was to announce the arrival of the seventh month in order to prepare the people for the Day of Atonement which was ten days later. This was the "Great Day of Judgment" when God would judge the sins of the nation. The Feast of Trumpets reminded the people that the Day of Atonement was at hand.

The day was not marked by any special events other than the blowing of trumpets and the offering of sacrifices (Numbers 29:1-6). The type of trumpet blown was the ram's horn, for which the Hebrew word is *shofar*.

God used trumpets in the First Testament as a means of communicating with His covenant people. God could not speak directly to the people without them being terrified. So He spoke to them through the use of trumpets.

To the Hebrews, the sound of the trumpet represented both the voice of God and the might of God in warfare. A good summary of how trumpets were used is provided in the tenth chapter of the Book of Numbers.

One of the clearest demonstrations of the use of trumpets in warfare is the story of Joshua at the battle of Jericho. (See Joshua 6.)

When the people blew the *shofar*, God gave them victory. The Jews began to call God the "horn of their salvation."

King David was the great warrior who said to God, "…I will love you, O LORD, my strength. The LORD is my rock and my fortress and my deliverer; my God, my strength in whom I will trust; my shield and the horn of my salvation; my stronghold. I will call upon the LORD, who is worthy to be praised; so shall I be saved from my enemies" (Psalm 18:1-3).

Jesus is the "Horn of our Salvation" who defeats the enemies of our soul. Zacharias said of Jesus, "Blessed is the Lord God of Israel, for He has visited and redeemed His people, and has raised up a horn of salvation for us in the house of His servant David, as He spoke by the mouth of His holy prophets, who have been since the world began, that we should be saved from our enemies and from the hand of all who hate us" (Luke 1:68-71).

By His death and resurrection, Jesus defeated Satan, sin, and death. He gives His followers the Holy Spirit who lives the overcoming life of Jesus through them so they can have a victorious life.

We Christians cannot live this life within our own strength. We must draw our strength from the Spirit of God who comes to live in us. It is the Spirit of God who enables us to overcome the sins of the flesh and temptations of Satan. John wrote, "You are of God, little children, and have overcome them, because He who is in you is greater than he who is in the world" (1 John 4:4).

Paul wrote to believers everywhere, "Finally, my brethren, be strong in the Lord and in the power of His might. Put on the whole armor of God, that you may be able to stand against the wiles of the devil. For we do not wrestle against flesh and blood, but against principalities, against powers, against the rulers of the darkness of this age, against spiritual hosts of wickedness in the heavenly places" (Ephesians 6:10-12).

The armor of God is a description of Jesus Himself. He has defeated sin, Satan, and death. It is His very own life given to us and lived out of us that enables us to live the overcoming life. Thank God for Jesus who, as the horn of our salvation, has overcome the enemies of our soul.

The prophetic fulfillment of the Feast of Trumpets is the return of Jesus, which is described in Revelation 19. It is announced by the use of trumpets. John writes, "Then the seventh angel sounded: And there were loud voices in heaven saying, 'The kingdoms of this world have become the kingdoms of our Lord and of His Christ [Messiah], and He shall reign forever and ever!'" (Revelation 11:15).

John goes on to say that when Jesus returns He will be coming to make war (Revelation 19:11). He will crush all of His enemies and rule with a rod of iron over a kingdom that will never end. This is the Messianic Kingdom of God that all true believers, be they Jew or non-Jew, long for—when King-Messiah establishes the righteous rule of God on the earth.

Atonement

The next feast after Trumpets is the Day of Atonement. It is on the tenth day of the month of *Tishri*. This was the great day of national cleansing and repentance from sin. It was on this day that God judged the sins of the entire nation of Israel. In view of this, the Day of Atonement became known as the Day of Judgment.

Leviticus reads, "Also the tenth day of this seventh month shall be the Day of Atonement. It shall be a holy convocation for you; you shall afflict your souls, and offer an offering made by fire to the LORD" (Leviticus 23:27).

The Day of Atonement was the one day of the year when the High Priest would go behind the veil into the Holy of Holies with the blood sacrifice and sprinkle it on the Mercy Seat. This offering of the innocent substitutionary sacrifice made possible the atonement for the sins of the nation.

The word atonement means "to cover." On the great Day of Atonement, the sins of the nation were covered by the blood of the sacrifice. This dramatic procedure is described in detail in Leviticus 16.

Because this was the Day of Judgment, it was a time of great soul affliction. It was a day of godly sorrow, godly repentance, and confession of sins. It was a time of mourning before God with a broken spirit and contrite heart. It is the only required day of fasting in the Bible.

The Jews believed that the final judgment and accounting of the soul would come on the Day of Atonement. On this day, the future of every individual would be sealed and the gates of Heaven would be closed.

In light of this belief, the Jews perform many good deeds during the ten days between the Feast of Trumpets and the Day of Atonement. This ten day period is known as the "Awesome Days" or the "Ten Days of Repentance."

As the people prepare themselves for the Day of Atonement, they greet each other with the phrase, "May your name be inscribed in the Book of Life."

Jesus fulfilled the spiritual aspects of the Day of Atonement when He went into the heavenly holy of holies with His own blood which He shed for the sins of the world.

Believers have been forgiven and made clean once and for all by the blood of Jesus. His blood did what the blood of bulls and goats could not do for us. His blood doesn't just cover our sins, it takes them away to be remembered no more.

We receive this great blessing of forgiveness once and for all when we repent of our sins and, with a broken and contrite spirit, accept Jesus as the innocent substitutionary sacrifice who died in our place. At that moment, our future is sealed by the Holy Spirit and our names are written in the Lamb's Book of Life. This is a finished work of redemption and salvation.

Even though God has forgiven us of our sins, this does not mean that Christians do not need a continuous cleansing in our daily lives. We must judge our sins daily for the purpose of maintaining fellowship with the Lord. In this regard, the blood of Jesus purifies us that we can have continuous fellowship with Him. This is the work of Jesus in purifying His bride.

John spoke of this need with the following words, "If we say that we have fellowship with Him, and walk in darkness, we lie and do not practice the truth. But if we walk in the light as He is in the light, we have fellowship with one another, and the blood of Jesus Christ [Messiah] His Son cleanses us from all sin.

"If we say that we have no sin, we deceive ourselves, and the truth is not in us. If we confess our sins, He is faithful and just to forgive us our sins and to cleanse us from all unrighteousness" (1 John 1:6-9).

Prophetically, the Day of Atonement points to the return of Jesus to judge the earth. This future event will literally be fulfilled on the final great Day of Atonement.

The prophet Zechariah spoke of the future literal fulfillment of the Day of Atonement. Zechariah wrote, "And I will pour on the house of David and on the inhabitants of Jerusalem the Spirit of grace and supplication; then they will look on Me whom they pierced; they will mourn for Him as one mourns for his only son, and grieve for Him as one grieves for a firstborn" (Zechariah 12:10).

Jesus also referred to this time when speaking about His return to earth. He said, "Immediately after the tribulation of those days the sun will be darkened, and the moon will not give its light; the stars will fall from heaven, and the powers of the heavens will be shaken.

"Then the sign of the Son of Man will appear in heaven, and then all the tribes of the earth will mourn, and they will see the Son of Man coming on the clouds of heaven with power and great glory" (Matthew 24:29-30).

Tabernacles

The last feast God gave the Hebrews to observe was the Feast of Tabernacles. It was also called the Feast of Ingathering because it was at the end of the harvest season, and the Feasts of Booths because the Hebrews slept in booths or shelters during the feast (Exodus 23:16; Deuteronomy 16:16). It was celebrated during the month of *Tishri* and lasted for seven days, from the fifteenth to the twenty-first. There was also a special Sabbath on the eighth day.

The Feast of Tabernacles celebrated the final ingathering of the harvest God had blessed the people with for the year. The fruit of the land had been reaped, so the people could rest from their labors and rejoice in the goodness of God.

Leviticus reads, "…The fifteenth day of this seventh month shall be the Feast of Tabernacles for seven days to the LORD. On the first day there shall be a holy convocation. You shall do no customary work on it.…On the eighth day you shall have a holy convocation and you shall offer an offering made by fire to the LORD. It is a sacred assembly, and you shall do no customary work on it.

"Also on the fifteenth day of the seventh month, when you have gathered in the fruit of the land, you shall keep the feast of the LORD for seven days; on the first day there shall be a sabbath-rest, and on the eighth day a sabbath-rest.

"And you shall take for yourselves on the first day the fruit of beautiful trees, branches of palm trees, the boughs of leafy trees, and willows of the brook; and you shall rejoice before the LORD your God for seven days. You shall keep it as a feast to the LORD for seven days in the year. It shall be a statute forever in your generations. You shall celebrate it in the seventh month.

"You shall dwell in booths for seven days. All who are native Israelites shall dwell in booths, that your generations may know that I made the children of Israel dwell in booths when I brought them out of the land of Egypt: I am the LORD your God" (Leviticus 23:34-36, 39-43).

We learn from these instructions that the LORD required the Hebrews to dwell in booths or tabernacles to remind them of the years their ancestors wandered in the desert for forty years living in shelters. They were always to remember that the wanderings were brought about by unbelief and disobedience. Yet, God was in their midst providing for their every need and eventually brought them into the land of rest He had promised them.

God required the Hebrews to live in booths during this feast. They were visual aids reminding the people that they did not enter God's rest because of their unbelief (Hebrews 3:7-11).

The shelters were loosely constructed and decorated and the roofs were covered with branches. This allowed the Hebrews to see through the roofs to Heaven and be reminded of an even greater rest and rejoicing when Messiah would rule on the earth.

Thus, the Feast of Tabernacles symbolizes the messianic age when Jesus returns to establish the Kingdom of God on the earth. At that time all the nations will go up to Jerusalem to worship the King and keep the Feast of Tabernacles (Zechariah 14:16).

To the believer, Jesus is the ultimate tabernacle or dwelling place of God in human flesh. John tells us, "In the beginning was the Word, and the Word was with God, and the Word was God. And the Word became flesh and dwelt among us, and we beheld His glory, the glory of the only begotten of the Father, full of grace and truth" (John 1:1,14). Jesus Himself said, "…He who has seen Me has seen the Father…" (John 14:9).

God came in human flesh to reveal Himself to us and give rest and rejoicing to our souls by redeeming us from sin. Jesus said, "Come to Me, all you who labor and are heavy laden, and I will give you rest. Take My yoke upon you and learn from Me, for I am lowly in heart, and you will find rest for your souls. For My yoke is easy and My burden is light" (Matthew 11:28-30).

Christians can apply this work of Jesus to their lives personally by walking with God in loving trust and obedience. Believers can experience God's rest in their lives today.

The writer of the Book of Hebrews says, "There remains therefore a rest for the people of God. For he who has entered His rest has himself also ceased from his works as God did from His. Let us therefore be diligent to enter that rest, lest anyone fall according the same example of disobedience" (Hebrews 4:9-11).

Hanukkah

Hanukkah was not one of the original Feasts of the LORD. In ancient times it was a relatively minor holiday commemorating the deliverance of the great victory of the Jews over Antiochus IV (Epiphanes) in the second century BC.

Antiochus made a systematic attempt to replace Jewish faith and culture with Greek culture. He was determined to destroy the Jewish people through assimilation. This happened in 174–167 BC and is recorded in the intertestamental book of 1 Maccabees. We learned about this story earlier in Chapter 3 when we studied the history of the Jews between the Testaments.

The highlight of the victory was when the Jews rededicated the Temple to God. Traditional Jewish writings explain that the Greek-Syrians desecrated all the oil purified for Temple use.

When the Temple was rededicated, only one small undefiled container was found with the seal still on it. It contained only enough oil to burn the *menorah* for one day. But after the *menorah* was kindled, it miraculously burned for eight days.[151]

Hanukkah was called the Feast of Dedication and the Feast of Lights. While it was not a biblical holiday, Jesus kept the customs of His people and celebrated this feast. We read in John, "Now it was the Feast of Dedication in Jerusalem, and it was winter. And Jesus walked in the temple, in Solomon's porch" (John 10:22-23).

How interesting that Jesus was at the Temple during the very feast that celebrated the Jews' victory over the enemies of God as well as the rededication of the Temple. In a way that baffled those

---

151. Dosick, 152.

listening, Jesus related the story of Hanukkah to Himself. He said, "...Destroy this temple, and in three days I will raise it up" (John 2:19).

Jesus was not talking about the literal Temple, which had taken forty-six years to build according to John 2:20-22. Instead, Jesus was talking about His own body. How often we confuse spritual truths with natural observations.

After His ascension, Jesus would build a spiritual temple in the hearts of His followers by sending the Holy Spirit to indwell them. They would then dedicate themselves to God as the light of His life burned brightly in their hearts.

Paul spoke of this to the believers in Corinth, "Or do you not know that your body is the temple of the Holy Spirit who is in you, whom you have from God, and you are not your own? For you were bought at a price; therefore glorify God in your body and your spirit, which are God's" (1 Corinthians 6:19-20).

Although Hanakkuh has been celebrated for centuries, it has only been recently that it has gained importance. This is probably due to the influence of Christmas, since Hanakkuh is celebrated in late December. The date on the Hebrew calendar is the twenty-fifth of *Chislev* because this is the date when the Maccabees rededicated the altar to God (1 Maccabees 4:52).

The central focus in celebrating Hanukkah is the eight-branched *menorah* called a *"hanukkiah."* The *hanukkiah* has a ninth candle called a *Shamash*. This word means servant.

The servant candle is used to light the other eight. The candles are placed in the *hanukkiah* each evening from right to left, with a new candle added each evening during the eight-day celebration. The candles are lit from left to right. So the *Shamash* is lit first and then the others are lit.

From a New Testament perspective, Jesus is the servant candle who lights our lives with the fire of God. He said to His followers, "You are the light of the world. A city that is set on a hill cannot be hidden. Nor do they light a lamp and put it under a basket, but on a lampstand, and it gives light to all who are in the house. Let your light so shine before men, that they may see your good works and glorify your Father in heaven" (Matthew 5:14-16).

On Hanukkah the foods are cooked in oil as a reminder of the miracle of the oil when the Temple was rededicated. Many households eat potato pancakes called "latkes" and jelly-filled doughnuts fried in oil to commemorate the occasion.

A special game is played on Hanakkuh. It is called "dreidel." A *dreidel* is a four-sided top which is spun. Each side of the *dreidel* holds a Hebrew letter. The four letters form an acrostic that means, "A great miracle happened there." It refers to the miracle of the oil that lasted for eight days when the *menorah* was lit at the rededication of the Temple.

In Israel, the last word is changed so that the phrase reads, "a great miracle happened here." The winner of the *dreidel* game gets the most Hanukkah gelt (chocolate money).

Purim

As with Hanakkuh, Purim was not one of the original Feasts of the LORD. The background for Purim is found in the Book of Esther. This book tells the wonderful story of how the Jewish Queen Esther interceded for her people to save them from the plot of Haman, a wicked man who wanted to destroy the Jews.

The story of Esther takes place in the period of Persian rule when Ahasuerus was king. This was approximately 485–476 BC. In the third year of his rule, King Ahasuerus had a big party and ordered Queen Vashti to attend so he could "display" her to his drunken male guests. Now, to the queen's credit, if not to her good judgment, she refused his demand.

The king called together his counselors who advised him to dispose of his queen and give her position to another more worthy. A young woman named Esther was made the new queen.

Jewish Religious Cycle—the Feasts

Queen Esther was a Jewish woman who had been raised by her cousin Mordecai, a man who feared the LORD. Mordecai had uncovered a plot to assassinate the king and told Esther who informed the king in Mordecai's name. The plot was foiled but Mordecai was never rewarded for his loyalty.

Haman was jealous of Mordecai and sought revenge by having the king issue a decree to kill all the Jews living under Persian rule. He cast a *Pur*, or lot, to determine the date to attack the Jews. The lot fell on the thirteenth of *Adar* on the Jewish calendar (February-March).

Esther found out about the plot and, at great risk to her own life, interceded with the king for her people. The key verse in the Book of Esther is the statement Mordecai made to Esther. He said, "…Do not think in your heart that you will escape in the king's palace any more than all the other Jews.

"For if you remain completely silent at this time, relief and deliverance will arise for the Jews from another place, but you and your father's house will perish. Yet who knows whether you have come to the kingdom for such a time as this?" (Esther 4:13-14)

Esther called for three days of fasting and prayer before approaching the king. King Ahasuerus received Esther, who exposed Haman and his plot to kill the Jews. The king commanded that Haman be hung in his own yard on the very tree which Haman had prepared for Mordecai. Mordecai was exalted and the Jews were given the chance to defend themselves when attacked. The Jews slaughtered their enemies and celebrated on the next day.

As a result of this great victory, Mordecai declared Purim to be a holiday of feasting and joy, with presents being exchanged and gifts given to the poor. The people accepted Mordecai's words, and to this day, they celebrate Purim. Purim was celebrated not only by the Jews but by all God-fearers who would join them (Esther 9:26-28). The holiday was called Purim after the *Pur* (lot) which was cast for the day of the annihilation of the Jewish people.

While Purim is not specifically mentioned in the New Testament, there is no doubt that the feast referred to in John 5:1 is Purim. The reason we can know this is Purim is because Purim was celebrated before Passover, which is described in John 6.

Followers of Jesus can certainly learn much from the story of Esther. As Esther risked her life to intercede for her people, Jesus gave His life to intercede for us. But as Mordecai was exalted, Jesus also was exalted in His resurrection and ascension. The writer of Hebrews says, "Therefore He is also able to save to the uttermost those who come to God through Him, since He always lives to make intercession for them" (Hebrews 7:25).

Believers must pray and intercede for the Jewish people and the nation of Israel. The Psalmist wrote, "Pray for the peace of Jerusalem; may they prosper who love you" (Psalms 122:6).

Isaiah declared, "I have set watchman on your walls, O Jerusalem; they shall never hold their peace day or night. You who make mention of the LORD, do not keep silent, and give Him no rest till He establishes and till He make Jerusalem a praise in the earth" (Isaiah 62:6-7).

Like Esther, perhaps righteous Gentiles have come into God's kingdom for such a time as this. God has commissioned us to comfort Israel (Isaiah 40:1) and bless the Jewish people (Genesis 12:1-3). If we do not help them in their time of need, God will bring them deliverance from another source.

But we must not be deceived to think that we, who have become part of the commonwealth of Israel (Ephesians 2:12), will be able to sit on the sidelines and watch without being noticed by the modern Hamans of our world.

Jews all over the world celebrate Purim. The day before is a fast day in remembrance of Esther's fast, but Purim is a day of rejoicing and celebration. The main activity is to read the scroll of Esther.

Since Haman represents the archenemy of the Jews, noisemakers called "groggers" are sounded whenever his name is mentioned to drown out the mention of his name. People send gifts to

Jewish Religious Cycle—the Feasts

their friends and contribute to the poor as recorded in the Book of Esther.

A special pastry called "Haman's ears" is prepared. It has three corners and is usually filled with poppy seeds. In some circles, Purim is celebrated in a carnival atmosphere with masquerades, costumes, and much drinking and partying.

Chapter 13—Personal Study Guide

1. How does the Jewish calendar differ from the Gentile calendar?

2. Discuss each feast and how it relates to Jesus and applies to the Christian life.

Chapter 14

The Time to Favor Zion

The last great work of redemption prior to the coming of Messiah is the ingathering of the Jewish people to Israel from all the nations. This will happen at the close of the age when the "times of the Gentiles" come to an end, and the Lord's favor is on the Jewish people and Israel.

Because we are living in the generation that is seeing this great ingathering take place, it seems proper to conclude this book with an explanation of the prophectic events that are unfolding before our very eyes. The information presented in this chapter is taken from the author's publication, *The Time to Favor Zion Has Come*.

The rebirth of the nation of Israel is one of the most important events of our times. Yet it is also one of the most controversial. While most Bible-believing Christians support the state of Israel and see it as fulfillment of Bible prophecy, the nations oppose a strong Israel.

The nations have chosen to express their anti-Semitism by lashing out against Israel. Some Christian ministers have spoken out against Israel and God's purposes for her. Whatever our views, we cannot ignore the fact that the Arab-Israeli conflict is a heavy stone burdening the whole world.

Centuries ago, the prophet Zechariah wrote of our times and said, "Behold, I will make Jerusalem a cup of drunkenness [trembling] to all the surrounding peoples, when they lay siege against Judah and Jerusalem.

"And it shall happen in that day that I will make Jerusalem a very heavy stone for all peoples; all who would heave it away will surely be cut in pieces, though all nations of the earth are gathered against it. It shall be in that day that I will seek to destroy all the nations that come against Jerusalem" (Zechariah 12:2-3, 9).

As we look at world events with Israel regathered and the battle for Jerusalem at hand, surely we must see that Zechariah was writing about our times. This author, along with many others, personally believes that the role of Israel in Bible prophecy is going to be the next and greatest division in Christendom. As one who has taught the Bible for many years, I can see this great split getting wider from year after year.

All of us are going to have to make a decision regarding our view on Israel. Either the modern ingathering of Jews back to their land is an act of God or it is nothing more than a political accident where the Jews "just got lucky." The view presented in this chapter is that the modern ingathering of the Jews to Israel is a sovereign act of God that requires our understanding and participation.

One of the most significant Scriptures that relates to this subject and applies to our times is found in the Book of Psalms. It says, "But You, O LORD, shall endure forever, and the remembrance of Your name to all generations. You will arise and have mercy on Zion; for the time to favor her, yes, the set time, has come. For your servants take pleasure in her stones, and show favor to her dust. So the nations shall fear the name of the LORD, and all the kings of the earth Your glory. For the LORD shall build up Zion; He shall appear in His glory" (Psalm 102:12-16).

This Scripture says that there will be a time in world history when God will favor Zion. He will arise and have mercy on Zion by building up Zion. After God builds up Zion, He will appear in His glory. People who believe this are called Zionists.

The word "Zion" appears in the Bible 159 times. It is found 152 times in the Hebrew Scriptures and 7 times in the New Testament.[152] The best we can understand is that the word Zion means "stronghold." It was a Jebusite fortress when King David captured it around the year 1010 BC, as recorded in the Bible

---

152. Booker, *The Time to Favor Zion Has Come* (Houston, TX: Sounds of the Trumpet, 1996), 23.

The Time to Favor Zion

(2 Samuel 5:6-9; 1 Chronicles 11:5). This was the southeastern ridge of Mt. Zion and was called the City of David.

First Chronicles says, "And David and all Israel went to Jerusalem, which is Jebus, where the Jebusites were the inhabitants of the land. But the inhabitants of Jebus said to David, 'You shall not come in here!' Nevertheless David took the stronghold of Zion (that is, the City of David). Then David dwelt in the stronghold; therefore they called it the City of David" (1 Chronicles 11:4-5,7).

Because King David was a worshipper of God, he brought the ark of the covenant to the City of David. He set up a tabernacle in the City of David as a place to worship God. David understood the heart of what God intended through the various rituals.

We read in Chronicles, "David built houses for himself in the City of David; and he prepared a place for the ark of God, and pitched a tent for it. So they brought the ark of God, and set it in the midst of the tabernacle that David had erected for it. Then they offered burnt offerings and peace offerings before God" (1 Chronicles 15:1; 16:1).

After King David died, Solomon succeeded him to the throne. King Solomon built the Temple on Mount Moriah and moved the ark there. (1 Kings 8:1; 2 Chronicles 3:1; 5:2). At that time, the name Zion was extended to include the Temple Mount.

This is the same Temple Mount that Islamic fundamentalists claim belongs to Islam. However, according to the Bible, it belonged to the Jews centuries before Islam came into existence. In spite of Islamic claims, Jerusalem is never mentioned in the Koran.

Eventually, Zion referred to the city of Jerusalem as well as to the people themselves. We read in the Book of Psalms, "The LORD loves the gates of Zion more than all the dwellings of Jacob. Glorious things are spoken of you, O city of God!" (Psalm 87:2-3) Isaiah wrote, "For the people shall dwell in Zion at Jerusalem..." (Isaiah 30:19).

While Zion clearly refers to the literal city of Jerusalem, it ultimately applies to the New Jerusalem in Heaven, which will one day be seen on the earth. This heavenly city will be the new literal Jerusalem on the earth.

The New Testament reads, "But you have come to Mount Zion and to the city of the living God, the heavenly Jerusalem..." (Hebrews 12:22). (See also Isaiah 24:23.)

This Scripture does not mean that the Church is now Zion. It simply means that the final destiny of all believers of all ages will be with God in the New Jerusalem on the earth. The present earthly Jerusalem is a witness to the existence of the heavenly Jerusalem which will come to the earth at the end of the age.

In the Bible, God promised to comfort and restore Zion. Isaiah writes, "For the LORD will comfort Zion, He will comfort all her waste places; He will make her wilderness like Eden, and her desert like the garden of the LORD; joy and gladness will be found in it, thanksgiving and the voice of melody.

"So the ransomed of the LORD shall return, and come to Zion with singing, with everlasting joy on their heads. They shall obtain joy and gladness; sorrow and sighing shall flee away" (Isaiah 51:3, 11).

When Messiah comes in power and glory at the end of the age, He will not be coming to New York, Paris, Moscow, London, etc. He will be coming to Zion at Jerusalem from where He will rule over the nations of the world. Psalm 2 is clearly speaking of our times, when all the nations will gather against Israel in the battle for Jerusalem.

In spite of the plans of the nations, the Almighty will place the King-Messiah, His Son, on the throne of David in Jerusalem at Mount Zion.

The Scripture reads, "Why do the nations rage, and the people plot a vain thing? The kings of the earth set themselves, and the rulers take counsel together, against the LORD and against His Anointed, saying, 'Let us break their bonds in pieces and cast away their cords from us.' He who sits in the heavens shall laugh; the LORD shall hold them in derision.

"Then He shall speak to them in His wrath, and distress them in His deep displeasure: 'Yet I have set My King on My holy hill of Zion.' I will declare the decree: the LORD has said to Me,'You are My Son, today I have begotten You. Ask of Me, and I will give you the nations for your inheritance, and the ends of the earth for your possession' " (Psalm 2:1-8).

Secular Zionism

The words "Zion" and "Zionism" mean different things to different people and this is a cause for great confusion. The secular Jewish understanding is that Zionism is a political movement to establish a national homeland for the Jewish people in their ancient land. Nathan Birnbaum, in 1890, was the first to use the word "Zionism" to identify this political movement.

The idea of Zionism being a political movement initiated by human effort was new. Previously, the Jews believed that the Messiah would have to gather the Jews and return them to Israel. It was not right for Jews to think they should initiate this movement themselves. They were supposed to wait on the Messiah to do this work of redemption.

However, because of anti-Semitic events taking place in Europe, some Jewish leaders began to speak and write about the necessity of establishing a national homeland in what was then called Palestine.

While there were several forerunners to this movement, the man who is universally considered to be the father of modern Zionism is Theodore Herzl. Herzl was born in Budapest in 1860 and was the son of a wealthy banker. Herzl himself studied law but later became a journalist. He was well assimilated into the Gentile world in which he lived and felt very comfortable in it.

Herzl believed that modern man had become so civilized and tolerant of others that Gentile prejudices against Jews would soon disappear. Herzl would soon have an experience that shattered his "rosy" view of mankind. That experience was known as the "Dreyfus Affair." Alfred Dreyfus was a captain in the French army. He was also a Jew. And when necessary, Jews were always good scapegoats.

Dreyfus was accused of giving French military secrets to the Germans. He was put on trial and sentenced to life imprisonment even though there was little evidence to support the verdict.

During the trial, the public demanded justice. But they were not concerned about justice. They hated Dreyfus simply because he was a Jew. Herzl was in Paris covering the story. When he heard the angry mobs shout, "Kill the traitor, kill the Jew," he knew the Jews would never be safe living among the Gentiles. They had to have their own country.

Two years later in 1896, Herzl wrote *The Jewish State*. Herzel described the problem and challenged the Jews to work towards the establishment of their own nation.

In 1897, Herzl called together the First Zionist Congress which met in Basil, Switzerland. The Congress was attended by 204 delegates. Amazingly, Herzl predicted that in fifty years the Jews would have their own state.

This seemed like an impossible prediction, since the Turks ruled over the ancient land of the Jews. However, World War I changed this situation. Turkey and England fought each other for control of the Middle East. England was victorious and had sovereignty over the land the Jews wanted for their homeland.

A Jewish chemist named Chaim Weizmann made a major contribution to the war effort for England. As a result of his efforts, the British Prime Minister recognized Weizmann's contribution and sought to reward him. Instead of seeking personal gain, Weizmann asked that England grant the Jews a national homeland in Palestine.

The Prime Minister agreed, and in 1903, England offered the Jews a safe haven in Uganda. The Zionists leaders were divided as to whether or not they should accept this offer, because so many Jews were being persecuted at that time in Russia.

However, for centuries the Jews had longed for Jerusalem. They couldn't accept, "Next year in Uganda." The Prime Minister agreed and in 1917 the British Foreign Secretary, James Balfour, issued the famous Balfour Declaration, which said that the British government viewed with favor the establishment in Palestine of a national home for the Jewish people.

The newly formed League of Nations gave its approval to the Balfour Declaration. Herzl's prediction that the Jews would have their own state within fifty years proved to be prophetic.

On November 29, 1947, the United Nations voted to officially establish the existence of the state of Israel. On May 14, 1948, the Jewish people declared their independence and called their new country—Israel.

Replacement Theology Zionism

Another view of Zion and Zionism is called "Replacement Theology." This understanding has been the traditional teaching of the historical Church from the fourth century until the time of the Puritans in the seventeenth century. It is strictly a spiritual view that teaches that the Church has replaced the Jews and Israel in God's plan of redemption.

Proponents of Replacement Theology believe that the Church is the "New Israel and Zion." This view is based on an allegorical interpretation of the Scriptures as opposed to a literal interpretation. I have disussed this view in an earlier chapter and in my book *How the Cross Became a Sword*.

As previously explained, the teaching of Replacement Theology began at the first Christian seminary in Alexandria, Egypt. Alexander the Great established this city in 331 BC. It became a major center of Greek learning, having one of the greatest libraries of the ancient world. The Greek method of interpreting literature was allegorical. The Christian school of learning at Alexandria used the Greek allegorical method of interpreting the Hebrew Scriptures.

To review, the first head of the school was a man named Pantaenus. His most famous student was Clement, who succeeded Pantaenus as head of the school. Clement was born in Athens to pagan parents. He was the man who blended Greek philosophy with Christianity in order to make Christianity acceptable to the Gentiles.

Clement taught that God gave philosophy to the Greeks to lead them to Jesus, just as He gave the Hebrew Scriptures to the Jews to prepare them for Messiah. Clement was more schooled in Plato than he was in Moses. He looked more to Athens and Greek philosophers for truth and inspiration than he did to Jerusalem and the prophets. Clement laid the foundation built on by his successors, which would emphasize Greek philosophy as the forerunner to Christianity rather than the Hebrew Scriptures.

Clement was succeeded by his famous pupil, Origen, who was the greatest scholar of his day. His knowledge of Greek philosophy and theology was unparalleled. He served as head of the school in Alexandra for twenty-seven years, where he taught the allegorical method of interpreting the Hebrew Scriptures.

This allegorical method of interpretation denies the literal meaning of the text so that people can make the Bible say whatever they want it to say and make it fit their philosophy of life and worldview. People use the allegorical method to justify their beliefs and actions which are clearly contrary to the Bible.

Origen looked for hidden meanings behind everything he read in the Hebrew Scriptures. Because he did not interpret the text literally, he arrived at conclusions that grew out of his own fertile imagination. Some of his interpretations and teachings were so absurd that many of his peers considered him to be a heretic.

Although many of Origen's interpretations were rejected by his peers, they did accept his allegorical method of interpreting the Scriptures as the standard for the Church. This method of interpreting the Scripture produced the teaching that the Church is the new spiritual Israel of God that replaced literal Israel in God's redemptive plans and purposes.

According to this teaching, the establishment of the modern state of Israel is nothing more than a "political accident," and the Jews are no longer God's chosen people because they have been replaced by the Church. The Church is considered to be the "new Israel of God."

Origen literally interpreted the Scriptures that promised judgment and curses on the Jews, but applied the blessings spiritually to the Church. In this way he spiritualized the Hebrew Bible, making it acceptable to the Church and the Gentile world.[153]

Origen established a theological school at Caesarea where he taught his views to the future leaders of the church. He was succeeded by his student Pamphilus who passed Origen's view to the next generation of leaders.

His most important student was Eusebius. Eusebius became the bishop at Caesarea and later was the advisor to Constantine, who embraced Christianity and established it as the official religion of the Roman Empire. Eusebius was a great admirer of Origen and is considered the "Father of Church History."[154]

Augustine was the foremost theologian of the next generation of scholars. In his classic work, *The City of God*, Augustine used Origen's allegorical method of interpreting the Bible and spiritualized the relationship between the Church and the Jews. Augustine's writings became the theological textbook for the Church, and his views are still taught today by the historical Christian churches as well as some newer groups that embrace Replacement Theology.

---

153. Booker, *How the Cross Became a Sword*, 26-27.
154. Ibid., 28.

Jesus said that a tree is known by its fruit (Matthew 7:16-20). The fruit of Replacement Theology has always been a prideful arrogance and hatred towards the Jewish people that is contrary to God's word and true Christian character. Although Christians don't want to acknowledge it, Hitler used centuries of anti-Semitic teaching by the Christian Church to justify the Holocaust.

The apostle Paul wrote, "I say then, has God cast away His people? Certainly not!...I say then, have they stumbled that they should fall? Certainly not! But through their fall, to provoke them to jealousy, salvation has come to the Gentiles. Now if their fall is riches for the world, and their failure riches for the Gentiles, how much more their fullness! For if their being cast away is the reconciling of the world, what will their acceptance be but life from the dead?

"Do not boast against the branches. But if you do boast, remember that you do not support the root, but the root supports you. And they also, if they do not continue in unbelief, will be grafted in, for God is able to graft them in again" (Romans 11:1, 11-12, 15, 18, 23).

Biblical Zionism

The biblical understanding of Zion is that it is both a spiritual and natural movement. Biblical Zionism can be defined as the return of the Jewish people to their national and spiritual roots as revealed in the Bible in preparation for the coming of the Jewish Messiah.

A biblical Zionist is one who believes that God chose the ancient nation of Israel to reveal His plans and purposes for the redemption of mankind and that the modern ingathering of the Jewish people back to their land is a sovereign work of God in fulfillment of Bible prophecy.

This great ingathering involves three divine phases. These are: 1) regathering Zion, 2) redeeming Zion, and 3) restoring Zion.

The Time to Favor Zion

Regathering Zion

There are many places in the Bible where God says He will regather the Jewish people back to the land He promised them. I have listed a few Scriptures below.

"...The LORD your God will bring you back from captivity, and have compassion on you, and gather you again from all the nations where the LORD your God has scattered you. If any of you are driven out to the farthest parts under heaven, from there the LORD will gather you, and from there He will bring you.

"Then the LORD your God will bring you to the land which your fathers possessed, and you shall possess it. He will prosper you and multiply you more than your fathers.

"And the LORD your God will circumcise your heart and the heart of your descendants, to love the LORD your God with all your heart and with all your soul, that you may live"(Deuteronomy 30:3-6).

"He will set up a banner for the nations, and will assemble the outcasts of Israel, and gather together the dispersed of Judah from the four corners of the earth..." (Isaiah 11:12).

"Fear not, for I am with you; I will bring your descendants from the east, and gather them from the west; I will say to the north, 'Give them up!' and to the south, 'Do not keep them back!' Bring My sons from afar, and My daughters from the ends of the earth" (Isaiah 43:5-6).

"For I will set My eyes on them for good, and I will bring them back to this land; I will build them and not pull them down, and I will plant them and not pluck them up.

"Then I will give them a heart to know Me, that I am the LORD; and they shall be My people, and I will be their God, for they shall return to Me with their whole heart" (Jeremiah 24:6-7).

"Hear the word of the LORD, O nations, and declare it in the isles afar off, and say, 'He who scattered Israel will gather him, and keep him as a shepherd does his flock.' " (Jeremiah 31:10).

"...Thus says the LORD God: 'Although I have cast them far off among the Gentiles, and although I have scattered them among the countries, yet I will be a little sanctuary for them in the countries where they have gone....

"I will gather you from the peoples, assemble you from the countries where you have been scattered, and I will give you the land of Israel....Then I will give them one heart, and I will put a new spirit within them, and take the stony heart out of their flesh,...that they may walk in My statutes and keep My judgments and do them; and they shall be My people, and I will be their God.'" (Ezekiel 11:16-20).

"I will bring back the captives of My people Israel; they shall build the waste cities and inhabit them; they shall plant vineyards and drink wine from them; they shall also make gardens and eat fruit from them.

"I will plant them in their land, and no longer shall they be pulled up from the land I have given them, says the LORD your God" (Amos 9:14-15).

"For Zion's sake I will not hold My peace, and for Jerusalem's sake I will not rest, until her righteousness goes forth as brightness, and her salvation as a lamp that burns. I have set watchman on your walls, O Jerusalem; they shall never hold their peace day or night.

"You who make mention of the LORD, do not keep silent, and give Him no rest till He establishes and till He makes Jerusalem a praise in the earth" (Isaiah 62:1, 6-7).

As staggering as it sounds, it is God's plan to regather all the Jews from the nations to Israel. Ezekiel says, " 'then they shall know that I am the LORD their God, who sent them into captivity among the nations, but also brought them back to their land, and left none of them captive any longer. And I will not hide My face from them anymore; for I shall have poured out My Spirit on the house of Israel,' says the LORD God" (Ezekiel 39:28-29).

The Time to Favor Zion

The total population of Jewish people in the world today is approximately fourteen million. As we see from the Scripture, God intends to regather them to Israel. Even now the Interior Ministry in Israel is preparing for a Jewish population of twelve million.

God has a special word to righteous Gentiles among the nations to partner with God by assisting the Jewish people in their return to the land.

Isaiah says, "Thus says the Lord God: 'Behold, I will lift My hand in an oath to the nations, and set up My standard for the peoples; they shall bring your sons in their arms, and your daughters shall be carried on their shoulders.'

"Surely the coastlands shall wait for Me; and the ships of Tarshish will come first, to bring your sons from afar, their silver and their gold with them, to the name of the LORD your God, and to the Holy One of Israel, because He has glorified you" (Isaiah 49:22,60:9).

The Bible also instructs Christians to comfort the Jews (Isaiah 40:1), to pray for the peace of Jerusalem (Psalms 122:6), and to bless them with material support (Romans 15:27).

Jesus said Gentiles would be judged based on how they treated the Jews. Here are His words:

" 'Come, you blessed of My Father, inherit the kingdom prepared for you from the foundations of the world: for I was hungry and you gave Me food; I was thirsty and you gave Me drink; I was a stranger and you took Me in; I was naked and you clothed Me; I was sick and you visited Me; I was in prison and you came to Me.'

"Then the righteous will answer Him saying, 'Lord, when did we see You hungry and feed You, or thirsty and give You drink? When did we see you a stranger and take you I, or naked and clothe You? Or when did we see You sick, or in prison, and come to You?'

"And the King will answer and say to them, 'Assuredly, I say to you, inasmuch as you did it to one of the least of these My brethren, you did it to Me' " (Matthew 25:34-40).

Redeeming Zion

As the LORD regathers the Jews to the land He promised them, He will also redeem them. God is now in the process of redeeming the Jews by calling them back to Himself. Today, there is a great hunger in the hearts of Jewish people for spiritual things.

While this awakening is still relatively small, it is rapidly growing into a significant movement of Jews returning to their God. I have listed below a few of the many Scriptures that mention the redemption of the Jews and Israel at the end of the age.

"The LORD your God will bring you to the land which your fathers possessed, and you shall posses it. He will prosper you and multiply you more than your fathers. And the LORD your God will circumcise your heart and the heart of your descendants, to love the LORD your God with all your heart and with all your soul, that you may live" (Deuteronomy 30:5-6).

"So the ransomed of the LORD shall return, and come to Zion with singing, with everlasting joy on their heads. They shall obtain joy and gladness; sorrow and sighing [mourning] shall flee away" (Isaiah 51:11).

"Break forth into joy, sing together, you waste places of Jerusalem! For the LORD has comforted His people, He has redeemed Jerusalem" (Isaiah 52:9).

"Behold, the days are coming, says the LORD, when I will make a new covenant with the house of Israel and with the house of Judah—not according to the covenant that I made with their fathers in the day that I took them by the hand to lead them out of the land of Egypt, My covenant which they broke, though I was a husband to them, says the LORD.

"But this is the covenant that I will make with the house of Israel after those days, says the LORD: I will put My law in their minds, and write it on their hearts; and I will be their God, and they shall be My people.

The Time to Favor Zion

"No more shall every man teach his neighbor, and every man his brother, saying, 'Know the LORD,' for they shall all know Me, from the least of them to the greatest of them, says the LORD. For I will forgive their iniquity and their sin I will remember no more" (Jeremiah 31:31-34).

"Behold, I will gather them out of all countries where I have driven them in My anger, in My fury, and in great wrath; I will bring them back to this place, and I will cause them to dwell safely. They shall be My people, and I shall be their God; then I will give them one heart and one way, that they may fear Me forever, for the good of them and their children after them.

"And I will make an everlasting covenant with them, that I will not turn away from doing them good; but…I will assuredly plant them in this land, with all My heart and with all My soul" (Jeremiah 32:37-41).

"I will give you a new heart and put a new spirit within you; I will take the heart of stone out of your flesh and give you a heart of flesh. I will put My Spirit within you and cause you to walk in My statutes, and you will keep My judgments and do them. Then you shall dwell in the land that I gave to your fathers; you shall be My people, and I will be your God" (Ezekiel 36:26-28).

"O Israel, hope in the LORD; for with the LORD there is mercy, and with Him is abundant redemption. And He shall redeem Israel from all his iniquities" (Psalm 130:7-8).

" 'The Redeemer will come to Zion, and to those who turn from transgression in Jacob,' says the LORD" (Isaiah 59:20).

"…All flesh shall know that I, the LORD, am your Savior, and your Redeemer, the Mighty One of Jacob" (Isaiah 49:26).

"…Say to the daughter of Zion, 'Surely your salvation is coming; behold His reward is with Him, and His work before Him.' And they shall call them The Holy People, The Redeemed of the LORD; and you shall be called Sought Out, A City Not Forsaken" (Isaiah 62:11-12).

Paul adds these words in his letter to the Romans, "And so all Israel will be saved, as it is written: 'The Deliverer will come out of Zion, and He will turn away ungodliness from Jacob; for this is My covenant with them, when I take away their sins' " (Romans 11:26-27).

Jesus spoke of these awesome days and said, "Now when these things begin to happen, look up and lift up your heads, because your redemption draws near" (Luke 21:28). As we see the Jews being regathered and redeemed, surely we will soon see the next phase of God's divine plan. The glory that God has for the Jews will be fully restored, perhaps in our times.

Restoring Zion

The last phase in building up Zion is restoring Zion. After God regathers and redeems Zion, He will restore Zion and the Jewish people to the full blessings of the covenant He made with their ancestors.

This glorious restoration will happen when King-Messiah Jesus rules as the "Greater Son of David" over the nation of Israel and the nations of the world. At that time, Jerusalem will be the world capital (Isaiah 2:2-3; Jeremiah 3:17; Micah 4:1-2).

The Messiah will rule with perfect righteousness (Jeremiah 23:5-6). Peace will finally come to the earth as the Messiah will be able to accomplish what the United Nations is incapable of doing (Isaiah 2:4; Micah 4:3). I have included a few Scriptures below that speak about the restoration of Zion at the end of the age.

"Arise, shine; for your light has come! And the glory of the LORD is risen upon you. For behold, the darkness shall cover the earth, and deep darkness the people; but the LORD will arise over you, and His glory will be seen upon you. The Gentiles shall come to your light, and kings to the brightness of your rising. And they shall call you The City of the LORD, Zion of the Holy One of Israel" (Isaiah 60:1-3, 14).

The Time to Favor Zion

"For Zion's sake I will not hold My peace, and for Jerusalem's sake I will not rest, until her righteousness goes forth as brightness, and her salvation as a lamp that burns. The Gentiles shall see your righteousness, and all kings your glory" (Isaiah 62:1-2).

"At that time Jerusalem shall be called The Throne of the LORD, and all the nations shall be gathered to it, to the name of the LORD, to Jerusalem. No more shall they follow the dictates of their evil hearts" (Jeremiah 3:17).

"Now it shall come to pass in the latter days that the mountain of the LORD'S house shall be established on the top of the mountains, and shall be exalted above the hills; and all nations shall flow to it.

"Many people shall come and say, 'Come, and let us go up to the mountain of the LORD, to the house of the God of Jacob; He will teach us His ways, and we shall walk in His paths.' For out of Zion shall go forth the law, and the word of the LORD from Jerusalem.

"He shall judge between the nations, and rebuke many people; they shall beat their swords into plowshares, and their spears into pruning hooks; nation shall not lift up sword against nation, neither shall they learn war anymore" (Isaiah 2:2-4).

" 'In that day,' says the LORD, 'I will assemble the lame, I will gather the outcast and those whom I have afflicted; I will make the lame a remnant, and the outcast a strong nation; so the LORD will reign over them in Mount Zion' " (Micah 4:6-7).

"...The LORD will again comfort Zion, and will again choose Jerusalem. 'Jerusalem shall be inhabited as towns with walls....'For I,' says the LORD 'will be a wall of fire all around her, and I will be the glory in her midst. I will return to Zion, and dwell in the midst of Jerusalem. Jerusalem shall be called the City of Truth, the Mountain of the LORD of hosts, the Holy Mountain.

" '...Behold, I will save My people from the land of the east and from the land of the west; I will bring them back, and they shall dwell in the midst of Jerusalem. They shall be My people and

I will be their God.'..."In those days, ten men from every language of the nations shall grasp the sleeve [*tzitzit*] of a Jewish man, saying, 'Let us go with you, for we have heard that God is with you'" (Zechariah 1:17; 2:4-5; 8:3,7-8,23).

Favoring Zion in the Latter Days

The Bible says that the LORD will build up Zion in the latter days. An angel told Daniel, "Now I have come to make you understand what will happen to your people in the latter days" (Daniel 10:14). Moses wrote, "When you are in distress, and all these things come upon you in the latter days..." (Deuteronomy 4:30-31).

The writer of Psalms was looking ahead to our times when he said the time to favor Zion has come. He explained, "This will be written for the generation to come, that a people yet to be created may praise the LORD.... To declare the name of the LORD in Zion, and His praise in Jerusalem, when the peoples are gathered together, and the kingdoms, to serve the LORD (Psalm 102:18, 21-22).

The English phrase, "generation to come" can be translated from one of two Hebrew words. *Dor haba* means, "a generation in time." *Dor aharon* means literally, "the last generation." The last generation is the people who are living to see Zion regathered, redeemed, and restored in preparation for the coming of the Messiah. The context of Psalm 102 suggests that the proper Hebrew word is *dor aharon*.

The disciples of Jesus asked Him what would be the sign of His coming and the end of the age (Matthew 24:3). By His answer, Jesus must have had Psalm 102 in mind. He said, "Now learn this parable from the fig tree: when its branch has already become tender and puts forth leaves, you know that summer is near.

"So you also, when you see all these things, know that it is near—at the doors! Assuredly, I say to you, this generation will by no means pass away till all these things take place. Heaven and earth will pass away, but My words will by no means pass away" (Matthew 24:32-35).

Jesus spoke a parable using the fig tree as a symbol of the building up of Zion. He said the generation of people who witnessed this would be the last generation living at the time of His coming.

We see this interpretation confirmed in the Psalms which says, "Oh, that the salvation of Israel would come out of Zion! When the LORD brings back the captivity of His people, let Jacob rejoice and Israel be glad" (Psalm 14:7).

Regarding the times in which we are living, Jesus gave the following words of hope to believers, "Now when these things began to happen, look up and lift up your heads, because your redemption draws near" (Luke 21:28).

As we wait for these incredible events to unfold, may the Lord bless you and keep you. May the Lord make His face to shine upon you and be gracious unto you. May the Lord lift up His countenance upon you and give you peace. Shalom!

Chapter 14—Personal Study Guide

1. Explain the meaning of Zion and Zionism.

2. What is secular Zionism?

3. What is "Replacement Theology" Zionism?

4. What is biblical Zionism?

5. Discuss the following phases of Zion:
   A. Zion Regathered

   B. Zion Redeemed

   C. Zion Restored

Epilogue: The Hebraic Roots of Christianity

Most people do not realize there was a vital connection between Christianity and Judaism that was severed by the Christian church centuries ago. Once that severing took place, biblical Judaism and biblical Christianity, which God intended to be one, went their separate ways with tragic consequences for both.

We are living at a time when the Lord is calling both Jews and Christians back to their biblical roots. The biblical root of Christianity is Jewish. This root grew from an everlasting covenant God made with Abraham. Christians become part of that root through genuine faith in Jesus as Messiah, Lord, and Savior. This faith is evidenced by unconditional love to God and humanity.

There were 2,000 years of Hebrew history, culture, language, traditions and customs that formed the root of Christianity. While some may not like it nor want to acknowledge it, Christianity is nourished from that Hebraic/Jewish root.

A Jewish rabbi from Tarsus, known as the apostle Paul, wrote these words to the Christians in Rome, "Do not boast against the branches [Jews]. But if you do boast, remember that you do not support the root [the Hebraic origins of Christianity], but the root supports you [Christianity]" (Romans 11:18).

While Christians in America view life with a Western mind and worldview, the Bible was written by Abraham's descendants who had an Hebraic culture, language, and worldview. This presents a real problem and challenge. We have a Middle Eastern Book that we seek to understand from a Western culture.

Our Western perspective can easily cause us to misunderstand the Bible. Furthermore, our mind has been more influenced by Greek philosophy than biblical, Hebraic thought. This is why we must study the Hebraic/Jewish roots of Christianity.

When we read the Bible through Hebrew eyes, our understanding becomes richer, deeper, and clearer with so much more detail than we could ever imagine. We gain new and powerful insights and clarity of vision because we are perceiving the Bible through the eyes of the writers. We see truths that we just cannot see with our Western eyes no matter how sincere our motives and intense our desires.

While Christians have a good understanding of the divinity of Jesus, few know Jesus the man. Every culture makes Jesus over into their own image. Westerners get upset when they discover that Jesus was not a European. Religious groups may take offense when they are told that Jesus was not a member of their denomination. The PLO is trying to make Jesus into a Palestinian.

Jesus was a Jew born into a Jewish family in the Jewish village of Bethlehem in the land of Israel. His heritage was Hebraic, and He kept all the laws of God. Jesus did not start a new religion called Christianity, but He sought to renew Judaism with fresh life from the Spirit of the Lord.

Jesus' followers were Jewish. The New Testament tell us that they worshipped on Saturday (the biblically appointed day), attended the Synagogue, kept the feasts, and were zealous for the *Torah*. They did not become Christians, but were Jews who acknowledge Jesus as the Jewish King and Messiah. They wrote the "Jewish" New Testament and lived *Torah*-observant lifestyles.

Jesus and His early followers were deeply rooted in the rich Hebraic soil of their ancestors. They thought, taught, and lived out of this soil. God planted Christianity in this soil, and Christians must return to it in order to be biblically nourished.

Jesus said to two of His followers, "…'O foolish ones, and slow of heart to believe in all that the prophets have spoken! Ought not the Christ [Messiah] to have suffered these things and to enter into His glory?' And beginning at Moses and all the Prophets, He expounded to them in all the Scriptures the things concerning Himself" (Luke 24:25-27).

Epilogue: The Hebraic Roots of Christianity

Luke recorded this story and went on to say, "Then their eyes were opened and they knew Him...And they said to one another, 'Did not our heart burn within us while He talked with us on the road, and while He opened the Scriptures to us?'" (Luke 24:31-32).

When Christians learn their Hebraic/Jewish roots, the Spirit of the living God will open their spiritual eyes to know Jesus more clearly and more intimately. God's words will burn within their hearts with a fresh fire that cannot be quenched. May it be so for all who love the God of Abraham, Isaac, and Jacob.

Selective Bibliography

Barbour and Company. *Josephus Thrones of Blood*. Uhrichville, OH: Barbour and Company, 1988.

Berenbaum, Michael. *The World Must Know*. Boston, MA: Little, Brown and Company, 1993.

Berkowitz, Ariel and D'vorah. *Torah Rediscovered*. Littleton, CO: First Fruits of Zion, 1996.

Blech, Benjamin. *Understanding Judaism*. Northvale, NJ: Jason Aronson, 1991.

Booker, Richard. *Blow the Trumpet in Zion*. Shippensburg, PA: Destiny Image, 1985.

____. *The Time to Favor Zion Has Come*. Houston, TX: Sounds of the Trumpet, 1996.

____. *How the Cross Became a Sword*. Houston, TX: Sounds of the Trumpet, 1994.

____. *Jesus in the Feasts of Israel*. Shippensburg, PA: Destiny Image, 1987.

____. *Shabbat Shalom*. Houston, TX: Sounds of the Trumpet, 1998.

____. *Here Comes the Bride*. Houston, TX: Sounds of the Trumpet, 1997.

Brown, Michael. *Our Hands are Stained with Blood*. Shippensburg, PA: Destiny Image, 1992.

Cate, Robert. *A History of the Bible Lands in the Interbiblical Period*. Nashville, TN: Broadman Press, 1989.

____. *A History of the New Testament and Its Times*. Nashville, TN: Broadman Press, 1991.

Charlesworth. James H. *The Old Testament Pseudepigrapha*. New York: Doubleday, 1983, vol. 1.

____. *The Old Testament Pseudepigrapha*. New York: Doubleday, 1983, vol. 2.

Cohen, Abraham. *Everyman's Talmud*. New York: Schocken Books, 1949.

Daube, David. *The New Testament and Rabbinic Judaism*. Peabody, MA: Hendrickson, 1956.

Dosick, Rabbi Wayne. *Living Judaism*. New York: HarperCollins, 1995.

Eckstein, Rabbi Yechiel. *What Christians Should Know About Jews and Judaism*. Waco, TX: Word, Incorporated, 1984.

Evans, Craig. *Noncanonical Writings and New Testament Interpretation*. Peabody, MA: Hendrickson, 1992.

Ferguson, Everett. *Encyclopedia of Early Christianity*. New York: Garland Publishing, 1990.

Flannery, Edward H. *The Anguish of the Jews*. New York: Paulist Press, 1985.

Flusser, David. *Jewish Sources in Early Christianity*. Tel-Aviv: MOD Books, 1989.

____. *Judaism and the Origins of Christianity*. Jerusalem: The Magnes Press, 1988

Fuchs, Daniel, and Sevener, Harold. *From Bondage to Freedom*. Neptune, NJ: Loizeaux, 1995.

Ganz, Yaffa. *Sand and Stars*. New York, NY: Shaar Press, 1994.

Goldberg, Louis. *Our Jewish Friends*. Chicago, IL: Moody Press, 1977.

Gruber, Daniel. *The Church and the Jews*. Springfield, MO: Assemblies of God, 1991.

Hargis, David. *The Talit: Garment of Glory*. Virginia Beach, VA: Zadok Scroll Works, 1993.

____. *The Constantine Conspiracy*. Virginia Beach, VA: Zadok Scroll Works, 1994.

Hay, Malcolm. *The Roots of Christian Anti-Semitism*. New York: Liberty Press, 1981.

Kaplan, Aryeh. *Tzitzith: A Thread of Light*. New York: National Conference of Synagogue Youth, 1984.

Selective Bibliography

Kasdan, Barney. *God's Appointed Customs*. Baltimore, MD: Lederer, 1996.
____. *God's Appointed Times*. Baltimore, MD: Lederer, 1993.
Kertzer, Rabbi Morris. *What is a Jew?* New York: Collier Books, 1993.
Kolatch, Alfred. *The Jewish Book of Why*. Middle Village, NY: Jonathan David Publishers, 1981.
____. *The Second Jewish Book of Why*. Middle Village, NY: Jonathan David Publishers, 1985.
Juster, Dan. *Jewish Roots*. Rockville, MD: DAVAR Publising, 1986.
Lindsay, Robert. *Jesus Rabbi and Lord*. Oak Creek, WI: Cornerstone Publishing, 1990.
Mason, Steve. *Josephus and the New Testament*. Peabody, MA: Hendrickson, 1992.
Moseley, Ron. *Yeshua: A Guide to the Real Jesus and the Original Church*. Hagerstown, MD: Ebed Publications, 1996.
Neusner, Jacob. *Judaism in the Beginning of Christianity*. Philadelphia: Fortress Press, 1984.
____. *Rabbinic Literature*. New York: Doubleday, 1994.
____. *Rabbinic Judaism*. Minneapolis: Fortress Press, 1995.
Nickelsburg, George. *Jewish Literature Between the Bible and the Mishna*. Philadelphia: Fortress Press, 1981.
Palatnik, Lori. *Friday Night and Beyond*. Northvale, NJ: Jason Aronson, 1994.
Patai, Raphael. *The Messianic Texts*. Detroit, MI: Wayne State University Press, 1979.
Patzia, Arthur. *The Making of the New Testament*. Downers Grove, IL: InterVarsity Press, 1995.
Peterson, Galen. *The Everlasting Tradition*. Grand Rapids, MI: Kregel, 1995.
Phillips, John. *Exploring the World of the Jew*. Neptune, NJ: Loizeaux, 1993.
Rausch, David. *Building Bridges*. Chicago: Moody Press, 1988.

_____. A Legacy of Hatred: *Why Christians Must Not Forget the Holocaust*. Grand Rapids, MI: Baker, 1990.

Riggins, Walter. *Jesus Ben Joseph*. Tunbridge Wells, England: Monarch Publications, 1993.

Russell, D.S. *Between the Testaments*. Philadelphia: Fortress Press, 1960.

Scott, Julius. *Customs and Controversies*. Grand Rapids, MI: Baker Books, 1995.

Shanks, Hershel. *Christianity and Rabbinic Judaism*. Washington, D.C.: Biblical Archaeology Society, 1992.

Sherbok, Dan Cohn. *The Jewish Faith*. Valley Forge, PA: Trinity Press International, 1993.

Steinsaltz, Adin. *The Essential Talmud*. Northvale, NJ: Jason Aronson, 1992.

Stern, David. *Restoring the Jewishness of the Gospel*. Jerusalem: Jewish New Testament Publications, 1988.

Sumrall, Lester. *Jersualem: Where Empires Die*. Nashville, TN: Thomas Nelson, 1984.

Tessler, Gordon. *Clean and Unclean Foods*. Raleigh, NC: Trumpet of Zion, 1991.

_____. *Did God Change His Mind?* Raleigh, NC: Trumpet of Zion, 1991.

Trepp, Leon. *The Complete Book of Jewish Observance*. New York: Behrman House/Summit Books, 1980.

Young, Brad. *Jesus the Jewish Theologian*. Peabody, MA: Hendrickson Publishers, 1995.

Wagner, Clarence H. *Lessons from the Land of the Bible*. Jerusalem: Bridges for Peace, 1998.

Wein, Berel. *Echoes of Glory*. New York: Sharr Press, 1995.

_____. *Herald of Destiny*. New York: Sharr Press, 1993.

_____. *Triumph of Survival*. New York: Sharr Press, 1991.

Wigoder, Geoffrey. *The Encylopedia of Judaism*. New York: Macmillan, 1989.

Selective Bibliography

Wilson, Marvin. *Our Father Abraham*. Grand Rapids, MI: Eerdmans Publishing, 1989.
Wright, Fred. *Words From the Scroll of Fire*. Jerusalem: Four Corners Publishing, 1994

Selective Index of Names and Subjects

A
Aaronic-Zadok 46
Abrahamic Curse 1
Aelia Capitalina 97
Agrippa I 71-75, 77, 83, 86-88, 101
Agrippa II 74-75, 77, 91, 93, 101
Agrippina 90
Akiba, Rabbi 97
Albinus 91, 101
Alexander the Great 39-40, 287
Alexander, T.J. 88, 101
Alexandra, Salome 54-55
Ambibulus 83, 101
Amenhotep II 31-32
Antigonus 57
Antiochus II 42
Antiochus III 42
Antiochus IV (Epiphanes) 44, 274
Antipater 56-60
Antony, Mark 43, 58, 79-80
Archduke Franz Ferdinand 125, 131
Archelaus 70, 72-73, 77, 82, 101
Aristobulus I 54
Aristobulus II 56-57
Aristotle 39
Ashkenaz (ic) (im) 17-18, 23
Augustine 120-121, 136, 289
Augustus Caesar 43, 58-59, 64, 67, 70-73, 79, 84, 87, 91-92, 113

B
Balfour Declaration 287
Balfour, James 287
Bar Kochba, Simon 97, 105
Bar/Bat Mitzvah 230-232, 244
Battle of Gaugamela 40
Battle of Ipsus 41

Beitar 97
Bernice 42, 74-76, 93
Bimah 188
Birnbaum, Nathan 285
Bouilon, Godfrey 123
Bridges for Peace viii, 7
Brit Milah 221
Brutus 58, 79

C
Caligula 71-74, 85-87, 101-102
Cassander 41
Cassius 58, 79
Chrysostom, John 107
Chumash 162, 173
Chuppah 233, 235-236
City of God, The 120, 283, 289
Claudius 74-75, 87-90, 101-102
Clement 106, 111-112, 136, 288
Cleopatra 43, 57-58, 80
Columbus 125
Constantine 95, 113-116, 118-120, 136, 138, 145, 250, 289, PB 304
Constantius 113
Conversos 125
Coponius 82-84, 101
Council of Nicea 115, 136
Crassus 58, 79
Crusades 2, 122
Cumanus 88-89, 101
Cyprian 107

D
Dead Sea Scrolls 109, 181
Dionysius Exiguus 65
Domitian 94, 101
Dreidel 276
Dreyfus Affair 286

Dreyfus, Alfred 286
Drusilla 74-75, 86

E

Edict of Milan 114
Edot HaMizrach 17-18, 23
Elazar 95
Eleazar 82
Enlightenment 19, 239
Epistle of Barnabas 106
Epistle to the Philippians 106
Erasmus 125
Essenes 51, 109
Eusebius 105, 107, 113-115, 120, 136, 289

F

Fadus 88, 101
Felix, Antonius 74-75, 89-91, 101
Ferdinand and Isabella 125
Festus 75, 91, 101
First Book of Enoch 183
Florus, Gessius 91, 95, 101
Ford, Henry 129
Frederick the Great 11

G

Gaius 85
Galba 92, 101
Gamaliel 21, 82, 98
Gamaliel II, Rabban 98
Gemara 99
Goedsche, Herman 129
Groggers 278
Grynszpan, Herschell 133

H

Hadrian Aelius 97
Haggadah 99
Halachah 99
Haman 276-279
Haman's Ears 279
Hananel 59

Hanukkah 50, 256, 274-276
Hasidic (im) 19, 46, 48, 51-52
Hasmonean 53-54, 58
Havdalah 251
Heliodorus 44
Hellenism 40, 48-49, 53
Herod 54, 56-60, 62-64, 67, 70-75, 77, 82-83, 87-88, 101
Herod Agrippa 71-75, 77
Herod Agrippa II 74-75, 77
Herod Antipas 70-71, 74, 77, 83, 87, 101
Herod Antipater 56-58
Herod the Great 54, 57, 71, 73-74, 88, 101
Herodias 71-72
Herodium 60
Herzl, Theodore 285-287
Heschel 176
Hillel, School of 98-99
Hitler, Adolph 1-2, 126, 130-134, 290
Holocaust 2, 6, 124, 126, 130, 133-136, 290, PB 304
House of Onias 43, 45
House Tobias (iad) 43, 45-46
Hyrcanus, John 53-55
Hyrcanus II, John 56-57

I

Ignatius 106
Inquisition 2, 124-125
Institute for Hebraic-Christian Studies 6, PB 314
Institute for Holy Land Studies 7
Irenaeus 106

J

Jannaeus 54-55
Jason 45, 161, PB 304
Jerome 107
John of Gischala 96
Joly, Maurice 129

Selective Index of Names and Subjects

Jonathan 51-53, 61, 202, PB 304
Joshua, Huna ben 190
Judah the Prince 99
Judas of Galilee 81-82
Julius Caesar 43, 58, 79
Jupiter 59, 97

K
Kaddish 240-241
Kashrut 207-208
Ketubah 232-234
Kippah 189-191, 219
Koran 168, 283
Kosher 20, 201-202, 207-211, 214-215, 217
K'tuvim 146, 162, 164

L
Ladino 18
Latkes 276
League of Nations 287
Leisingen, Count 123
Lepidus, Aemilius 58, 80
Livia 83
Lysimachus 41

M
Maccabees 47-52, 61, 180, 274-275
Maimonides, Moses 160, 169, 179
Marcellus 85, 101
Mariamne 59-60, 73
Marranos 125
Marullus 87, 101
Masada 57, 82, 95, 204
Massoretes 167
Mattathias 48-50, 53
Matzah 260
Maxentius 113
Megillot 164
Mein Kampf 2, 132
Menelaus 46
Menorah 274-276
Messiah Ben David 184

Messiah Ben Joseph 184, PB 304
Mikveh 203-207, 219
Minyan 188
Mishna 99-100, PB 304
Mithra 118
Mitzvah (ot) 97, 144, 146, 176-177, 221, 230
Modein 48-49, 52
Mohel 224
Moon-god 26
Morris, Kertzer 11, 166

N
Nachman, Moshe Ben 103
Nazi 124, 126, 131-132, 135
Nero 90-95, 101
Nerva 94, 101
Nevi'im 146, 162-163, 165
Night of Broken Glass 132-133
Nomos 152-153
Nuremberg Laws 132

O
Octavia 58
Octavian 58, 79-80
Onias 43, 45
Oral *Torah* 19, 99-100
Origen 106, 112-113, 119-121, 136, 288-289
Otho 92, 101

P
Pamphilus 113, 289
Pantaenus 111, 288
Pella 104
Peter the Hermit 122
Petronius 86-87
Philip of Macedonia 39
Pidyon Haben 227-228
Pilate, Pontius 68, 71, 83-85, 101, 258
Plato 105, 288
Pogroms 128-129, 136

Pompey 56, 58, 79
Priscilla 88
Protocols 129-130, 136
Ptolemy I, II, III. IV, V 41-42
Pur 277
Puritans 287

Q

Quirinius 64, 81-82
Qumran 51-52, 109, 204

R

Rabbinic Judaism 19, 65, 97-99, 102, 104, 138, 140, 175-176, PB 304
Radulf 123
Ramban 103
Ramses II 31
Rashi 173, 181
Rath, Ernst Von 133
Replacement Theology 113, 287, 289-290, 300
Retcliffe, Sir John 129
Romulus 79

S

Sabbath 7, 46-47, 56, 67-69, 99, 104, 129, 142, 163, 177, 194, 198, 205, 217, 223, 239, 242, 245-253, 255, 261-262, 264-265, 267, 272, PB 314
Saddok 81-82
Sadducees 53-56, 108, 238
Salome 54-56, 60, 71
Salomon, Haym 5
Sanhedrin 242
Seder 258
Sefer Torah 163
Sejanus 84
Seleucus I 41
Seleucus IV 44
Sepharad (im) 17-18, 23
Septuagint 42, 151

Shabbat 7, 216, 246, 251-252, PB 304, PB 314
Shamash 193, 196, 275
Shamma, School of 98
Shema 97, 166, 168, 170, 186
Sheol 239
Shivah 241
Shofar 234, 236, 267-268
Sica (rii) 89
Simchat Torah 163
Simon of Gerasa 96
Sofer 201

T

Tallit 191, 193-194, 197, 240
Talmud 99-100, 162, 165, 190, 221, 237
Tanakh 146, 148, 162, 164-165, 171, 173, 184
Tefillin 198-200
Tertullian 106
Theodosius 119
Thirteen Principles of Faith 160
Thutmose I 31
Thutmose III 31
Thutmose IV 32
Tiberius 67, 71-73, 83-86, 101
Titus 76, 93-95, 97, 101-102, 140, 142-143, 174, 206, 226
Torah 19-20, 32, 45-46, 48, 53, 66-67, 99-100, 104-105, 144, 146-157, 161-166, 170, 177, 183, 188-190, 195, 199, 203, 211, 214, 216-218, 221, 225-227, 230-231, 239, 250, 266, 302
Torquemada, Thomas De 125
Trajan 94, 101
Treaty of Apemea 44
Treaty of Versailles 131
Twain 21, 25
Tzitz (ot) 191-195, 197-199, 219, 240

Selective Index of Names and Subjects

V
Valerius Gratus 84
Vespasian 92-93, 95-96, 101-102
Vitellius 92, 101

W
Weizmann 286
Woolley 26

Y
Yad 189
Yarah 146
Yarmulke 189

Yavneh 98
Yiddish 17, 189
Yom Teruah 267

Z
Zadok 45-46, 51-53, 109, 114
Zakkai, Johanan Ben 98
Zbaszyn 133
Zealots 82-83, 89, 95, 97, 109
Zeus 41, 44, 46, 50
Zinzendorf 11
Zion 129, 136, 209, 281-285, 287, 289-300

The Institute for Hebraic-Christian Studies Vision and Resource Materials

As explained in this book, we are living at a time when the Lord is calling Christians to an awareness of the Jewish roots of their faith, a desire to establish new relationships of love and understanding between Christians and Jews, and an active role in blessing the Jewish people and the state of Israel.

The goal of the Institute for Hebraic-Christian Studies is to assist believers in fulfilling this calling. IHCS is a unique Christian educational organization with a biblical worldview. We are not political, and we do not proselytize. We seek to promote love, understanding, and mutual respect between Christians and Jews through emphasizing our common heritage.

Our vision is to educate Christians in their Hebraic-Jewish roots, build relationships between Christians and Jews, and bless Israel and the Jewish people. We do this through celebration events, seminars, educational materials, joint meetings between Christians and Jews, tours to Israel, helping Jews home to Israel, providing social assistance to immigrants, and numerous other activities.

If the Lord has put this vision in your heart, we invite you to contact us about how we may assist you. Perhaps you can order some of the books listed on the following page. We also have some exciting celebration videos you can order. You may also study our courses as a correspondence student and earn a diploma in Hebraic-Christian Studies.

Additionally, the IHCS ministry team is available to conduct a conference in your area. There are many other ways you can get involved. Don't just read about prophecy, be part of it. Contact us for a complete list of resource materials. Shalom!

Book Order Form

You may order these books by copying this Order Form or through our website at: www.rbooker.com. Sounds of the Trumpet, 4747 Research Forest Drive, Suite 180-330, Woodlands, TX 77381. Or you may write for a complete catalog of all of our books and ministry resources.

- ☐ _____ copies *No Longer Strangers* at $15.00 each
- ☐ _____ copies of *The Miracle of the Scarlet Thread* (the blood covenant and Messiah) at $10.00 each
- ☐ _____ copies of *Blow the Trumpet in Zion* (Israel and Bible prophecy) at $10.00 each
- ☐ _____ copies of *Jesus in the Feasts of Israel* (how the festivals point to Messiah and believers) at $10.00 each
- ☐ _____ copies of *How the Cross Became a Sword* (the events that separated Christianity from its Jewish roots) at $5.95 each
- ☐ _____ copies of *Islam, Christianity and Israel* at $5.95 each
- ☐ _____ copies of *Here Comes the Bride: Jewish Wedding Customs and the Messiah* at $5.95 each

(Please add $2.00 per book for shipping)

Name _____

Address _____

City _____ ST _____ Zip _____

Foreign Orders please send an additional $3.00 per book ordered in U.S. funds only for surface mail

Book Order Form

You may order these books by copying this Order Form or through our website at: www.rbooker.com. Sounds of the Trumpet, 4747 Research Forest Drive, Suite 180-330, Woodlands, TX 77381. Or you may write for a complete catalog of all of our books and ministry resources.

☐ _____ copies of *Shabbat Shalom: A Guide for Christians to Understand and Celebrate the Sabbath* at $5.95 each

☐ _____ copies of *Time to Favor Zion* (modern ingathering of Jews to Israel) at $5.95 each

☐ _____ copies of *The Shofar: Ancient Sounds of Messiah* at $5.95 each (information about the shofar and its meaning to our lives today)

☐ _____ copies of *Torah: Law or Grace?* at $5.95 each (explains the biblical meaning of law and grace and their significance to our lives today)

☐ _____ copies of *The Battle for Truth: Middle East Myths* at $5.00 each

☐ _____ copies of *The Root and Branches: An Introduction to the Jewish Roots of Christianity* at $10.00 each

(Please add $2.00 per book for shipping)

Name _____

Address _____

City _____ ST _____ Zip _____

Foreign Orders please send an additional $3.00 per book ordered in U.S. funds only for surface mail